The Green Crusade

Rethinking the Roots of Environmentalism

Charles T. Rubin

ROWMAN & LITTLEFIELD PUBLISHERS, INC.
Lanham • Boulder • New York • Oxford

ROWMAN & LITTLEFIELD PUBLISHERS, INC.

Published in the United States of America
by Rowman & Littlefield Publishers, Inc.
4720 Boston Way, Lanham, Maryland 20706

12 Hid's Copse Road
Cumnor Hill, Oxford OX2 9JJ, England

British Library Cataloguing in Publication Information Available

The Free Press edition of this book was previously catalogued by the Library of
Congress as follows:

Rubin, Charles T.
    The green crusade : rethinking the roots of environmentalism / Charles T. Rubin.
        p. cm.
    Includes bibliographical references and index.
    1. Green movement. 2. Environmentalism. I. Title.
    GE195.R83 1994   93-48858
    333.7'2—dc20   CIP

ISBN 0-8476-8817-8

Printed in the United States of America

☉™ The paper used in this publication meets the minimum requirements of American
National Standard for Information Sciences—Permanence of Paper for Printed Library
Materials, ANSI Z39.48–1984.

TO LESLIE, AND TO OUR CHILDREN

with the hope that they will be able to make our mistakes

Contents

Acknowledgments

A work whose genesis extends back as far as this one presents the danger of a list of acknowledgments of unseemly length, combined with the possibility that some important people will be overlooked. To avoid both errors, I would like to extend blanket thanks to teachers, colleagues, and friends whose help over the years is reflected in the pages that follow.

A more manageable number of people deserve recognition for the smaller, yet far more intense, task of bringing this book to precisely its present form. Adam Bellow, editor at the Free Press, worked patiently with me to do what I could not have done alone—make this an interesting book for his press and for a nonspecialized audience. Research assistance was provided by Melanie Maurer and Kathy Toulson, both graduate students at Duquesne University's Graduate Center for Social and Public Policy. Ben Franklin's advice that you make a friend when you ask someone to do you a service was entirely vindicated by the generous willingness of Dr. Jeffrey Salmon, executive director of the George C. Marshall Institute, to comment on a draft of the book; it should be less heavy going for the reader as a result of his efforts. Dr. Thomas L. Short provided the same service and gave me the incisive criticism that I have long had the pleasure of relying on.

As they always do, my family came through in numerous ways. My brother, Bill, helped get the footnotes under control (assisted by his son, Eli), my sister, Betsy, picked at my arguments, and my parents, Alan and Audrie Rubin, lovingly supported me and at crucial moments took care of my children. My wife, Leslie, did *all* of these same things and combined them with the functions of editor, research assistant, cook, adviser: the list could go on but I will spare her modesty. There would be no book without her.

Over the years, the sinews for the research behind this book were provided by a number of foundations (critics, please note). Thanks to Dr. Robert H. Horwitz and Dr. Anthony Sullivan, the Earhart Foundation was willing to support me when I had little to show why they should. Dr. Philip N. Marcus and Dr. Kenneth M. Jensen at the Institute for Educational Affairs were equally willing to assist the work of a largely untested scholar. The John M. Olin Foundation provided help at a critical juncture, allowing me to keep an academic career alive; in this connection, I owe much to Dr. Christopher Bruell and Dr. Walter Berns. Finally, the Lynde and Harry Bradley Foundation allowed me to have the necessary time off to pull many years of effort together into this finished form. I hope this book, however belated, is fitting thanks to these farseeing institutions and individuals.

Forest Hills, PA
July 1993

INTRODUCTION

Green in Judgement

1985. A Metromedia production. Distributed by CCM Films, Inc. . . . 1970. 56min., $550 . . .

. . . in this dramatization of international catastrophe in the year 1985 . . . [o]n-the-scene reporters from Los Angeles to New York detail the degree of pollution and its dire consequences—mass panic, violence, and death . . . What first appears to be a belabored subject with a sensational approach eventually turns into one of the most realistic portrayals of a tragic possibility as the entire world crumbles simply because no one thought it possible. At the end of the program, Evans asks for possible ways out of the crisis, but the reporters only give bleak outlooks as communications slowly end with one sudden blackout after another. A desperate call to action, the film is recommended for all junior and senior high school classes and college courses dealing with ecology and pollution, for public library programs, and for groups or individuals concerned with environmental destruction. Ages 12–adult.

The Booklist, 4/1/71[1]

POSTCARDS FROM THE CUTTING EDGE

Unless there is somewhere a Museum of Fast-Food Packaging, the McDonald's polystyrene "clamshell" is already nothing but a memory. Developed in the late 1970s, it was for over ten years a model of corporate environmental responsibility. It was potentially recyclable, saved trees and energy, used up what would otherwise be by-products of oil refining, and cost less to manufacture to boot. Furthermore, at a time when it seemed like trash burning would help solve both the energy and the landfill "crises," polystyrene was an energy-productive material to burn.

All that began to change in the late 1980s. Starting in Vermont and New Jersey before spreading nationwide, the Citizen's Clearinghouse for Hazardous Waste initiated a boycott of McDonald's. The bill of particulars against the clamshell was impressive. If it were burned, who knows what toxic materials it would release? If it were landfilled, who knows how much space these remnants of the millions of McDonald's products sold each year would take up? Furthermore, its manufacture involved HCFCs, chemicals linked both to ozone depletion and the greenhouse effect. McDonald's tried to respond first by speeding efforts at recycling the offending item. But costs were high, the quality of the material recycled poor, and skeptics wondered how much good restaurant-based recycling would do when so much of McDonald's business was take-out.

So with the help of the Environmental Defense Fund, McDonald's came up with a new plan: paper wrapping. Not recycled paper, because FDA regulations would not permit it, and not plain paper, but plastic-coated paper. Why the EDF and McDonald's together came up with this alternative is not entirely clear, except that it did lift the boycott and silence the clamshell's critics. The new wrap cannot presently be recycled in either the plastic or the paper recycling stream. Will it then merely take up room in landfills, or produce unknown toxins if burned? How many trees will die to feed the nation's hunger for a Big Mac? The Environmental Action Coalition may perhaps be laying the groundwork for future anti-McDonald's agitation, having pointed out that the wrap is a problematic choice because the paper has been chlorine-bleached.

McDonald's, on the other hand, is looking into whether it can be composted, the currently fashionable method of dealing with organic trash.[2]

Along with Love Canal, the city of Times Beach, Missouri, has become emblematic for toxic contamination. In 1982, the Environmental Protection Agency permanently evacuated and bought out its 2,242 residents at a cost of some $40 million because the roads had been coated with dioxin-contaminated oil. Dioxin was regarded at the time as an extremely potent carcinogen. The entire town was fenced off, pending a cleanup estimated to cost $120 million, but still not completed.[3]

Jump ahead to spring 1991. In the interim, the government has spent some $400 million researching dioxin's effect on human health. The results are startling: Vernon Houk, assistant surgeon general and director of the Center for Environmental Health at the National Centers for Disease Control (and one of the same officials who recommended the evacuation of Times Beach), announced new information suggesting that the levels of dioxin at Times Beach are unlikely to be harmful: "Given what we now know about this chemical's toxicity and its effect on human health, it looks as though the evacuation was unnecessary."[4]

Yet only one year later, another chapter is added to the dioxin story. New claims start appearing that dioxin might be even more dangerous than we thought. Cancer is no longer the focus of attention, but rather the possibility that low doses of dioxin "may deal a stunning blow to the immune system," as it "whips up widespread chaos in the body's hormonal messenger system."[5] As is almost always the case with such medical pronouncements about toxic chemicals, most of the results are drawn from study of animals other than humans. But, as one researcher put it, "The fact that you can't clearly show the effects in humans in no way lessens the fact that dioxin is an extremely potent chemical."[6] Neither is the issue of carcinogenicity completely dead. In the course of news coverage of the controversy, the same study published in the *New England Journal of Medicine* is cited by both those who want to minimize dioxin's dangers and those who want to emphasize them.[7]

<hr>

Shellfish, like mussels, are well-established indicators of environmental quality. As they feed by straining water, they tend readily to pick up and concentrate bacteria and contaminants. They are also a problem when they accumulate on offshore oil rigs. And, of course, for years offshore oil rigs have been a problem for environmentalists, concerned about water pollution from oil spills or other kinds of contamination.

Today, however, many of the mussels served in San Francisco restaurants are harvested from oil platforms. Weekly tests have found no contamination by bacteria, heavy metals, or hydrocarbons. Are environmentalists rethinking their opposition to offshore drilling? Not at all. The issue now is not water pollution but whether a national energy policy should encourage new exploration and drilling instead of focusing on energy conservation. Besides, oil is part of the carbon-based energy economy that we all know is causing global warming.[8]

<hr>

By early 1992, it was hard not to know about the "ozone hole" over Antarctica, but for those of us in the north, it seemed a distant problem. Suddenly the threat came much closer to home. Newspapers reported that a NASA study found that a "new ozone 'hole' could open over densely settled areas of the Northern Hemisphere, exposing the population to increased amounts of harmful radiation."[9] The results were "so disturbing" that the NASA team released them before the data had been completely analyzed, let alone before they had waited for peer review. "Everybody should be alarmed by this," said a NASA manager. "It's far worse than we thought."[10]

Al Gore, then a senator, immediately introduced legislation to force a faster phaseout of CFCs, the culprit chemical in ozone depletion, expressing the hope that "an ozone hole over Kennebunkport" would finally move President Bush to see the urgency of the problem.[11] The *New York Times* editorialized about "The Ozone Hole Over Mr. Bush's Head" while the *Washington Post* contented itself with noting that ozone depletion was occurring "even faster than the pessimists expected."[12] The Senate passed a speeded phaseout bill by 96 to 0; on February 11 the White House agreed to accelerate the process.[13] Even CFC producers agreed that faster was better. *Time* was almost behind the times when its February 17 cover featured a burning sky to symbolize its story on ozone loss, but a special sidebar did provide useful information about what to do "as ozone depletion gets worse."[14]

Surely this episode vindicates the ability of both U.S. business and government to respond decisively to a crisis. If only there had really been a crisis. Already by March 10 a NASA scientist could state, "There is no ozone hole over Kennebunkport. There never has been an ozone hole over Kennebunkport. And I don't really expect one."[15] Throughout the summer of 1992 no hole developed anywhere in the north. And it was only as the furor died down that certain key details began to emerge—like the fact that even had there been a hole, the increased ultraviolet radiation at a given site below it would have been comparable to normal levels of ultraviolet radiation a few hundred miles south of that site.[16]

Such anecdotes remind us that environmentalism is a powerful movement in the United States and elsewhere, and is getting more powerful. We are constantly on the lookout for man-made threats to nature and to ourselves, using ever more sensitive measures and ever more refined understandings of just what constitutes such threats. Our ability to explore nature ever more finely means that dangers we might once have missed can now be found everywhere. It is the power of environmentalism that propels us on the restless quest for ever greater sophistication and sensitivity in identifying hazards to ourselves and to nature.

Not that you would get many environmentalists to agree that they are powerful. But their testimony is perhaps not the most reliable. "Power denial" is a common feature of American politics, where our democratic ideals make it important that individuals or groups not appear to stand too much apart from the crowd. And environmentalism is not powerful in the sense that environmentalists can always prevail in the political arena; in a pluralistic society such as ours, with so many different and conflicting interests, a 100% success rate is simply not to be expected. It is powerful because not so slowly, and quite surely, it is changing people's minds. Environmentalism is becoming the lens through which we look at our relationship to nature.

In an astonishingly short time environmentalism has passed from the fringes to the mainstream of society. There are many signs of this transformation. Barry Commoner, once called the "Paul Revere of ecology" when he appeared on the cover of *Time*,[17] was still regarded as something of an odd duck when he ran for president on a third-party ticket in 1980. But in 1993, we have in Al Gore a vice president who has decided that the environment is *the* crucial issue facing mankind in the post–cold war world. And some of his thinking on that topic makes a "fringe" candidate like Commoner look like a moderate.

Another measure of environmentalism's growing place in the public mind can be seen by examining citations under "environment" in the *New York Times Index*. In 1955 the word is not indexed; in 1960 there is one citation to a story about environmental science and the aerospace industry. The point is not that the *Times* didn't cover stories about pollution and humans' effect on nature in this period, but rather that they were considered stories about discrete if serious problems, not about grave threats to some overarching entity called "the environment." In 1965 the word is first found as a heading in its present, familiar—if amorphous—sense, and there are two citations. By 1970, the year of the first Earth Day, there were 86 paragraphs under the heading, taking up nearly two pages of the index, many paragraphs containing citations to more than one story. (The *Times* provides not just citations but brief summaries of stories.) After that things settled down a bit: 30 paragraphs in 1975, 73 in 1980, 41 in 1985. In 1990, however, the twentieth anniversary of Earth Day, there were 172 paragraphs, some two-and-a-half index pages, just under the heading "environment" (i.e., not counting other related stories about energy policy or oil spills or toxic waste, and so on).[18]

We are a society—and a world—transformed by concern about the environment. The 1972 United Nations Conference on the Human Environment in Stockholm saw the attendance of two heads of state or government, not the over one hundred that came to the Earth Summit in 1992. Not long ago the desire to "save the planet" would have been dismissed as the hysterical pretensions of a crank. Today, it has become a motto by which businesses attempt to capture market share. Environmentalism has its own credit cards, mutual funds, travel services, catalogs, and computer networks. You know something is up when various organizations quarrel over whose "green mark" on products is the best guarantor of environmental quality. Environmental regulation is no longer something that only big business has to worry about when laws mandate recycling and prevent people from, or imprison them for, improving their property if that means draining swamps—or rather, "wetlands."

We should not be too surprised at such changes. They happen when millions of good-hearted people become worried by problems as close as a bulldozer in the adjoining property, or as far away as a threatened species in Madagascar shown on TV. And worry they do. A 1991 Gallup poll of adults nationwide showed that 80% of the population by their own estimation worries "a great deal" or "a fair amount" about loss of natural habitat for wildlife. Some 86% showed the same levels of concern about pollution of drinking water, 64% about acid rain; 69% worried that much about contamination of soil and water by radioactivity from nuclear facilities, 83% about contamination of soil and water by toxic waste, 62% about global warming, 67% about the loss of tropical rain forests, 87% about air pollution, 88% about fresh water pollution, 79% about ocean and beach pollution. Furthermore, in each case those who are "a great deal concerned" were a higher percentage than those who worried "a fair amount."[19] Since these topics are almost an exhaustive listing of the environmental agenda of the past 30 years, it can hardly be said that the message has not come across.

The motives that prompt such concern are surely as various as the concerns themselves, as are people's actions in response to them. Growing up in suburban Cleveland, Ohio, I know a good deal about such motives firsthand; a late baby boomer, I am of the first generation educated to look around and see "environmental problems" as such. In 1964–65, my fifth-grade teacher, Miss Spere, taught us about what were becoming the two prongs of the environmental movement. She is one of the best teachers I ever had. Under her tutelage we became young experts in ecology, learning about plant succession, eutrophication of lakes, weather, birds, and all kinds of wonderful things. But we lived, after all, on the shores of "dying" Lake Erie. The city was often fouled by air pollution (although it produced spectacular sunsets) and was cut in two by a river that—no surprise to any Clevelander—would a few years later catch fire. It wasn't enough just to learn about nature. As a Junior Audubon project, our class embarked on a campaign to save Lake Erie. Somewhere or other we set up a table with information and bumper stickers. We wrote letters to our congressman. For me, the high point of the campaign was Richard Grossman's birthday party. Rather than go see a movie or go bowling (the two usual options), his mom arranged a visit to the local sewage treatment plant.

What I was learning helped make sense of earlier childhood experiences. I began to understand why there were fewer animals around after the woods at the back of our yard was torn out and houses were built on it. Additional runoff from the same kind of development all over my suburb probably had something to do with the torrential flood on nearby, and aptly named, Meadowbrook Road, a flood that left only huge jumbled chunks of asphalt where once there had been a street. So by the time in junior high school when I bought my first book by an environmentalist, Barry Commoner's *Science and Survival*, I was ready to hear what he had to say, even if I was too young to understand it completely.

I mention such experiences only because I believe them to have been common for my peers. They help explain why I and so many others fulfilled our college science requirements in the 1970s with "relevant" courses that stressed the environment. One of my most enjoyable college experiences was sitting in a small rowboat in the Cuyahoga River navigation channel (the part that burned) trying to take water samples from the disgusting sewage outfall of a steel plant. (The guy who finally just took hold of the bottle and plunged it into the water got a truly terrible rash as a result.) I was a child of my time; I had no conception that environmentalism could be anything but a Good Thing.

I am no longer so sure. Where once I saw a movement founded in science, now I see a utopian political program. Where once I felt that the problems were obvious to all, now I understand that different situations can appear to people to be problems depending on how they want the world to be in the future. Where once I knew exactly what grand solutions would solve all environmental ills, now I believe there is a great deal to be said for modest expectations and muddling through.

This book takes a fresh look at the transformation in our thinking that popular environmental writers like Rachel Carson, Barry Commoner, Paul Ehrlich, and E. F. Schumacher have produced. Unlike many books about environmentalism, critical or otherwise, its focus is not on environmental science, the history of the movement, or its political victories and defeats. Neither is it a work of "environmental philosophy," as that term is ordinarily understood. It *is* a look at how what is now called common sense was constructed. How do "we all know" that the earth is in danger, that everything is connected to everything else, that too many people live here, that smaller is better? Where do the ideas come from that hold up the ediface of our growing environmental concern, and what are we agreeing to when we accept them? It is time to pay attention to the man behind the curtain and find out who will run this Emerald City we are building. For if, as all environmentalists seem to agree, our future must look very different from our past, there is good reason to make sure it isn't all just humbug, or a fevered dream.

PROVIDING PROBLEMS

How did the green transformation of our thinking come about? We all know at least part of the answer: "environmentalists" did it. The word has become such a part of the language that we forget what a new, and rather strange, word it is. It doesn't even appear in my 1966 *American College Dictionary*. The latest (1987) supplement to the *Oxford English Dictionary* includes the word; the first example they provide of its now popular sense comes from 1970. What does it mean? One critic has called "environmentalism" an essentially meaningless term because it does not distinguish any distinct concern or point of view. Who does not want clean air and water, or a variety of wildlife and beautiful places?[20] But a sympathetic student of environmentalism is closer to the mark when he suggests that environmentalists are the "vanguard for a new society."[21] Being an environmentalist, in other words, means being part of a political or moral crusade for a better world.

Environmentalism is heir to the antislavery and temperance movements and thus a part of the ongoing saga of evangelical reform that has characterized American history.[22] Indeed, it is not so far off the mark to say that environmentalism is the temperance movement of our time. We know it wants to save the earth. But we forget just how much, in the spirit of its predecessor, it seeks to save us from ourselves. The parallels between the two movements are instructive.

Vast quantities of "ardent spirits" were consumed in nineteenth-century America; Portland, Maine, had two daily bell ringings to signal the time of drinking breaks.[23] "Common sense" alone would suggest there is something wrong with this situation. Alcoholic beverages were a normal part of daily life for people of all ages, and by the turn of the century the medical science of the day already testified to many of the dangers of such consumption. The problem was obvious; temperance workers just wanted to get out there and solve it.

But was the problem so obvious? The various temperance groups that grew up in the course of the nineteenth century—and particularly before the Civil War they proliferated wildly—had some very different ideas about just what made alcohol consumption a problem. Was it the bad effects on health? Or that it undermined family life? Was drinking wrong because the grog shops were so often centers of disorderly behavior and crime? Or because drinking itself was a sin? Perhaps the problem was that it interfered with productivity at work. As Abraham Lincoln once asked, was a good thing being abused, or a bad thing used?[24]

If there was incomplete agreement about the problem, there was also wide divergence about the solution and how to achieve it. Should more moderation be all that was aimed at? Or should individuals "take the pledge" not to drink at all, and thus set an example? Should they abstain from wine as well as liquor—or even unfermented apple cider? Should the movement focus on shutting down taprooms, and how should that be done? Through legal prohibition, by praying the owners into submission (i.e., sit-ins), or by destroying the vice dens with axes? Should temperance activists seek "local option" legislation, statewide bans on liquor sales, or national prohibition? Should they act through existing political parties, or should they form an independent temperance party? Should they court the votes of legislators who were drinkers themselves, or only those who were teetotalers?

These many differences did not always prevent men and women of goodwill from working together in a common cause, although it did produce intrigues and factions. It might seem these disagreements would have led people to formulate a more moderate policy when they attempted to build coalitions. But we know that something quite different happened. The shared yet amorphous sense that drinking was *somehow* a problem, and the widely felt need to do *something* about it, led ultimately to the triumph of the movement's most extreme elements. Chance—in the form of World War I—may also have contributed to the victory of national prohibition. But chance favors the prepared party. The triumph of the extremists was prepared when, in a remarkable transformation of language, it became possible to attack moderation in the name of temperance—two words that had previously meant much the same thing. The extremists, those who, having the clearest vision of what they wanted, were willing to work hardest, and not always scrupulously, to get it, seemed to take the strongest and most consistent stand, compared with which anything else was tainted with compromise and expediency. These were also the people who could make the most effective use of public hopes and fears.

Prohibition failed. Not, however, because it was a new idea that was foisted on an inattentive public; temperance had been on the public mind for well over 75 years. And not only because it was not really what most people wanted, whatever they may have imagined.

More telling for the failure of prohibition is the fact that this extremist policy was built on extreme hopes of a millennial change in human affairs. Evangelist Billy Sunday's jubilation was not atypical: "The reign of tears is over. The slums will soon be a memory. We will turn our prisons into factories and our jails into storehouses and corncribs. Men will walk upright now, women will smile and children will laugh. Hell will be forever for rent."[25]

With such expectations, it is hard to imagine how prohibition could have succeeded even if no drop of liquor were subsequently consumed in the United States. And that difficulty, as much as the failure of the policy on narrower grounds, helps account for the subsequent view of prohibition as an archetype of legal lunacy.

Any comparison between the temperance movement and environmentalism is not likely to be viewed with much favor. We would retrospectively expect temperance workers to disagree, since they were motivated by religious and moral sentiments that we "know" now to be ultimately matters of personal choice, and in any case ill suited, or downright unconstitutional, as the foundations of public policy. Science, on the other hand, which is often taken as the root of environmentalism, seems to offer objective knowledge of the world, and bears no constitutional taint. Or again, the existence of environmental problems is taken to be simply a matter of common sense; people don't need to be passionately committed to a cause to see that smog is bad. As a result, there may seem to be an important difference between environmentalism and other American reform movements. That difference may be represented by the fact that those at the forefront of prohibition were often religious figures; the great environmentalists are generally thought of, and generally are, *scientists*. Their métiers are not poetry, piety, or politics, but such things as biology and chemistry.

But are environmental problems simply a matter of common sense? Twice Environmental Protection Agency Administrator William Ruckelshaus seems to think so: "most people do not need a scientific panel to tell them that air is not supposed to be brown, that streams are not supposed to ignite and stink, that beaches are not supposed to be covered with raw sewage."[26] But there is less truth to this truism than meets the eye. Most people did not need the temperance movement to tell them they did not like being accosted by drunks, but that didn't tell them what was to be done about the problem. Not all that long ago, the stink of raw sewage was simply a fact of life, and within the memory of my generation the belching smokestack was a symbol of progress and power. As I was growing up, drainers of swamps were still accounted net bene-factors of humanity. Here in Pittsburgh, many did, and some still would, agree with the barber who said, "When smoke is pouring people get a haircut. When there isn't smoke, people don't spend money."[27] A 1915 Congregational hymn contains the lines, "The Wilderness is planted, the deserts bloom and sing; On coast and plain the cities; their smokey banners fling." Changing the public perception of such things required not only that they come to be seen first and foremost as "pollution." It also required adoption of a perspective from which brown air and smelly streams were all part of the *same* problem.

If "common sense" can be thus benighted, then surely modern natural science is responsible for its enlightenment. The progress of science is seen as intimately connected with our national pres-tige and well-being, whether it comes in the form of improved medical knowledge or ever faster computers. As befits the provider of so many goods things, science becomes an increasingly powerful public authority. Stephen Hawking can write a speculative best-seller on the beginnings of the universe itself, and Richard Dawkins can write a popular book deriving moral imperatives from "the self-ish gene," while Genesis and the Ten Commandments languish in public obscurity. Even Carl Sagan seems to have unlimited access to *Parade* magazine, whether he wants to talk about international relations or the threat of earth-asteroid collision.

That most people can't take their science straight creates a cen-tral role for the environmental popularizer. The reign of science does not require that the general public be scientists; indeed, per-haps the contrary is true. It does require that the public have some appreciation for what science can do for them, in order that they support its efforts on their behalf.

How does the public know about global warming? People don't go out and buy the computer models that predict such warming, and run them on their PCs. They don't study journals of meteorology and atmospheric physics. A few members of the general public might read about warming in a journal like *Science* or *Nature*, a few more will read articles in *Scientific American*. The process of popularization continues in places like *Natural History, Popular Mechanics, Discover*, and *Science Digest*, and ends with Carl Sagan in *Parade*, or a TV news special report with talking heads and computer graphics.

The link between environmentalism and science that the popularizers convey seems to be its strongest claim to moral and political authority. Yet something more is needed. As we have seen in the temperance case, agreement that there are problems does not mean there is agreement on what those problems are, or on what makes them problems, or on what to do about them.

"The environment" is, of course, all-encompassing. If we are to pay attention to it, there must be selectivity in focus. Why do some situations appear to us as urgent problems, while others seem to be matters we can afford to downplay or ignore? After all, the world is full of people who, if they have homes at all, live in hovels, do not have enough food to eat, cannot drink the water they walk miles to get without risking disease and death, and have no choice but to fry in the heat and shiver in the cold. In other words, the world is full of people who live under conditions of discomfort or environmental disaster that, for us, are only projections of some distant past or dreadful future. Yet far more attention was paid at the Rio Earth Summit to a treaty on a speculative concern—global warming—than to increased aid for improvement of water supplies. Millions—hundreds of millions—lack ready access to the most basic drugs we take for granted, yet "biodiversity" becomes a hotly contested issue, in part because of the prospects for, and profits from, new and exotic pharmaceuticals.

I am not suggesting that there is anything arbitrary about what we call a problem. Yet problems do not announce themselves. For ages nobody thought that infant mortality was a problem; it was a fact of life, part of the human condition. It became a problem only when people began to imagine that things didn't have to be that way, and when they gained the power to change them. Gravity, on the other hand, is *still* not a problem; no one seriously anticipates doing anything about it. Until very recently the fact that an asteroid or comet could collide with the earth was simply a fact of life well known to astronomers and geophysicists. Now it is being taken up by experts and popularizers as a problem requiring public action.[28]

All "problems" are situations that become unsatisfactory when we begin to think that a better alternative is possible. The task of the popularizers is thus to call attention to situations and suggest how and why they should be changed, thus creating a problem. To do so, they need more than science; they need some "vision of how we want the world to be,"[29] some ideal against which the present is found wanting.

Consider urban air pollution. How did the popularizers take the existence of certain substances in the air, a fact that can be ascertained by science, and turn it into a problem that now "everyone agrees" we should do something about? Are those substances a problem because they threaten human health or the health of other living beings? Because they might harm everyone, or because they are bad for some already weakened by disease? Is smog a problem because of a hubristic modification of a God-given atmosphere? Is it a problem because of the aesthetic revulsion it so often creates? Or do we want our grandchildren to be able to see the great spectacle of the city laid out before us that is now only visible on a "good day"?

And what is the cause of the problem? Let us assume that it has a great deal to do with cars. Does urban air pollution exist because we have too many people driving too may cars, too many people altogether, too many badly designed cars, or a badly designed transportation system that puts too much reliance on cars? Is it caused by a dangerous individualism that makes us like cars in the first place? By industries that seek profit at the expense of the environment? Or by industries that are behaving rationally, given that they are allowed to treat the environment as a commons, rather than having to internalize the costs of pollution? Perhaps the problem is that we have cars and industry at all.

In each case, a different goal or end point of policy is suggested by the different understanding of the problem. It's not enough to say we want clean air, or even only cleaner air. If the problem is too many people, we would want population reduction policies. If it is badly designed cars, we need technological regulation. If we want to protect human health, we would focus on some kinds of pollution before others; if we want a pristine atmosphere, we need to take on everything at once. To say we all want cleaner air does not tell us what that means and how much change is required, nor when we want it and at what cost, nor how to weigh this goal against others—all issues that actually define policies.

Are all these considerations just quibbles? Why not just say, "All of the above"? Perhaps it all comes down to a feeling that something is terribly wrong, and that we delay making it right at our peril. Such vague but deeply felt dissatisfactions are precisely the sentiments that leave us vulnerable to the extremes, for these tend to offer the simplest explanations of our fears, and the greatest hopes for overcoming them.

So despite the fact that the influence and public legitimacy of environmentalism is connected with that of modern natural science, this link does not tell the whole story. If environmentalism's hope of avoiding the divisions and excesses of the temperance movement is founded there, it has been building on sand.

The first indication of the failure of science to provide a unified perspective from which to view environmental problems is the increasingly open secret that many environmental laws and regulations have only the slimmest scientific foundation. The situation for federal regulation is typical. In May 1991, EPA Administrator William K. Reilly commissioned a four-member panel to examine how his agency uses scientific data in its decisions about environmental policies. The result was a report highly critical of the EPA for failing to take the appropriate science into account, and for failing to employ the best scientists. In other words, while there is widespread agreement that the best available science should inform environmental policy, the EPA is weak in its ability to generate or even use such information. Reilly vowed to change all that by reorganization and special efforts to attract better scientists to the agency.[30]

This finding would come as no surprise to the EPA's more perceptive critics,[31] nor is it a weakness that the agency itself has only just been made aware of. As early as 1985 then EPA Administrator Ruckelshaus was admitting that EPA science was inadequate and promising improvements.[32] This admission is particularly ironic, since as the agency's first administrator he turned the EPA away from making scientific research the foundation for its policy recommendations.[33]

Better science will take the EPA only so far. For whatever aspiration *science* may have to speak with one voice about the natural world, *scientists* show a marked tendency to disagree—a propensity that is more to their credit than anything else, since it is out of such past disagreements that increasingly fruitful understandings of nature have always developed. This propensity is no less present in the specialties relevant to environmental questions than it is in any other branch of the sciences. How could it not be, given the scope of scientific concerns comprehended by "environmental issues," ranging from cell biology to global meteorology? The methods of science, properly understood and rigorously adhered to, may be our best hope for eventually coming to grips with some of the problems environmentalism has brought to light. But at present we can have no assurances that the results of specific research programs will decisively define or solve a given environmental problem.

Nor could it, for it is not the business of science to generate or choose among ideals that describe how we want the world to be. Such visions of a good life are not mere academic abstractions; they are central to environmental debate, as witnessed by the existence of environmental sectarianism. "Radical" groups like Earth First! and Greenpeace exist because (once radical) groups like Friends of the Earth no longer "go far enough"; Friends of the Earth is itself an offshoot of the once-fringe Sierra Club, while the Audubon Society is so much a part of the establishment as to be viewed by some as part of the problem. Some of these organizations can and do cooperate despite their differences. But because they have some very different "visions" of how the world should be, they are fragmented in a way that keeps open the tendency to move to the extreme that ultimately discredited the temperance cause.

CREATING THE CAUSE

Environmentalism, no less than the temperance movement, requires those who can rouse people to join the fight. The necessary ideas about how the world should be rarely, if ever, fall ready-made from heaven. It is usually given to only a few human beings to set the agenda, tell us what we're doing wrong and how to right it, tear the veil from our eyes, and move us to act. Such are the popular environmentalist writers whose skill at presenting the environmental message in a powerful and accessible way makes them the key to the success of their movement. Harriet Beecher Stowe may not have been the most profound thinker of the Abolition movement, but she moved people to sympathy with the cause in a way that few others could. Martin Luther King, Jr., may have borrowed from a variety of sources in his writings and speeches, but those sources lacked in themselves the clear and brilliant passion that King achieved for them. Environmentalism too requires those who can provide the clarion calls and dark warnings, and it has such people in authors like Rachel Carson, Paul Ehrlich, Barry Commoner, and others we will examine.

These are the figures who educate and activate the small army of lawyers, doctors, scientists, managers, and sundry other professionals who lead, staff, and fill the membership rolls of the hundreds of environmental organizations that exist in the United States. It is the popularizers who provide the basis for the studies, films, and news releases, lawsuits and lobbying, testimony and policy recommendations. Even "grass roots" social movements do not magically spring up of their own accord one fine day. Somebody has to activate the public so that they will help buy property; arrange marches, demonstrations, and various other media events; and solicit funds for all of the above.[34]

Environmental popularizers fill so many functions it is difficult to find one word that adequately characterizes them. They act as scientific researchers, radical politicians, moral prophets, aesthetic judges, social critics, historical analysts, technical experts, and prognosticators about anything and everything. But whatever they are describing, criticizing, or proposing, the discussions must share one characteristic: they must be popular. For each great environmentalist author there may be hundreds of experts who know more about a given subject, or have thought and written more profoundly about it. But they do not bring to that subject the same accessibility and sense of urgency.

What makes a popularizer? The impression the public would get from, say, a book review or a talk-show interview is something like the following. In the course of research or in observing the work of colleagues, the author becomes increasingly aware of the importance of some neglected issue or problem. But this problem typically requires him to transcend "narrow, disciplinary boundaries" and cover ground well outside of his particular expertise. Public spiritedness combined with the scientific conscience leads him to take this risk and bring the matter to the attention of fellow citizens. This outline can be followed in a book or an article, in testimony before a congressional committee—just about anywhere but in the various forums in which scientists speak to each other using the strict canons of method, evidence, and inference that are the backbone of scientific research and self-scrutiny.

The general form of such a popularizing effort is pretty well established. Too long we have been able to ignore . . . problem X, but in an increasingly complicated and interdependent world, that is no longer possible. The bad effects of our ignorance or complacency are evident anytime we see . . . this or that situation. But now that science has finally begun to reach an understanding of problem X, we no longer need to tolerate these potentially dire consequences. Whereas in the past problem X was mistakenly thought to be caused by . . . something or other—or indeed, not even appreciated for the evil it is—recent discoveries in . . . this branch of science strongly suggest that it is really caused by . . . whatever it turns out to be. Thus we have an unprecedented opportunity to do something about problem X. While as a scientist I don't claim to be an expert in law (or government, or economics, or social science), it seems to me that we could solve this problem if only the government and the people would work together to do . . . something. If we don't act now, we will certainly face a more difficult situation in the future.

An alternate form goes something like the following. Human beings have for ages pondered the meaning of . . . moral or metaphysical problem Y. Recent advances in the sciences have exciting new possibilities for throwing light on this age-old conundrum. These advances are . . . whatever they are. Their implications for how we understand ourselves and the world around us are startling. Philosophers and moralists have always said . . . this about problem Y, but now we can see that really we must understand it to be . . . that. So a whole new kind of ethics or politics or world view will clearly be required, now that this new scientific understanding of problem Y is available to us.

The ease with which the popularizers' efforts can be parodied does not one whit diminish their importance. Contemporary environmentalism would not exist without them. Any society requires an authoritative public voice that can explain the world and how we fit into it. To see just how much the science that has been brought to the fore by environmental popularizers imbues our way of looking at the world, it is helpful to recall the power once held by an alternative authority. Stendhal found nineteenth-century Italian peasants so molded by Catholicism that "nothing occurs in nature without a miracle. Hail is invariably meant to punish a neighbor who has neglected to bedeck with flowers the cross that stands at the corner of his field. A flood is a warning from above, intended to bring a whole countryside back on the right path. Should a young girl die of fever in the middle of August, it is a chastisement for her love affairs. The curate is careful to say so to each of his parishioners."[35] We, of course, know better. A drought or heat wave is a precursor of global warming. Premature death or disability points to environmental contamination. A change in a species' numbers is caused by some human act. Scientist popularizers are careful to tell us so.

If my own students and members of the public I talk to are any indication, the popularizers have reached what is perhaps the highest possible peak of achievement. When asked what my book is about, I usually list the authors I am discussing; I am normally met with blank stares except perhaps when I mention Rachel Carson. But in any discussion of an environmental question, it's only a matter of time before someone mentions "limits to growth," "small is beautiful," "everything is connected to everything else," or like notions. The popularizers' ideas have *become* commonsense categories, detached from any knowledge of their origins.

PASSIONS AND POLITICS

There is nothing wrong with attempting to make the often difficult and complex findings of science available to a wider audience; much about our form of government calls for it. Nevertheless, the environmental popularizers' deficiencies illustrate perfectly the superficial and profound weaknesses of the scientific reed.

Their deficiencies are more often remarked upon to forgive than condemn. They occur when the popularizer presents a one-sided picture and hides important scientific disagreements on issues relevant to environmental quality. The zeal to draw firm conclusions from the results of scientific research frequently prompts speculative matters to be left out or presented with greater authority than they deserve. The partisanship implicit in these failures is most often excused by the originality of the author's perspective on the subject or a passionate commitment to do good. How could one regret the "minor" obfuscations that might arise from such noble impulses?

But using one-sided and incomplete accounts of the state of scientific knowledge has led to projections, predictions, warnings, and sundry essays into the future that, not surprisingly, have been falsified by events. No one knows what the future may hold. But reports that Lake Erie and the oceans would be dead by now were surely greatly exaggerated. The United States is wracked neither by food riots nor a great epidemic of pesticide-induced cancers. Birds continue to sing in the mornings, and they do not have to face the rigors of either a man-made ice age or of a global warming caused by the heat of increased energy production and consumption. With what confidence should we look upon the projected horrors of global warming, rain forest destruction, or toxic waste, given the record of the past?

This failure of prophecy may be an intellectual weakness, yet prophecy continues because it provides the popularizers a profound rhetorical strength: it releases the power of both fear and hope.[36] The central role these sentiments can be made to play in political rhetoric has long been understood. Arousing fear, though, is not always easy. Even as far back as Aristotle it was observed that we fear things less the more distant they are. Hence when Churchill sought to rouse the British, he brought the Germans to the beaches, landing grounds, fields, streets, and hills of "our island." So, too, to arouse fears the popularizers have to present pictures of imminent calamities that could befall their relatively comfortable and well-off readers. Environmental disasters like endemic water-borne disease due to inadequate sewage treatment in the Third World do not fit this category. The prospect of my getting skin cancer due to ozone depletion does. Oil fires were a major story during the Gulf War, until word got out that their pollution would not be felt in the United States. Now that there is a possibility that they caused longer-term health problems for service personnel, we will doubtless see attention returning to them. Without such immediacy, one could only arouse a sentiment like compassion, which is not so strong as fear, and even by some accounts environmentally problematic.

Fear's counterpart is hope, the "comforter in danger."[37] The popularizers arouse hope when they supply vague and rosy pictures of future happiness, if we do whatever is called for to avoid disaster. If we limit population, says one, we can have "Cadillacs, symphony orchestras, wooded wilderness." If we have the right values, says another, we can feed and shelter all humanity on a healthy earth. Having been threatened with pictures of the multitude of disorders that would result from environmental collapse, we are soothed with glimpses of harmony, peace, and plenty that make even the present—not yet the worst state of affairs—look hellish. How much more, then, does the possibility of having our heart's desire "if only" give us something to fear if we fail to act as we are told?

Thus hopes and fears, the ecological disaster of the week, and the promise of environmental perfection are crucial components of the success of environmentalism and the rhetoric of its popularizers. The risk that some few members of the public may become cynical in the face of such rhetoric and start muttering about Chicken Little appears to be worth running, if only because in comparison with the widespread, visceral power of hope and fear, cynicism is a weak and effete sentiment. While it is a useful corrective to know just how often such fears prove unfounded, to expect therefore that such prognosticating will not have an impact the next time around is to think that we can overcome our propensities to fear and hope. Yesterday we were supposed to be worried about airborne particulates, today it is CFCs or carbon dioxide. Although no doubt part of the explanation of such things would have to include love of novelty, fickleness, and the perversity of public and/or elite opinion, this unwillingness to be satisfied is also a sign of the passions that environmentalism depends on. The scientific particulars of global warming, for example, and the policies that might be implemented to address it are controversial, obscure, technical, and dry to all but the scientist or "policy wonk." But the fear that we are going to destroy the earth, and the hopes for a new order of things that we would need to prevent this destruction, can excite interest and passion. Interest and passion are powerful motives for action. Long after people have forgotten the scientific details of what produces smog, they will remember that it exists because of the exploitation of the environment by capitalism, or because of the inability of liberal political institutions to make coherent policy, or because we have chosen to develop the wrong kind of technology.

Such explanations bring us to the second characteristic defect of the popularizers. Even were we to assume a meticulous presentation of the state of scientific knowledge about an environmental issue, it is a rare popularizer indeed who knows how to move from there to a prescription for public policy or private efforts. The popularizer, to turn a fact into a problem, must have some vision of how the world should be that the fact does not fit. But while many of them recognize that this part of their project is important and confidently call for new values and new social systems, the particulars are rarely well thought through. As a result, the central place of politics and morals in the popularizers' thought has not been adequately appreciated. The picture of their thinking that results from missing this point and focusing only on science or common sense is rather like the understanding of human life that can be gained by an autopsy. You can achieve a certain knowledge of the parts and their relationships, but the animating character is lost.

Are we asking too much of popularizers to expect them to be both scientifically accurate and fully cognizant of the moral and political implications and underpinnings of their enterprise? The request might be unreasonable were it not for the fact that they themselves introduce the subject and call for changes in ethical belief or political institutions with abandon. The problem is not that they attempt criticism in this realm. The problem is the pronounced tendency for the ideals described to be at best utopian and at worst totalitarian in character.[38]

Temperance expected widespread social and economic transformations from a radical change in *one* kind of behavior. To that extent, environmentalism seems the less utopian of the two movements; it expects a similarly sweeping transformation from radical changes in *many* kinds of behavior. Yet this many-sided project pushes it toward totalitarian thinking, as it works "to set a new agenda for life on earth," Friends of the Earth's task for the Rio Summit.[39]

That is a tall order for beings who (as I once heard a TV minister describe us) cannot even organize our sock drawers. But how could it be otherwise? The prohibitionists could only threaten individual damnation, family destruction, or at (worldly) worst, social decay. Environmental popularizers have made the price of failing to change our ways nothing less than the destruction of human life— perhaps most life—on earth. The scope of the means must be total, to match the scope and urgency of the end. Hence we see global schemes of economic and political control, sweeping revisions of value structures, vast increases in the powers of government. Building a sewage treatment plant is not nearly as interesting.

The charge that environmentalism has a utopian strain has been heard with increasing frequency over the years. Neither is it a charge all environmentalists would reject; for some, "utopian" has a decidedly positive connotation. But for the critics, "utopian" is too often shorthand for "I don't think it will work" (i.e., lack of imagination), and "it's against human nature" (i.e., my opinions about what people want). For the advocates, it seems to mean something like "creative."

In what follows, "utopian" thinking should be understood to have two characteristics. In the first place, it suggests a goal that *by the admission of its advocates* requires fundamental changes in or destruction of present human relationships, institutions, and ways of life. One could think the change justified or unjustified and, so far, admit the possibility of utopianism. But in the second place, "utopian" means that the thinking in question contains internal contradictions or conflicts—known or unknown to its author—that would make it impossible or unlikely for it ever to come into being, or accomplish its end. This usage returns us to the literal Greek meaning of the term: no place. To say something is utopian is to point out that the purposes it tries to achieve are in some way at odds with one another. In this respect, there is a frequent failure among the popularizers. While nearly all profess some concern for freedom, the thoroughgoing reforms they propose are most likely to involve powerful, centralized, and intrusive institutions of governance either at the global level or within individual societies.

Even after the welcome demise of so many totalitarian governments, the word "totalitarian" must be used with caution. The following characterization would probably be relatively uncontroversial: totalitarians see no obstacles in principle or practice to the achievement of forms of human life that conform to the model of an organic whole. In such a whole, the nature and functioning of the parts are determined by their place within the larger entity; they have their life by being parts of that entity. Totalitarians believe that human social, political, and economic arrangements can and should have a like unity of purpose.

To say that some environmental popularizers have a totalitarian vision is not to suggest that environmentalism is some leftist conspiracy, or a form of communism, fascism, or national socialism. Still less am I suggesting that the many good-hearted people who adhere in so many different ways to the cause of environmentalism are a cadre bent on the destruction of freedom. But totalitarianism obviously has great attraction in our time, with its promise to explain, organize, and unify lives that often appear to be meaningless and out of control. The problem is not only that the well intentioned and moderate if they are incautious can be used by the extremes, but also that totalitarianism seems to be an ongoing temptation that like most serious temptations, it is perfectly consistent with good intentions.

Americans consider themselves a moderate people, not given to ideological excess. To the many decent citizens whose environmentalism consists of cleaning up waste along a riverbank, taking the bus instead of driving, faithfully recycling whatever they can, or caring about the fate of the parks they hike and camp in, the portrait of crusading utopian moralism just painted will probably not be immediately familiar. We need to look again. The lessons from the temperance movement about how easily prudent moderation and moderate prudence can be abused by extremes should not be forgotten. Those who want genuine moderation can't know why they don't "buy" the whole agenda, unless they know exactly what it is.

The Plan of This Book

This overview of the role of the popularizer suggests how environmentalism, no less than the temperance movement, is intimately bound up with normative judgments about ethics and politics, about the ways the existing world fails to live up to some ideal. Its ultimate reliance on a normative vision deepens the significance of the political role of the popularizer in a liberal democracy. Since the popularizers are dealing with what are fundamentally political and moral questions, they must be regarded as political educators, whose diagnosis of our environmental situation creates important expectations about the kind of world we should want to live in.

In the first three chapters of the book, we look at some of the most influential environmental popularizers of the past three decades: Rachel Carson, Barry Commoner, Paul Ehrlich, Garrett Hardin, E. F. Schumacher, and the Club of Rome. To see how that reputation arises, we will examine how their books were received.

To be a popularizer, a popularizer must be popular. Of particular interest will be the source of their authority, the moral and political principles that animate their work and engender zeal in their followers. In the course of this examination of key popularizers, we will see how a variety of "schools" of environmental thought have come into existence, as science and politics combine to produce partisan positions.

Each chapter pairs a very popular author who may be less aware of the normative ramifications of his or her thinking, with one who provides the missing elements in a more self-conscious way. Chapter 1 begins with Rachel Carson, who need take second place to none in her ability to move her readers. It is Barry Commoner, however, who supplies a more complete account of the technological optimism and political centralization that remains implicit in *Silent Spring*. Chapter 2 takes up Paul Ehrlich, who likewise thrills his readers with the terrors of overpopulation, but we then turn to Garrett Hardin, because he has given more thought to the moral principles that would be needed to justify radical reductions in population. Chapter 3 opens with a look at *The Limits to Growth*, almost certainly the most popular and influential book ever written by a computer, but proceeds to E. F. Schumacher, who has given thought to the political institutions and ethical ideals that would justify the now popular vision of "sustainable development" to which *Limits* pointed.

Schumacher is a transitional figure, for his influence elevated the status of moral and political concerns to a new level of sophistication. In so doing, he helped set the stage for the rise of another kind of popularizer of environmental issues, the environmental moralist. These authors bring environmentalism to a near perfect likeness with the moralism of the temperance movement. Chapter 4 examines the movement called deep ecology as the "cutting edge" of this tendency, focusing on the work of its founder, Arne Naess. His project has been to develop common ground for different environmental sects, welding together a worldwide party of moral reform.

For the moment, deep ecology is the "radical" fringe of environmental thought, just as Carson, Ehrlich, or any of those studied here would once have deserved that title. The fact that deep ecology is now regarded as "extreme" is no indication that it is not the future of environmentalism. Progressive thought practically requires that today's extreme be tomorrow's moderation. Few mainstream "conservationists" would have imagined in 1960 that such future as their movement had was to be found in "environmentalism."

No look at the passions aroused by the environmental popularizers would be complete without consideration of those who have opposed and criticized the movement. Chapter 5 examines some of these writers but suggests that they have by and large missed the real moral and political sources of environmental enthusiasm, and thus failed to provoke a useful debate about environmental issues. The green crusaders have begged the most serious questions, and their critics have allowed them to get away with it. It is time that all sides acknowledge that questions about how to lead our lives should be the beginning of our concern about the environment.

Brightest Heaven of Invention

It is a mark of a mean capacity to spend much time on the things which concern the body.

Epictctus, *Enchiridion* XLI[1]

. . . it is possible to reach knowledge that will be of much utility in this life . . . and so make ourselves the masters and possessors of nature. This would not only be desirable to enable us to enjoy the fruits of agriculture and all the wealth of the earth without labor, but even so in conserving health, the principal good and the basis of all other goods in this life.

Descartes, *Discourse on Method* Part Six[2]

SHADOWY BEGINNINGS

Poisoning, with its potential for subtle, drawn-out, or excruciating and convulsive death, is, murder mysteries would have us believe, the method of choice for intelligent killers bent on revenge. What is more calculatingly deceptive than the gambit that conceals poison in a favorite treat of the victim? To think that some slight but familiar enjoyment hides so great an evil touches something deep. Fear of poisoning seems as universal as fear of death, yet it is more likely to come out in some circumstances than in others. People in battle or facing imminent threats like famine or disease do not generally fear poison, fast or slow. One fears poison most when conditions are most favorable to the poisoner (i.e., when there is a certain regularity, sufficiency, and leisure in life). Speaking metaphorically, we can say that the evildoer has to be able to purchase the Turkish delight, have time to spike it, and wait patiently, knowing that it will be consumed.

A comfortable middle class, therefore, is likely to be particularly susceptible to fear of poison, just as it will be the main consumer of the mystery stories that provide the vicarious thrill of that fear. And that brings us to an unacknowledged master of the murder mystery, Rachel Carson.

Those who commend Rachel Carson and those who condemn her agree that it is impossible to conceive of today's environmental crusade without her best-selling *Silent Spring* (1962).[3] As her editor and biographer, Paul Brooks, wrote, it is "one of those rare books that change the course of history—not through incitement to war or violent revolution, but by altering the direction of man's thinking."[4] But the precise nature of her contribution is not easy to pin down. Was it her literary ability to evoke a sense of wonder at the beautiful complexities of nature? Yet such nature writing was a well-established and popular American genre since long before her best-selling *The Sea Around Us* (1951),[5] let alone *Silent Spring*. Was she the first to notice the problematic side of pesticide use? In fact, *Silent Spring* involved no original research but was a compendium of over ten years of ongoing investigations by scientists and researchers. Was it her fanatical attacks on DDT and modern chemical technology that set the tone for the subsequent excesses of environmental fearmongering? Yet she acknowledged the need for chemical insect control, making her position significantly more moderate than many who came after her. Was it by promoting regulation of pesticides that Carson left her mark? A 1962 government study was prompted by *Silent Spring*; it acknowledged that until the publication of that work, "people were generally unaware of the toxicity of pesticides."[6] But government regulation of pesticides was not, in fact, new.

By her own admission, Carson was not a likely crusader: "once in a lifetime, she remarked, was enough."[7] By all accounts an intensely private person, she was evidently a fine friend to those who got to know her, in whom she inspired intense love and loyalty for her combination of intelligence and reserve with "zest and humor."[8] Born May 27, 1907, in Springdale, Pennsylvania, she grew up on a farm and showed an early interest in writing. She intended to pursue that career, but while attending what is now Chatham College in Pittsburgh, she developed her interest in biology and graduated in 1928 with a degree in zoology. There followed graduate work at Johns Hopkins, where Carson taught summer school in addition to receiving her M.A. in 1932. She also taught at the University of Maryland and spent several summers at the Marine Biological Laboratory at Woods Hole. But she kept up her writing, doing science features for the Baltimore *Sunday Sun*.

In 1936 Carson began her work in government that continued until her success as a writer allowed her to resign in 1952. At the Bureau of Fisheries (now the Fish and Wildlife Service) she started out as a scriptwriter and became editor in chief of their publications in 1949. Meanwhile, she continued free-lance writing, which led to her first book, *Under the Sea Wind* (1941).[9] Although a critical success, the book sold well only after her reputation was established with her second, and best-selling, book, *The Sea Around Us*. First serialized in *The New Yorker*, the book was in first place on the *New York Times* best-seller list for 39 weeks, and on the list for 86 weeks in all.[10] It was joined by a reissued *Under the Sea Wind*.

There followed another best-seller—*The Edge of the Sea* (1955)[11]—before *Silent Spring* came out in the fall of 1962, much of it having already been serialized in *The New Yorker*. From the very first it generated passionate controversy, and the impact of the book's message, as well as that controversy, continues to this day.

Silent Spring takes its name from the book's first chapter, in which Carson presents "A Fable for Tomorrow." An "evil spell" settles over a once beautiful and vibrant rural community; animals and human beings sicken and die, vegetation withers, livestock can no longer reproduce, there is no morning bird song. We have a mystery—"What has already silenced the voices of spring in countless towns in America? This book is an attempt to explain." But like any dramatic author, Carson has already foreshadowed the solution to the mystery in the fable. "No witchcraft, no enemy action had silenced the rebirth of new life in this stricken world. The people had done it themselves."[12]

The central theme of *Silent Spring* is that the thoughtless use of insecticides and herbicides (Carson called them "biocides," for she saw them as indiscriminate destroyers of life) at least threatens the health of nature and humanity, and possibly puts life on earth itself in jeopardy. These miracles of modern science are systematically poisoning us, interfering with reproduction, and causing cancer. Even in the unlikely event that we do not come into much direct contact with these dangerous substances, Carson notes, they spread throughout the ecosystem, destroying life as they go and upsetting the balance of nature. While much of the power of the book, for all the facts and footnotes, depends on arousing fear at this threat of being poisoned, it is a two-pronged attack: direct threats to our health, and threats to the environment on which all life depends. Within this context, Carson conveys many of the teachings that have become staples of environmental arguments: about the balance of nature, the interconnections that make up ecosystems, the role of genetics in disease, and the subtle danger of small doses of toxins over a long period of time.

If arousing the fear of being directly poisoned could be called the "low road" taken by *Silent Spring*, then the vision of ecological fitness and a moral reevaluation of our relationship to nature is the "high road." But the ease with which Carson's brilliant writing allows the reader to travel down these paths also conceals pitfalls.

Both cases depend on seriously flawed arguments. The result is that what Carson is against turns out to be much clearer than what she is for.

CHALLENGE AND RESPONSE

Carson admits at the beginning of *Silent Spring* that there is an "insect problem" in need of "control." She makes quite clear that it was not her "contention that chemical pesticides must never be used."[13] Instead, she says, she seeks to provide more knowledge of the harm they can do and spur further research into their effects. She wants their use to be based on "realities" and not "mythical situations."[14]

Given the insidious effects Carson believes that even small doses of pesticides produce, and the way they spread, and the terrible toll they take on innocent animal life, it is understandable if by the end of the book, the reader has quite forgotten this opening admission. Perhaps she makes it only as the price of being heard, or because of the already "irrecoverable" and "irreversible" "contamination of air, earth, rivers, and sea with dangerous and even lethal materials."[15]

Yet Carson is quite enthusiastic about some methods for insect control; she sees great promise in "biological" techniques like the use of natural predators, lures, repellents, or the release of great numbers of sterilized males.[16] However problematic it might be to make any sharp distinction these days between "biological" and "chemical," it seems that Carson does not believe that nature is in all respects something we must let stand in whatever form it comes to us. She is, for example, against the wholesale application of herbicides to control plant growth at roadsides, but she is not against selective spraying to keep down large, woody plants and trees.[17] She is for the use of radiation to produce sterile male insects as a means of pest control, even though when she wants to foster our fear of poison, she likens the effects of pesticides to the effects of radiation.[18]

It seems Carson wants to strike *some* kind of balance on the question of pesticides, and the larger question of our relationship to nature, but the character of that balance, and the elements that enter into it, are not immediately clear. The scientists who developed the pesticides Carson excoriates did not set out to create "biocides." Indeed, part of the impetus for their creation was a search for more specific poisons for use against pests. Whatever these scientists' extreme expectations about their ability to eliminate those pests,[19] their aim of providing a safe and secure food supply is not, it would seem, one that Carson objects to. Why did they go wrong—or more to the point, why have they failed to change direction? Carson summarizes the situation as she prepares to solve the mystery of who is poisoning us:

> Who has made the decision that sets in motion these chains of poisonings, this ever-widening wave of death that spreads out, like ripples when a pebble is dropped into a still pond? Who has placed in one pan of the scales the leaves that might have been eaten by the beetles and in the other the pitiful heaps of many-hued feathers, the lifeless remains of the birds that fell before the unselective bludgeon of insecticidal poisons? Who has decided—who has the *right* to decide—for the countless legions of people who were not consulted that the supreme value is a world without insects, even though it be also a sterile world ungraced by the curving wing of a bird in flight?[20]

The same thing keeps biocides on the market and produces scientists willing to develop and defend them: big business profits. Carson speaks of "an era dominated by industry, in which the right to make a dollar at whatever cost is seldom challenged."[21] Furthermore, "major chemical companies" are deeply involved in supplying funds to universities for pesticide research; "certain outstanding entomologists" support pesticides because they dare not "bite the hand that literally feeds them."[22] Having thus "poisoned the well" as regards her potential critics, Carson continued to put great weight on this ad hominem argument when they became her actual critics after the book was published.[23]

To deal with such problems, Carson speaks of increased government regulation of pesticide use, establishing zero-tolerances for pesticide residues in food, and substitution of relatively safer for more dangerous pesticides.[24] By implication, she also seems to believe that private funding of scientific research at universities should be limited. But such measures would clearly be only makeshift. *Silent Spring* provides numerous examples of government regulatory agencies and researchers being part of the problem, not the solution.[25] No merely institutional or legal changes could be assured of providing the safer pest control Carson advocates, so long as the basic outlook of those who hold the offices and do the research does not change.

It is for this reason that Carson ultimately calls for a moral revaluation of our relationship with nature. It is widely and not unreasonably believed that Carson should be credited with bringing the public to understand nature in terms of ecology, food chains, the "web of life," and the "balance of nature," thus promoting greater respect for nature and more cautious interventions in it.[26] Indeed, this accomplishment reveals the moral vision that plays so prominent a role in her work, about which more shortly.

Whether they liked it or not, little of Carson's frightening message was lost on readers of the book. *Silent Spring*, wrote the noted anthropologist Loren Eisley in *Saturday Review*, is Rachel Carson's "account of those floods of insecticides and well-intentioned protective devices which have indiscriminantly slaughtered our wildlife of both forest and stream. Such ill-considered activities break the necessary food chains of nature and destroy the livelihoods of creatures not even directly affected by the pesticides."[27] Her book, added the *New York Times Book Review* in an essay aptly titled "There's Poison All Around," "is a cry to the reading public to help curb private and public programs which by use of poisons will end by destroying life on earth."[28] From the start, sympathetic reviews such as *Christian Century*'s "Elixirs of Death" have pictured Carson as having made her case on the basis of "impeccable" scientific credentials.[29] "[S]he is no hysterical Cassandra," noted *Commonweal* in "Varieties of Poison,"[30] but for all that *Christian Century* correctly noted that she had produced "a shocking and frightening book."[31]

Those who praised the book were often quite open about its essentially polemical character: "No one is in a better position than Miss Carson to arouse the indignation of the public," noted *The Nation*.[32] While Lamont Cole, writing in *Scientific American*, was "glad this provocative book has been written," he admitted that it was not a "fair and impartial appraisal of all the evidence" but "a highly partisan selection of examples and interpretations that support the author's thesis." This tactic is apparently justified, to his mind, by the fact that "the extreme opposite has been impressed on the public by skilled professional molders of public opinion."[33] Such hostility to the existing business, scientific, and governmental establishment, which is only now showing signs of abating among some environmentalists, created a sense that ecological PR needs to fight business PR. That, at least, is what *Commonweal* might have had in mind with this otherwise cryptic lead for its review: "*Silent Spring* represents a major breakthrough in the communications industry."[34]

Praise was not the only thing Carson met with. The book was widely and vociferously criticized as well. Many such responses came more or less directly from the chemical industry she had attacked, and they often matched Carson in the intemperateness of their tone, without her elegance of expression. Monsanto published a parody of the book, called "The Desolate Year," in its house organ, picturing the poverty and disease of a world without pesticides; 5,000 copies were sent to editors and book reviewers around the country.[35] The Nutrition Foundation, a trade group of food and chemical industries, developed a critical and widely distributed "Fact Kit."[36] The Velsicol Chemical Corporation is said to have made efforts to have Houghton Mifflin suppress the book, but that claim is debated.[37]

Carson's critics certainly used some unscientific arguments against her. *Chemical and Engineering News* claimed that she had ignored "the sound appraisals of such responsible, broadly knowledgeable scientists as the President of the National Academy of Sciences, the members of the President's Scientific Advisory Committee, the Presidents of the Rockefeller Foundation and Nutrition Foundation," as if mere arguments from authority would settle the issue.[38] But Carson herself may have invited them by suggesting that scientists who favor present pesticide practices "prostitute their professional work in order to win lucrative research fellowships," as a review in *The American City* put it. "This callous smear of the professional integrity of those who disagree with her is ugly. Miss Carson would be indignant if they countered that she based her writings on what would sell the most books rather than on what is fair and impartial analysis. But one suggestion follows another."[39]

Critics typically accused the book of being one-sided, presenting none of the benefits to health and food production that had been wrought by pesticide use. *Science* argued that the book was not "a judicial review or a balancing of the gains and losses; rather, it is the prosecuting attorney's impassioned plea for action against the use of these new materials which have received such widespread acceptance, acceptance accorded because of the obvious benefits their use has conferred."[40] Carson's attitude toward technology, *Chemical and Engineering News* noted, would mean "disease, epidemics, starvation, misery and suffering incomparable and intolerable to modern man."[41]

Most seriously, Carson was accused of misrepresenting or misunderstanding the evidence she cited. A review in *Archives of Internal Medicine* asserted that *Silent Spring* "as science, is so much hogwash."[42] I have not been able to locate any review that attempted to take up her errors in the presentation of scientific material in any great detail. Still, the general points that are mentioned are far from trivial, such as Carson's assertion that birth-to-death exposure to "dangerous chemicals" is a new phenomenon,[43] or her failure to appreciate that the dose makes the poison.[44] Lamont Cole's generally favorable review treats this question in a very curious way: "Errors of fact are so infrequent, trivial and irrelevant to the main themes that it would be ungallant to dwell on them." He mentions one or two, but more to the point he finds two of Carson's main conceptual foundations highly suspect: her assumption that there is a "balance of nature," and that insects who exhibit resistance to pesticides will turn into super bugs.[45] Other Carson partisans and critics have pointed to different factual errors.[46]

As is so often the case, the controversy was not exactly bad for sales. Houghton Mifflin printed 100,000 copies, editorials and editorial cartoons on both sides appeared in newspapers across the country, the book was selected by Book of the Month Club, and Consumer's Union sponsored a special edition.[47] Within a short time, the book was published in at least 17 countries and 10 languages. Carson, having known since 1960 she was ill with the breast cancer that took her life in 1964, participated selectively but importantly in the intense controversy the book sparked, appearing on TV, testifying before congressional committees, and giving widely reported speeches on the occasion of receiving the awards that showered down on her.

What did this remarkable woman do to inspire such intense emotions and engage the imagination of not only the public at large but of politicians and policymakers? Carson's admirers have had two important insights into her accomplishments. On the one hand, they note that part of the effectiveness of her case was in overcoming scientific specialization so that she could give an overview of the problem posed by the increasing use of pesticides and herbicides.[48] It could be said that before Carson, scientists studied many problems: insecticide problems and herbicide problems, problems of human health effects and livestock health, impacts on this kind of plant or that kind of insect. It is only a slight exaggeration to say that after Carson, the public began to believe there was only one issue: the environmental problem.

In assessing Carson's contribution, her supporters are also on target when they admit that there was little new in *Silent Spring*. Instead, as her friend Shirley A. Biggs put it, "Her role was to put together a diffuse and variable body of data and to shape it into a clear account that would not only educate the public but also reach people in authority."[49] In other words, Carson was a wildly successful popularizer.[50]

SELECTING THE EVIDENCE

As capable as she was of making a clear and moving case, was she as capable of fulfilling the demand on a popularizer for accuracy and truthfulness? This question has been debated heatedly ever since the publication of the book. It is central to understanding how she so powerfully aroused our fear of being poisoned—the "low road" of *Silent Spring*.

Latter-day critics are able to point out that some of Carson's claims have not held up to subsequent research. For example, it is very unlikely that DDT is a carcinogen.[51] Changes of medical or scientific outlook subsequent to the book's publication mean that many parts must now be taken with a grain of salt. But it would hardly be Carson's fault if, having honestly presented the legitimate scientific opinions of her day, those opinions have since been abandoned. Yet *was* her presentation uniformly accurate? Her advocates have been able to take advantage of a characteristic critical blind spot. The main focus has always been on what Carson did *not* say, on her failure to admit the usefulness of pesticides in promoting human health and food production. Thus, despite much huffing and puffing about expert opinion disagreeing with Carson, critics rarely give specific or well-documented instances of where Carson was wrong *in terms of the evidence available to her at the time*. As Shirley Biggs notes, while there is often vague talk of exaggerations and errors, as of 1987 "[w]e at the Rachel Carson Council have yet to be shown a valid example, despite the sketchy state of much of the information available at the time. This accuracy shows the value of her very conservative approach."[52] It justifies calling her " 'the greatest biologist since Darwin' " for the shift in our values and way of understanding the natural world that she helped bring about.[53]

It is beyond the scope of this work to examine all of Carson's sources and how she used them. But a closer look at her treatment of some of the human health effects of pesticides is in order, given the theme of poisoning. This theme was a "no lose" proposition for Carson, since no honest critic could deny that under some circumstances, the "biocides" she was discussing were indeed poisonous. In addition, we may focus on human health effects because, as Carson noted in a letter to Paul Brooks, "As I look over my reference material now, I am impressed by the fact that the evidence on this particular point outweighs by far, in sheer bulk and also significance, any other aspect of the problem."[54]

If the Rachel Carson Council had not yet seen a "valid" case of something not unreasonably called an "error," it is not for want of such examples. It is indeed possible to document material that is misrepresented or used out of context. The result is to make the harm of pesticides seem greater, more certain, or more unprecedented than the original source indicates.

A major theme of Carson's book is that one reason for the "silent spring" of the future is that pesticides obstruct reproduction. The culmination of a lengthy discussion of how DDT interferes with the ability of cells to produce energy is the remark, "Some indication of the possible effect on human beings is seen in medical reports of oligospermia, or reduced production of spermatozoa, among aviation crop dusters applying DDT."[55] Her citation (at the back of the book) is to a 1949 "letter to the Editor" of the *Journal of the American Medical Association* (JAMA).[56]

This short sentence reveals a great deal about Carson's rhetorical skill. While Carson says "reports," the citation is to a single report; because that report cites more than one case, the use of the plural is technically justified even if misleading to someone who does not check her references. Note also that "possible effect" is ambiguous; does it mean an effect that might be caused by DDT or a known effect of DDT (as in "it is possible to contract a cold from a handshake")? Finally, there is an ambiguity about how widespread the observation of oligospermia is. The sentence could imply the results of a large-scale study of crop dusters, but the source is nothing of the sort. It is a letter in the Queries and Minor Notes section of JAMA, where doctors sent in questions for referral to "competent authorities." In this case, a doctor from Phoenix writes to ask whether oligospermia he has noted in three crop dusters could be caused by DDT or its xylene solvent. The answer begins, "Neither xylene nor DDT is known specifically to impair spermatogenesis." It goes on to suggest that "real exposure to xylene" would produce symptoms sure to provoke "medical comment" and that the doctor investigate repeated low-dose exposure to carbon monoxide or pituitary gland malfunction. The answer notes in conclusion that an "adequate exploration" of this case might be "an outstanding contribution," since there is not much clinical data in the area.[57] In other words, the source cited denies the very connection Carson suggests, although with proper scientific caution it would not affirm that DDT could *not* be the cause. But that caution is quite different from Carson's attempt to represent this source as supporting her position that DDT is a "possible" cause of low sperm production.

Carson also discusses neurological effects of DDT exposure on human beings, citing reports by three British scientists who dosed themselves by exposure through the skin. The list of symptoms they experienced included aching limbs and joint pain that was "quite violent at times." Carson goes on parenthetically, "Despite this evidence, several American investigators conducting an experiment with DDT on volunteer subjects dismissed the complaint of headache and 'pain in every bone' as 'obviously of psychoneurotic origin.' "[58] American investigators are thus presented as incompetent and heartless. Note also that "the complaint" is grammatically ambiguous; it could refer to a single complaint that many subjects reported or to a single complaint from one subject. The immediate reference to "volunteer subjects" clearly suggests the former.

The source is a report whose publication in JAMA was authorized by the Council on Pharmacy and Chemistry of the American Medical Association.[59] It studied relatively low doses of DDT given to prisoners over an extended period of time. One of its conclusions was that "During the entire study, no volunteer complained of any symptom or showed, by the tests used, any sign of illness that did not have an easily recognized cause clearly unrelated to exposure to DDT." Further, "The results indicate that a large safety factor is associated with DDT as it now occurs in the general diet."[60] These are two propositions that Carson is entitled to dispute, but she does not so much as mention them. What about the bone and joint pain? Do the researchers draw their conclusions having ignored it? It is worth quoting the source of "the complaint" at length, for it comes from a single individual:

> He had participated for 155 days and had received 138 doses of DDT. He had several complaints, including pain every day in every bone, occasional headache, and tearing of the right eye. He submitted to complete physical and laboratory examination, and all findings were normal. His complaints obviously were of psychoneurotic origin, and even the man himself did not seem to take them seriously.[61]

Thus does Carson manage to misrepresent, and by implication discredit, a report whose conclusions decisively undercut her own.

In other instances, Carson places her sources in a context that radically changes their original meaning. One case can be found in connection with another major example of how we are being poisoned, the carcinogenic properties of pesticides. She argues that pesticides act like radiation in impairing cell division. Leukemia, she notes, is "one of the most common diseases to result from exposure to radiation or to chemicals that imitate radiation." She then discusses how benzene, a common insecticide solvent, "has been recognized in the medical literature for many years as a cause of leukemia."[62] Immediately following, she points out how the "rapidly growing tissues of a child would also afford conditions most suitable for the development of malignant cells." Indeed, Sir Macfarlane Burnet has shown an increasing incidence of early childhood leukemia. "According to this authority, 'The peak between three and four years of age can hardly have any other interpretation than exposure of the young organism to mutagenic stimulus around the time of birth.' "[63] She then continues to discuss the carcinogenic effects of urethane, neither an insecticide nor a solvent but a chemical related to certain herbicides. One would be forgiven for believing, then, that Burnet and Carson have the same kinds of things in mind when they speak of "mutagenic stimulus."

The source here is an essay Burnet published in the *New England Journal of Medicine*, first delivered as a speech at the Harvard School of Public Health in 1958.[64] He documents a rising incidence of leukemia, particularly among children. While he does not doubt radiation can cause leukemia, he also suggests that in the United States, among urban whites, "Only an insignificant portion of the increase is due to ionizing radiation."[65] Hence, he believes, some other mutagenic stimulus must be found, just as Carson quotes him as saying.

Burnet admits he can only speculate about what that stimulus is. What is interesting is just how different his speculations are from Carson's. He argues that since the increase is not seen "in colored persons" in the United States, it seems unlikely that the stimulus is "some all pervading element associated with advancing civilization such as traces of carcinogens in the air from combustion processes of various types."[66]

It is the point of *Silent Spring* that "biocides" are precisely all-pervading elements of advancing civilization. Did this passage, then, give Carson any pause? What did she make of the fact that when Burnet discusses possible sources of "mutagenic chemicals," he talks about increased coffee and tea drinking, cigarette smoking, pharmaceuticals prescribed during pregnancy, and some hitherto unknown by-product from the production of artificial infant formula?[67] None of these sources is fully satisfactory for him; all of them are speculative. But he does not mention pesticides and herbicides at all.

We know what Carson made of this part of Burnet's argument. She suppressed it. She bracketed his point with observations that made it appear that his thinking in the article cited moved in the same direction as her own. Furthermore, Carson claims to know what Burnet only speculates about and attributes that certainty to him as well. But Burnet's open-mindedness is precisely what characterizes the "meticulous" scientists among whose ranks Carson's defenders would like to place her.[68]

Sometimes Carson neglects to tell the whole story in other ways. In making the case for the neurotoxic effects of organic phosphate insecticides, she notes that the "severe damage" they cause to the nervous system would make one expect them to be implicated in "mental disease."[69] A study from Australia supplies her that link, documenting mental illness in 16 individuals with "prolonged exposure" to such insecticides.[70] But Carson neglects to note some important qualifications on this study. The author admits he performed no statistical analysis showing that the apparent correlation between exposure and mental illness was not due to chance. When the author investigated two fruit-growing districts to see if an increase in "mental ill-health" could be found in the field, only 3 of 16 physicians surveyed reported any such increase. Of these, two could support their impression with case records.[71] In short, the study Carson uses to "nail down" her speculations is more speculative than she admits.

Carson does *not* misrepresent *all* her sources. Furthermore, there is no question that pesticides and herbicides can be extremely dangerous to human beings if misused or used carelessly. There would certainly be nothing wrong if Carson wished to disagree with or reinterpret her sources in light of her own understanding of the nature of the "biocide" problem. What is wrong is for her to have failed to do so openly. Of course, there would have been a cost to this kind of honesty. The book would be far less rhetorically powerful if Carson were frequently saying, "So-and-so reports his results that way, but I think they should be interpreted this way." As matters stand, her citations of authorities lead the reader to believe that scientific opinion is consistently on her side. As we have seen, that is not necessarily so. There are indeed "valid" examples of inaccuracies or mistakes to be found in *Silent Spring* and, further, these lapses do not occur at random but fit within a pattern that is necessary for Carson's case to be presented in the most effective and affecting way.

EXIT HUMANITY?

It is evident from Carson's obviously one-sided treatment of the topic—omitting any serious discussion of the benefits of pesticides—and by the less obvious pattern of distortion of her sources that she herself did not think that the facts of the matter spoke entirely for themselves. Since most people do not have to worry about acute pesticide poisoning, the "low road" fear had to be aroused by the presentation of threats whose subtlety makes them seem all the more insidious. That means her information had to be carefully selected and filtered. But there is another filter, the high road of her call for a moral revaluation of our relationship to nature, that Carson's supporters not only do not deny but celebrate. We turn now to that vision.

The idea of a "balance of nature," which Carson is often credited with popularizing, has had great persistence among the general public. Ironically, already in 1962 LaMonte Cole could assert that the balance of nature "is an obsolete concept among ecologists."[72] Nevertheless, one sees in Carson some of the reasoning that makes so many people think there is a delicate and static balance of nature, and that "upsetting" it is a particularly reckless thing to do. At the same time, a look at Carson's own metaphors and examples suggests some of the difficulties and ambiguities of this concept and that Carson herself may not have been clear on just how she wanted human beings to act in relationship to nature.[73]

Following the implications of the concern that we are both poisoners and poisoned, Carson suggests that the balance of nature can no more be ignored than a "man perched on the edge of a cliff" can defy the "law of gravity."[74] In other words, we face a dangerous situation in which the slightest misstep will bring final disaster. After all, it took "eons of time" for life to reach "a state of adjustment and balance with its surroundings" that we see around us.[75] In a moment, it would seem, humanity can disturb this delicate balance. And because "in nature nothing exists alone," such disturbance may be expected to have the most far-reaching consequences.[76]

If everything is connected to everything else in a finely tuned balance, then physically problematic and temporally remote consequences of pesticide use, on which Carson places a good deal of stress, become a plausible substitute for looking at positive immediate consequences such as prevention of epidemics or increased crop yields. The argument that small, repeated doses eventually can have widespread and dangerous consequences also becomes more plausible. Carson must develop this argument because however tragic the acute cases of pesticide poisoning she cites, they were relatively rare and often linked to flagrant misuse.

When nature comes to be seen as a seamless web and a delicate balance, human activity is more easily painted as the violation or destruction of that balance. Instead of a variety of potentially distinct human/nature relationships, each to be judged on its own merits, all interactions come to be viewed in light of the manifold impacts of the most intrusive and disruptive. Thus diverse situations come to be simplified into one "environmental crisis." Looking at the destruction we have shown ourselves capable of causing, we find it hard to see that there is any place for human beings within nature, leading some to wonder whether Carson has created an ideal of nature in which human beings have no place.[77]

Yet this notion of a natural balance of nature is precisely the one that has least ecological support. To her credit, it is not Carson's final word on the topic, however much the emotional force of some of her arguments depends on it. For she also likens the present interaction between humans and nature to the "rumblings of an avalanche."[78] While this image retains the idea that small beginnings can have disastrous and unstoppable consequences, it makes human interventions seems less "unnatural." We are not the only cause of avalanches. Furthermore, nature recovers from avalanches; they are an ongoing aspect of ecosystem change.

Despite her sometime use of static imagery, at other times Carson recognizes that, if we are to speak of a "balance" at all, it is better understood in dynamic terms: "The balance of nature is not a *status quo*; it is fluid, ever shifting, in a constant state of adjustment. Man, too, is part of this balance."[79] Over time, changes, even vast changes, are normal. Species and habitats disappear. Life adjusts to hostile or dangerous situations and takes advantage of favorable conditions.[80]

Might it not be argued, then, that human beings, as participants in this ongoing, dynamic balance, are simply promoting the same kind of changes that are always going on in nature? Why any special concern about our modifications? Carson tries to explain the peculiar danger human actions pose even to the dynamic balance of nature. Human-induced changes, she argues, work much faster than nature normally works on its own.[81] Such speedy changes mean that ecosystems may not have time to adjust to them, and that in turn raises the specter of a dominolike collapse of the system as a whole.

This argument from collapse due to rapid change has proven increasingly popular. It is a staple, for example, with those concerned about the greenhouse effect. They admit that life on earth has flourished during periods even warmer than those they are projecting. But if we were to make a transition to such a warmer world in a mere hundred years, as opposed to hundreds of thousands, there would be no chance for various biota to adjust to the change, with terrible consequences.

Still, we know that natural ecosystems can undergo vast and

rapid changes due to things like volcanoes, earthquakes, fires, floods, and hurricanes, any of which can produce destruction on a scale that dwarfs just about anything humans can do at any speed. The question is, is the effect even of such great changes amplified over time and through space, as the avalanche metaphor suggests? Or does the balance of nature dampen the effects of such disturbances?

Carson is well aware that in fact the avalanche likeness is not entirely appropriate for what human beings are doing to nature. In yet another metaphor, she suggests how the consequences of our actions expand "like ripples when a pebble is dropped into a still pond."[82] But the ripples, even as they widen, have less and less of an impact on the still pond. What may be a tidal wave to the water strider next to the pebble's point of impact is hardly felt by the tadpole near shore. The sudden collapse of the ecosystem surrounding Mt. St. Helens did not cause a dominolike fall of surrounding and dependent systems, in turn spreading out an avalanche of destruction.

Is there any reason to believe that the way humans interact with nature is likely to weaken nature's ability to dampen the impact of our changes to it? Carson believes so, despite her use of the pebble metaphor: "Nature has introduced great variety into the landscape, but man has displayed a passion for simplifying it."[83] This argument is also now well established in environmental thinking. Carson associates what has come to be called "biodiversity" with ecosystem stability. The consequences of human-induced changes become more severe rather than less over time if the net result of those changes is to destabilize ecosystems by simplifying them.

Now, as we will see shortly, Carson is well aware that human activity can also create richer and more complex ecosystems. However, as plausible as the association of diversity and stability might seem, within the discipline of ecology it is not taken quite as a matter of course.[84] If diversity uniformly bred stability, it would be hard to understand how tropical rain forests, widely regarded as the greatest reservoirs of biological diversity, would be as fragile as they are said to be.

Thus, while the fear of poisoning that is the "low road" of *Silent*

Spring is perfectly clear, the "high road," or Carson's attempt to popularize the significance of ecology and the "balance of nature," is less coherent. We began this examination by noting that Carson's advocates celebrate the existence of an informing moral vision in her work. It was not enough for her merely to catalog the various potential or actual dangers posed by the use of pesticides and herbicides. She also sought to provide an overarching lesson that could be learned from those particulars. But if that vision is clouded, how are we to know what to do or refrain from doing?

DOING THE RIGHT THING

Early in the book Carson notes that for the most part, the environment has shaped life on earth, and not vice versa. Over "the whole span of earthly time" the ability of life to modify its surroundings has been "relatively slight"—until humans came along.[85] And only in the last century have human beings gained "significant power" to "alter the nature of [their] world."[86] From this outlook, modern humans appear as a kind of rogue species, an unnatural product of nature. We are back to the edge of the cliff. But later in the book, when Carson discusses soils, we get a different picture. Without soils, neither land plants nor land animals could survive. Yet soils are "in part a creation of life, born of a marvelous interaction of life and nonlife long eons ago."[87] This modification by life of its surroundings hardly seems "relatively slight," since it makes possible the natural world as we know it today. Compared with this accomplishment, it is human intervention that, so far, seems "relatively slight."

Still, Carson might say, it is human beings whose impact has been dangerous to life, rather than creative. For in "less than two decades," synthetic pesticides have become "so thoroughly distributed" that "for the first time in the history of the world, every human being is now subjected to contact with dangerous chemicals, from the moment of conception until death."[88] The implication is that there was a time when the "balance of nature" meant that human beings were not routinely exposed to potentially dangerous substances. Critics have pointed out what nonsense this statement is, since there have always been chemicals in the environment that, in some dose, are dangerous.[89] But more to the point, even Carson herself provides evidence that nature was not simply benign prior to the last two decades, when she talks about pesticides "derived" from naturally occurring substances—some of which she knows to be extremely dangerous.[90] Nature was not a safe place that human actions made dangerous.

Perhaps human beings have used their ingenuity in such a way as to introduce entirely new kinds of dangers into nature. That seems to be the suggestion when Carson talks about "systemic insecticides," chemicals that kill insects by converting "plants or animals into a sort of Medea's robe by making them actually poisonous."[91] Such insecticides produce "a weird world, surpassing the imaginings of the Brothers Grimm . . . where the enchanted forest of the fairy tales has become the poisonous forest where an insect that chews a leaf or sucks the sap of a plant is doomed."[92] Yet in the very next paragraph, Carson admits that the "hint" for such pesticides came from nature itself, where plants defend themselves by the synthesis of substances poisonous to their predators![93] The vision of nature as an "enchanted forest" where such things do not happen is, as Carson says, a "fairy tale"—but this fairy tale forms the basis for her excoriation of systemic insecticides.

Even if the human ability to modify nature is not as radically new as Carson sometimes makes out, even if nature is not "by nature" as safe as Carson sometimes suggests, it might still be true, as we will see Barry Commoner suggest later, that "nature knows best," and that human beings should therefore impose minimally on natural processes, lest the balance of nature be disturbed. Clearly, this lesson is one Carson wants to get across, as the book's epigraph by E. B. White suggests. White laments that the human race "is too ingenious for its own good" in its efforts to "beat" nature "into submission." He hopes that we could accommodate ourselves "to this planet" and view it "appreciatively."[94] Yet we have seen how Carson admits that there is an "insect problem" in need of "control," and that there is a legitimate use of herbicides to control plant growth along highways. *Control* is very different from the *accommodation* White calls for.

The highway-spraying case is quite telling. Here, nature is being controlled not for some essential purpose like food but for creating marginal increases in safety and aesthetics by keeping large plants well back from the road. Such efforts may be important for many reasons, but they hardly represent an "accommodation" to planet earth.

Carson's stand on roadside spraying suggests in another way that nature does not always know best. Wholesale spraying is wrong in part because it destroys wildflowers that make the road beautiful.[95] But surely Carson knew two things about those roadside wildflowers: most of them are there *because* the road exists; many wildflowers do best on disturbed ground, which they take over and colonize. And that in turn is true because a great many North American wildflowers are aliens brought from Europe; they do well in disturbed ground because there they have less competition from native species. Finally, left to itself, the roadside would tend to exhibit ecological succession; the larger, woody plants that she is willing to see sprayed would force out many of the wildflowers that do well on open ground. In other words, in defending roadside wildflowers, Carson is defending a "natural" state that is in three ways a result of human intervention: the importation (accidental or otherwise) of the wildflowers, the building of the road, and the maintenance of conditions suitable for wildflower growth. It thus appears that human beings, while conquering nature, can at the same time *increase* biological diversity.

Carson's case shows how love of nature, which by all accounts she felt deeply, by no means guarantees that one has a clear view of the beloved. Careful writers about Carson have already recognized that her thinking about nature is more complex than at first meets the eye. Her failure to tease out the various strands of that complexity is probably a net rhetorical gain. It makes it possible for there to be "man" and "destruction" on one side of the ledger, and "nature" and "danger" on the other side. Because there is no clear picture of when humans intervene properly in nature, Carson can maintain both her pessimism about a future "where no birds sing" and her optimism that the right science and the right agricultural technology can provide many of the benefits of existing pesticides without their grave costs.

Carson's lack of clarity about humans' relationship to nature is summed up in her view of modern natural science. As much as she must rely on science for the better methods of pest control she wants to see put to work, she condemns its arrogance and seeks a new humility. She says that science must waken to the fact that in dealing with living beings, it is dealing with a world of "pressures and counterpressures . . . surges and recessions."[96] Only by taking this complexity into account will science be able "cautiously" to "guide" such "life forces" into "channels favorable to ourselves."[97]

> The "control of nature" is a phrase conceived in arrogance, born of the Neanderthal age of biology and philosophy, when it was supposed that nature exists for the convenience of man. The concepts and practices of applied entomology for the most part date from that Stone Age of science. It is our alarming misfortune that so primitive a science has armed itself with the most modern and terrible weapons, and that in turning them against the insects it has also turned them against the earth.[98]

Carson's last book is widely seen as an attempt to describe the kind of education children should have to produce the right relationship to nature. The title, *A Sense of Wonder*, already describes the essentials of that outlook.[99] Wonder, as she suggests, is indeed a good thing. But wonder and humility do not have to spring from the same sources as caution, nor would they necessarily have the same outcomes. Wonder is most consistent with a contemplative stance toward nature, a stance Carson clearly had an affinity for. Caution suggests an active stance. To channel nature cautiously is not to give up on control of nature; it is to control it better than we do now, as the slighting references to the stone age of philosophy and science suggest. Yet that age might have had a clearer picture than Carson of the difficulty of reconciling the activist and contemplative requirements she places on a more "modern" perspective.

By now, nothing can detract from *Silent Spring*'s immense contribution to the rise of the green crusade. But as our discussion suggests, it is not a fully coherent or completely worked out line of argument. While critical of the impact of the profit motive on government and science, it presents no complete critique of the American economic and political arrangements that produce such a result. While advocating humility toward nature, it maintains the necessity for human intervention, without fully articulating what constitutes legitimate and illegitimate intervention. While critical of one instantiation of modern science and technology, it relies on another. These tensions are not unique to Carson; we will see them again in others who have advanced the environmental crusade. But these others have paid more attention to the attempt to resolve and explain them; one such attempt, along with its consequences for humans and nature, can be found in the work of Barry Commoner.

SCIENTIFIC BEGINNINGS?

If Rachel Carson is a founding mother, Barry Commoner is a founding father of today's environmentalism. The sheer ubiquity of his writings would suggest such status; author of five books, Commoner has also published in journals and magazines ranging from *Science* to *The New Yorker* to *Field and Stream*. He ran for president on the left-wing Citizen's Party ticket in 1980. By 1991 he had at least 11 honorary degrees, 8 literary or public service awards, and was founder, board member, or adviser to 20 organizations and 5 publications. One hint of his status in environmental circles was revealed when this persistent critic of federal environmental policies received a standing ovation after castigating an audience of Environmental Protection Agency officials.[100]

The son of Russian immigrants, Commoner exemplifies the American dream. Born in 1917 in Brooklyn, he graduated with honors in zoology from Columbia University in 1937. He continued his studies at Harvard University, receiving his doctorate in biology in 1941. His naval service in World War II ended with a stint in Washington, D.C., working for the Senate Military Affairs Committee. There he was active in the passage of the Mahon Act in 1946, which "mandated civilian control of atomic energy and highlighted its peaceful aspects."[101]

Commoner spent most of his teaching career, from 1947 to 1981, at Washington University in St. Louis. He established there the Center for the Biology of Natural Systems (CBNS), which in 1981 moved with him to Queens College. Today the center engages in a variety of studies (e.g., of intensive solid waste recycling, risk assessments for trash-burning incinerators, and evaluation of degradable plastics). Prior to 1980 CBNS operated with some federal funding, but since then it has received none, and the bulk of its work is supported by private foundations and contracts with state or municipal agencies.

While Commoner's early work focused on conventional biological research, already by the mid-1950s his long-standing attachment to progressive causes had brought him to be concerned with radioactive fallout and a nuclear test ban. As the discipline of biology moved in the direction of molecular biology after the discovery of DNA, a transformation Commoner strongly criticized as it was happening, he more and more took on the role of what has been called a "politico-scientist."[102] He was a founder of the St. Louis Committee for Nuclear Information. This "public interest" science organization developed a nationwide baby tooth survey that proved the human ingestion of radioactive fallout nationwide, helping to promote an atmospheric test ban treaty. The organization put out a mimeographed newsletter, titled at first *Information* and then *Nuclear Information*. Its subsequent metamorphoses seem to symbolize Commoner's own development. It became *Scientist and Citizen* in 1964 under the auspices of the Scientists' Institute for Public Information, for which Commoner served on the board of directors. In 1968 it became the well-known glossy magazine *Environment*, put out by the Helen Dwight Reid Foundation. Commoner was on the editorial board until 1984.

The Closing Circle[103] may be Commoner's best-known book, although he was already a noted public figure when it was published in 1971. In its review, *The Economist* could call him "the father of the environmental movement."[104] This book is typical of his approach to environmental problems: a combination of an exposition of general scientific principles, particular case studies of environmental problems, and diagnoses of social, political, or economic sources for these problems. These three parts are usually taken to form an obvious whole. Science examines our relationship with nature and uncovers problems in what we are doing to it. Science also tells us the policies that will avoid these problems. But as we will see, this understanding does not nearly do justice to the argument Commoner is making.

The Closing Circle begins with background information on the biological and ecological bases for life on earth, including the four "laws of ecology." In effect an attempt to systematize Carson's observations, these "laws" have become central to the popular presentation of environmental issues: "everything is connected to everything else," "everything must go somewhere," "nature knows best," and "there is no such thing as a free lunch."[105] Commoner then considers case studies of how human actions that ignore these laws disrupt the essential biological processes. Adopting the Greek fourfold division of elements, he discusses destruction of agricultural land, Los Angeles smog, nuclear testing and fallout, and the pollution of Lake Erie.[106] After presenting and rejecting arguments that these problems are caused either by excessive affluence or population, Commoner presents his own analysis of their source: the search for ever-increasing business profits since World War II.[107] He concludes with some guidance about how ecological imperatives will need to guide our political and economic decision making in the future if we want to prevent the increasing degradation of the planet.

If the argument of *The Closing Circle* is vintage Commoner, so is the way the book was received, with numerous, and nearly always favorable, reviews. It appeared to many to be a breath of fresh air on the environmental scene for a number of reasons. First, there is the question of tone. As Michael Crichton, writing in the *New York Times Book Review* saw it, *Circle* was perhaps "the best book on ecology ever written." Commoner's analysis is "sober, rigorous, and well organized." Furthermore, he does not speak in the prevailing tone of environmentalists: not a "high, thin hysterical shriek, or a deep rumbling anticipation of doom" but rather a tone of "near-detachment and great calm."[108] "Dr. Commoner is a scientist, not an evangelist," as *The New Yorker* put it in its brief notice.[109] "[C]almest, most convincing call to alarm in years," noted *Newsweek*.[110] Even the *Wall Street Journal* had to bow to this sober and reasonable tone: "He takes great care to avoid accusations, hysteria or sermonizing, but in a carefully measured way sets about tightening down his argument, forcing the reader along until at the end he is confronted with . . . some extremely unpleasant realities."[111] "[N]ot a Doomsday book at all," said the daily *New York Times*.[112]

A few reviewers called it differently; they saw fearmongering playing a more central role. *Choice* labeled the book "that type of presentation" where the author is "crying doom."[113] *Bookworld* seemed to *like* the book at least in part for its "fund of scary examples."[114] In another favorable review in *Commonweal*, Victor Ferkiss likewise noted how "Commoner repeats the by-now familiar claims that the world is on the eve of destruction: we have perhaps fifty years before it is too late to turn back—before pollution in its widest sense makes it impossible to sustain large-scale human life on the globe."[115] (*The American Scholar* thought he gave us a "grace period" of only about 25 years before "'serious large-scale catastrophe overtakes us,'"[116] while *The Spectator* thought a strength of the book was that Commoner avoided such prediction and could distinguish between things that "might" happen and those that "will."[117])

Crichton also liked the book because of its gift for presenting scientific information "briefly and clearly and without oversimplification."[118] Here too he was widely echoed. *The Living Wilderness* found Commoner's arguments "fortified by his professional competence as a biologist and ecologist,"[119] while *Publishers Weekly* found the case studies and the chapters on the laws of ecology to be "written with scientific authority and the kind of clarity the lay reader appreciates."[120]

What does this sober, scientific analysis tell us needs to be done? *The New Republic* read a book that said "mere survival will require a political revolution,"[121] while *Natural Resources Journal* commented that "he offers no prescription" for what is to be done, only a diagnosis.[122] Many reviews were simply silent on Commoner's politics. As among these options, *Library Journal* offered a prudent mean: "The solutions offered are not easy,"[123] it said, without mentioning what these hard solutions are. *Commonweal* was a little more specific: "capitalist and socialist" nations will need "social, economic and political revolutions" to create "social mechanisms that will control technological innovation and use for the public good."[124] *American Forests* also picked up the theme of environmental equivalence between socialism and capitalism; while noticing that Commoner found profits to be the cause of increased pollution, it also saw him reject "state socialism."[125] Yet *Life* magazine, in a review titled "The Totalitarian Ecologist," warned that "To satisfy his demands for a self-perpetuating society, we apparently need a bureaucratic control mechanism that doesn't sound much like a democracy."[126]

In sum, the vast majority of reviews of *The Closing Circle* saw it as the popular presentation of rigorous scientific analyses of environmental problems. When it was even acknowledged that the cure for these ills was of a radical nature, the assumption was that the cure was as well grounded in science as the analyses of the disease. A popularizer could hardly ask for more appropriate grounds on which to be praised. But while the mere fact of the praise means that it is deserved from the purely rhetorical point of view—Commoner always makes an extremely convincing case—what about the substantive questions? In fact, Commoner himself would never claim that all of his judgments about environmental problems can be derived from scientific analysis. A political program to develop a technocratic socialism plays a large role in his diagnosis of and proposed cure for environmental ills.

WHAT NATURE KNOWS

In *The Closing Circle*, Commoner admits that the "laws" of ecology are "informal," and not like the laws of physics.[127] He does not specify in what sense, then, they deserve to be called laws at all; certainly not all ecologists find them satisfactory as such. His first law—"everything is connected to everything else"—is surely the hallmark of what it means to think about "the environment," and obviously requires the most inclusive possible definition of environmental problems. To establish this interconnectedness as completely as possible, Commoner is thoroughly egalitarian; one finds no hint that connections can be closer or more tenuous, that some parts may be more important than others. As a result, more explicitly than Carson, he argues that the first law means ecosystems are amplifiers, so that small changes can produce "large, distant, long-delayed effects."[128] Yet in the very same discussion he suggests that unless they are "overstressed," ecosystems tend toward stability.[129] Surely for most ecosystems a "small perturbation" is not enough to overstress it; therefore, the impact is likely to be dampened, not amplified. But Commoner wants the reader to come away with the impression that any change is likely to be for the worst: his third law is that "nature knows best." He explains by arguing that through billions of years of "R & D" (i.e., evolutionary change), nature has tended to come up with an arrangement that is "'best' in the sense that it has been so heavily screened for disadvantageous components that any new one is likely to be worse than the present ones."[130] He likens nature to a watch, and our present interventions in it, to the extent that we lack proper knowledge, to poking a pencil into the works. We are not likely to improve the watch thereby.[131] It is as if there were no difference between poking the balance wheel of a watch and poking a main gear—or between poking the watch with a pencil and hitting it with a hammer. We are back to the notion of a static balance that Carson used so effectively, even as she denied its truth.

Or again, Commoner has shown a long-standing concern with the supposed problems caused by declining availability of "nonrenewable" mineral resources and the use of nonrenewable energy sources.[132] Yet if the second law is true—"everything must go somewhere"—then no material resource can be "used up." Commoner admits as much; the problem, he says, is actually that metallic resources will be scattered and can be recovered and concentrated only by the use of energy, which is itself a limited resource, in order to make them useful again.[133] Never mind that human activities can concentrate metallic resources, which is what makes things like aluminum and steel recycling as compared to mining economically feasible. Never mind that Commoner admits that metals considered precious are readily recovered, suggesting that any metal could be recycled if market conditions were favorable.[134] Never mind that solar energy is renewable, hence overcoming the problem of the supposed limit on energy available to recycle mineral resources. Never mind that it is Commoner himself who wants to see more extensive materials recycling.[135] Everything must go somewhere, except we are running out of metallic resources.

Finally, the last and best of Commoner's four laws—"there is no such thing as a free lunch"—is the one he takes least seriously. He is very good at using it against the pretensions of those who would defend the present constellation of politics, technology, and economics. But when he comes to presenting his own recommendations, he is nearly silent on any possible costs that will be associated with his suggested gains. Commoner leaves it to others to argue the costs of "going solar" or of recycling sewage into the soil.

The four laws do not add up to a picture of nature any more conceptually consistent than Carson's less formal presentation of similar ideas.[136] Laws that are not themselves rigorous could hardly produce analyses that are rigorous, however much Commoner relies on the rhetorical impact of bringing "laws" of ecology to the fore. Perhaps that is why *The Poverty of Power* (1976) begins with an explanation of the laws of thermodynamics.[137] In his analysis of energy problems, he has here a much more solid starting point. Without understanding these laws, we are told, it is impossible to understand the energy crisis.[138] Yet the conclusions he apparently draws from the laws of thermodynamics are remarkable; the book is an attempt to argue on behalf of solar power by showing that Marx's predictions about the final crisis of capitalism were coming true in the mid-1970s energy crisis.[139] In this instance, there was some greater degree of critical skepticism than we saw in the case of *The Closing Circle*. The *Times* opined that in his conclusions Commoner had "lost his way" and shifted from "rationality to muted outrage"; but the *Christian Science Monitor* was convinced there was an "inexorable chain of logic" by which Commoner arrived at his conclusions.[140] Does Commoner make any better use of the laws of thermodynamics than he does of the "laws" of ecology?

The answer here is a little more complicated. Commoner wants us to start thinking about energy efficiency in a new way. Some energy sources, he suggests, are better matched for doing some jobs than others. Just as one would not use a blowtorch to warm a baby bottle, so he argues it is foolish to use nuclear power to boil water to make steam to drive turbines to produce electricity to heat water in a home water heater.[141] "Energy is efficiently used when the quality of the source is matched with the quality demanded for the task."[142]

Commoner argues that this point is missed in traditional calculations of energy efficiency and commends a new method of measurement by which existing technologies turn out to be much less efficient than we had thought. Energy source is not being properly matched to purpose. This failure requires an explanation; why have we chosen such inefficient technologies? Because, Commoner argues, they tend to be more profitable than the technologies that would be more efficient.[143]

Commoner did not invent this alternative method of calculating energy efficiency. If one goes back to his sources, a rather different picture of its purpose emerges. Some of those who advocate its use are much more open about its practical limitations than Commoner is. The Study Group on Technical Aspects of Energy Efficient Utilization, in an article published in *Physics Today*, noted that the measure "provides immediate insight into the quality of performance of any device *relative to what it could ideally be* showing how much room there is for improvement *in principle*."[144] Commoner slides very quickly from "in principle" to "in practice."

Indeed, while the study group is as enthusiastic as Commoner about the potential usefulness of this measure, they also note, "In economic terms, there may be no *reason* to press for efficiency beyond a certain level. Nevertheless, as physicists, we must think in terms of what Nature permits."[145] Yet Commoner uses the measure precisely to raise economic questions, not as an exercise in seeing what Nature permits. He thus is prompted to create an explanation for something the study group suggests may not require an explanation. It is one thing to say that energy is not always used efficiently in the United States. It is quite another to use an idealized measurement technique to lay the supposedly scientific groundwork for the thoroughgoing critique of capitalist economics that is the heart of *Poverty of Power*.

That Commoner's scientific foundations begin to show such cracks under examination is an important point, given the weight reviewers have put on his scientific credentials. But to focus too much on this question is not to appreciate sufficiently another central aspect of Commoner's thinking. He has maintained it from his first book, *Science and Survival*[146] (which deals with the relationship between science and society, with particular emphasis on the issue of nuclear testing), to his most recent *Making Peace with the Planet*[147] (a re-presentation of the argument of *The Closing Circle*, with lessons drawn from the environmental policy failures of the intervening years). For Commoner has all along been quite open about the limited extent to which modern natural science can provide a rational foundation for any belief that we face an environmental crisis.

SCIENCE AND VALUES

Commoner certainly presents science as a major part of the solution to environmental problems. Scientific research, he argues, can indicate the actual or likely risks, along with the benefits, of any action we take, particularly any technical innovation that might have "environmental impact." While we need more such analysis, a crucial limitation on the scientist's ability to give authoritative answers to risk-benefit questions reveals why objective scientific analysis of environmental problems cannot be the final source of Commoner's arguments. For while science can give us an accurate picture of the risks that will follow the introduction of something new into the environment, it can never *weigh* these risks against the benefits that might be gained. It is possible to decide where to put the balance between risk and benefit only on the basis of "a value judgment; it is based on ideas of social good, on morality or religion—not on science."[148]

Hence, any threat to the environment posed by this or that technology, Commoner argues, should be dealt with by a careful balancing of risk and benefit by the public. In this "Jeffersonian" democracy (as he calls it), scientists will provide citizens with the best information they can, and citizens will, on the basis of that information, make all the decisions for which there are no scientific answers.[149]

The judgment about what constitutes a risk or a benefit in the first place may be far more value-laden than Commoner's account suggests, since what is considered a benefit and what a risk or cost are products of social forces and political decisions that change over time.[150] But even as far as he has taken the "unobjective" aspects of cost-benefit analysis, Commoner has undermined his own attempt to prove scientifically that we are facing an environmental "crisis." To call something a crisis is a "value judgment." Any talk of an "environmental crisis" in Commoner's work is the result of the way *his* values—not only scientific information—lead him to weigh risks and benefits.

Indeed, he goes so far as to argue that scientific objectivity itself is "perhaps" illusory; scientists have interests and "values" that inevitably determine what work they seek to do and how they approach it. These interests and values reflect things like the relation of the scientists to "major segments of society" and their "vested interest" in their own work. Such positions, he notes, cannot be "defended, or criticized, on *scientific* grounds." Science uncovers the truth not by the attempt of scientists to achieve "'objectivity' " (the quotes are Commoner's), but by "open discussion and publication. Whatever his personal aims, values and prejudices," when a scientist publishes, "he has done his service to the truth." It is less necessary to avoid "personal bias" than to be willing to display it in public, where it "can be corrected."[151]

Just how far Commoner intends to go with these criticisms of scientific objectivity as a reasonable standard to which individual researchers might be held is not entirely clear. Perhaps he only means that objectivity is not to be expected in the individual's choice of research topic. A more shocking possibility is that under circumstances of open discussion and debate, it is not *necessary* that individual researchers be objective in interpreting the results of their research in order that science as a whole reach true results.

To free individual scientists from an expectation that research results be interpreted objectively (i.e., that scientists work hard to see results for what they are, not for what they might be wished to be) is bad enough, as a recent flurry of books on "politicized science" suggests.[152] But it is worse when such results reach the public before the process of discussion within the scientific community has had a chance to "objectify" them. The weight Commoner puts on discussion as the source of scientific objectivity would seem to put a premium on presenting results and interpretations first for peer review. But why submit one's own biases for judgment to a tribunal that will merely judge according to their own? Freed in principle from a requirement for individual objectivity, why not choose in cases of public controversy to bring preliminary results and interpretations first to the general public, in hopes of producing an immediate and specific personal or political result? As numerous cases suggest, subsequent discussions within the scientific community will be so technical, restrained, narrowly circulated, and late as to be ineffective in overcoming the initial impression gained by the public. The process of making public policy will certainly suffer. Science will suffer as well. Research stimulated by premature, sloppy, tendentious, or falsified results is hardly likely to be a sound expenditure of time or money.

Commoner is not wrong to think that scientific facts alone cannot prove there is an environmental crisis and that values play a central role in any such judgment. He errs in using this same argument to undermine the possibility of scientific objectivity, and in implicitly rejecting the possibility of rational discussion or investigation into moral and political values. As a result, all we are left with is interest-based politics and persuasion. It is not surprising that Commoner made a stab at electoral politics, even if he aimed high in running for the presidency as his first office.

In *Making Peace with the Planet*, it appears that Commoner has had second thoughts on the usefulness of the risk-benefit analysis that formerly he equated with the scientific treatment of environmental problems. With what must have been for him painful irony, risk-benefit analysis had been increasingly adopted by the Environmental Protection Agency during the Reagan years. Commoner remarks that it "has achieved the status of a fad, often with peculiar results,"[153] and he calls it the "risk/benefit game."[154] He notes how it has produced results that exhibit "outrageous" morality.[155] But Commoner has not in fact turned against his earlier arguments. His main objection goes back to his earlier political judgment. Instead of openly submitting the task of balancing risk and benefit to the moral consideration of the public, the EPA has made its own implicit moral judgments and tried to conceal them with the appearance of objective quantification.[156] The EPA has taken on "deep moral and political issues"[157] that "only the public, hopefully with the aid of their elected representatives, ought to deter-mine" for themselves.[158]

Thus, Commoner the democrat. But there is a long-standing tension in Commoner's picture of how politics, interests, and expertise are to be related. He is caught between an adherence to the good of democracy and freedom, and arguments that push him to call for expertise-driven central planning.

Qua scientific expert, he admits that it is "tempting to call in the scientific expert" when faced with ecological problems but main-tains that because they are "matters of morality, of social and politi-cal judgment . . . [i]n a democracy they belong not in the hands of 'experts,' but in the hands of the people and their elected represen-tatives."[159] Commoner's argument shifts ground slightly in this pas-sage. Perhaps the role for scientific expertise need *not* be so limited in other political systems as it must be in a democracy; perhaps *only* a democracy needs to avoid the temptation of calling in scientific experts. Perhaps "Jeffersonian" democracy is not, after all, the best form of government for solving environmental problems.

That Commoner has entertained such doubts is indicated by his pre-*perestroika* praise of central planning in the then Soviet Union. In *The Closing Circle* he admitted that it faced pollution difficulties remarkably like the capitalist West but noted that "a strong ecolog-ical movement seems to be developing in the USSR."[160] The gov-ernment responded by asserting ecological control over industrial development:

> Here, of course, the socialist system in the Soviet Union does have an important practical advantage over the private enterprise system. Nationwide, all-encompassing plans for industrial and agricultural development—indeed, for nearly every aspect of economic life— are an intrinsic feature of the Soviet system. The advantage of such planning in any effort to alleviate environmental problems hardly needs to be demonstrated to anyone familiar with the chaotic envi-ronmental situation in the United States . . .[161]

In *Making Peace with the Planet*, Commoner tacitly admits how absurd this picture of the actual workings of the Soviet Union was, because "social interests such as environmentalism have not been free to comment on, let alone influence, government decisions."[162] But there is a deeper issue than his qualifications as a Sovietologist. "All-encompassing" planning is hardly Jeffersonian democracy by anybody's definition. What other advantage would it have than the opportunity for expert-driven control over choices that remain private in a capitalist economy? The fact that this advantage "needs hardly to be demonstrated" frees Commoner from having to assert directly the usefulness of freeing experts from having their judgments, however much based in values, mediated through shifting public opinion.

In any case, it is important not to confuse even Commoner's advocacy of Jeffersonian democracy with approval of anything like existing American liberal democracy. Frequent criticisms of the United States pervade his books, particularly *The Poverty of Power*. The energy and environmental crises, he says, reveal (along with racism and colonialism) the truth about our "deeply faulted institutions" and the "deep and dangerous fault in the economic system."[163] Energy and environmental problems cannot be solved by regulatory or reformist measures. Rather, our social, political, and economic arrangements must be revolutionized.

SOCIALISM LIVES!

Unlike many of his reviewers, Commoner makes no bones about the fact that some brand of socialism is behind this revolution.[164] But while rhetorically, Commoner's argument proceeds *from* environmental problems *to* socialism, as if socialism were called for by the scientific analysis, we have already seen how logically it is the other way around. Strictly speaking, Commoner's socialist "values" are the source of his judgment that certain things represent environmental problems. This is not to say that only socialists believe that there are environmental problems. But as noted in the Introduction, environmental problems do not come with labels on them saying, "I am an environmental problem." The sorts of situations Commoner considers problems, and the reasons he considers them problems, must, by the logic of his own argument, be bound up with his understanding of socialism.

Thus, he focuses on problems that could be linked to his thesis that technological development in the postwar period has been distorted by the profit motive of free enterprise. Although Commoner concedes that not *every* new technology is more polluting than the one it replaces, he concludes that pollution is connected to capitalism because profit, and not ecological soundness, is the criterion on which decisions about what to produce are made.[165] In the second place, there is the problem of "externalities," where the producer does not have to bear the cost of environmental degradation but passes it off onto society as a whole as when, for example, river water is taken into the plant and wastewater returned to the river.[166]

I have argued elsewhere that the statistical "proof" Commoner offers for these propositions is incomplete and circular.[167] Others have shown how Commoner's discussion of the economics of oil consumption and production, or of solar energy, are also seriously flawed.[168] Surely externalities exist. Surely some new technologies pollute more than some old ones. Surely businesses seek to maximize profits. But Commoner wants to suggest far more: capitalism succeeds only if it can pollute. Thus, the only way to solve pollution problems is to abolish capitalism.

No mere regulatory system, such as that used to control pollution in the United States, can do much good. In *Making Peace with the Planet* Commoner looks back on nearly two decades of widespread public concern for the environment to assess the accomplishments of the environmental movement. He is not happy with what he sees. Little progress, he says, has been made in air and water pollution, while toxic chemicals and radioactive materials are only beginning to get the necessary attention. Meanwhile, the greenhouse effect and ozone destruction lurk in the background as global environmental problems. To Commoner, these failures mean the general failure of government to address the real causes of pollution. Environmental successes have been won, Commoner says, only when "the relevant technologies of production are changed to eliminate the pollutant" (e.g., the banning of PCB, DDT, or the change in the method of chlorine production to remove mercury from the process).[169] Pollution control technologies are simply ways to continue to pollute; we need the technology of pollution elimination. But this will require that hitherto private choices about production be brought under public control (as well as a 50% cut in military spending).[170] Commoner criticizes major elements of the environmental movement for failing to realize the revolutionary political and economic implications behind this necessity.[171]

Commoner claims that it is the economic decentralization of capitalism that cannot cope with the challenges of environmental degradation and technological development. Rather than be directed by private choices, economic activity requires guidance by a unified vision of the public good. "If we are to survive, ecological considerations must guide economic and political ones."[172]

Commoner's understanding of socialism is, so far as one can tell from his writing, not profound. In one version of how this guidance will work, Commoner speaks of the necessity of governing production by "social thrift," or "the rational use-value of the final product rather than by the value added in the course of production."[173] This principle "is likely to be in conflict with private gain."[174] Who is to make the decisions about "rational use-value" that will govern production (i.e., what people can and cannot have)? Commoner may think that an informed public will be capable of making the necessary rational decisions concerning the governance of production. Through representative government, plebiscitary democracy, sophisticated survey research, or even electing Commoner as president, it may be possible for the public as a whole to decide what are the "social needs" of the moment. But in his books, Commoner never proposes such measures as means of decision making about "rational use-value."

Commoner could argue that this silence does not mean he is against making such decisions freely and democratically. He engaged in an extended and bitter polemic with Paul Ehrlich—it became something of a scandal in environmental and scientific circles—about the sources of environmental pollution, a dispute based in part on his criticism of those "population minded ecologists" who advocate coercive measures to bring down the birthrate.[175] But when he speaks in this context of the problem of political repression, he thinks of the repression of a majority by a minority.[176] Whether Commoner understands that political repression can also involve a majority coercing a minority is less clear.

He is unwilling to have the private choice of childbearing governed publicly because he assumes that it would mean a few controlling many. But it does not seem to occur to him that the governance of hitherto private choices of consumption and production by public needs or decisions would be just as coercive or repressive, even if it represents the will of many imposed on a few. The problem of coercion implicit in governing hitherto private choices by public decision is made only more severe by the fact that Commoner suggests that certain rights may be "*political* luxuries" we can no longer afford.[177] When he says we can no longer have wealth serving the interests of a few, or "self-serving propaganda" that obscures "issues revealed by logic," he is saying more than that people can misuse their property and be misled by advertising—he is attacking private property and free speech.[178] The one right he does explicitly believe in is the "right of political governance," that is to say, the right to determine hitherto private decisions by public means.[179]

When, in *The Poverty of Power*, Commoner acknowledges Marx as a source of his political analysis,[180] we see how the "right of political governance," the criticism of certain liberal rights, and the governance of production in accordance with a unified, "rational" view of the public good draws him back to authoritative central planning. We must be prepared to govern production by "social need"; this task is impossible to achieve within capitalism, where emphasis on profit wastefully works against "socially desirable ends."[181] "At least in principle," socialism is a system that allows the production of goods to be "consciously intended to serve social needs" and values those products "by their use."[182]

At least in principle. Commoner admitted in the 1960s that existing socialist regimes were hardly ecological paradises. The collapse of communism in the Soviet Union and Eastern Europe brought the full public revelation of ecological horrors that were once known or suspected in the West only by specialists. Commoner blames them in part on the use by the East of flawed Western technologies.[183] But more to the point, these revelations allow him to repeat earlier criticisms of socialist regimes like the USSR, China, and Cuba. On the one hand, they had failed to avoid being excessively enamored of growth. On the other hand, they were "rigorously planned, highly centralized, and therefore incompatible with the individual freedom that is the foundation of U.S. democracy."[184] Here again, the qualification is interesting; the fact that such planning is incompatible with U.S. democracy, which Commoner clearly believes to be quite defective, does not mean it is wrong simply. Can Commoner show how he plans to avoid planning with enough clarity to make us think that he is doing anything more than paying lip service to a freedom he finds dangerous?

His answers to the problems of growth and planning are remarkably similar. On the one hand, "the *theory* of socialist economics does not appear to require that growth should continue indefinitely"[185]; on the other hand, "there appears to be nothing in basic socialist theory that *requires* the establishment of a totally centralized economy, or of political repression to enforce it."[186]

Here it is evident that Commoner is not widely read in socialist theory, which abounds both with promises of growth and the extolling of centralization. Even so, what is remarkable is how both of these "undesirable" aspects of existing "socialist" regimes turn out, by assertion, to be nonproblems; the fact that "no existing example of a socialist society" conforms to Commoner's picture simply means that "wholly new political forms would need to be created." Still, it is "unrealistic . . . to categorically reject a socialist economy" simply because we have never seen one work the way Commoner says it should.[187] Such "realism" (i.e., choosing to leap into the unknown rather than being guided by experience) creates legitimate doubt about how Commoner intends to protect freedom and what he *is* advocating under the name of socialism.

Such doubts are not removed in more recent writings. Commoner has acknowledged that "a critic" may wonder just how social governance is to work, given that it has failed to materialize in existing socialist regimes.[188] "It will be pointed out," he notes, that "ecologically sound production decisions would need to be implemented through some form of planning," and the record here is likewise not good.[189] Instead of directly answering these objections, Commoner enters upon an extended paean to global democratization. (That in most parts of the world this trend is a reaction *against* planning is left to the reader to remember.) We should "expect the unexpected from the inherent impulse to extend democracy . . . it is an impulse that generates novelty . . . Recent history is a powerful assurance that the common democratic impulse can be translated into new, practical forms."[190] His stress on its unfathomed creative powers frees him from having to commit himself to any political good that democracy might entail. One gets little sense of what all those people in Poland, Czechoslovakia, or East Germany were actually fighting for except change, a lacuna made all the larger by Commoner's attempt to maintain a strict moral equivalence between East and West.[191] Commoner is still not willing to face up to the likelihood that "social governance" means centralized, expert-driven planning. If he wants freedom and democracy, he cannot have extensive social governance; if he wants social governance, freedom and democracy must be curtailed. The tension is the first indication of the utopian character of the standard by which he judges what constitutes an environmental problem.

TECHNOLOGY SAVES THE ENVIRONMENT

Indeed, behind that familiar label of socialism, the core of Commoner's argument is that we need social, political, and economic arrangements that conform to the dictates of efficient and rational technical organization. In *The Poverty of Power* the real standard, and the animating force behind Commoner's "socialism," is a "rational ideal" that makes the "production system" conform to the "ecological system" and the "economic system" conform to the "production system."[192] The ambivalence between an authoritative role for scientific expertise and "Jeffersonian democracy" has been resolved. How could scientists be merely advisers in this new society? To mold such a world will require accepting the authority of those who can articulate and implement the "rational ideal."

It is precisely here that Commoner's reliance on the promise of modern technology comes to the fore.[193] His description of the technological sophistication necessary to address ecological problems is remarkable; those who paint him as calling for "de-development," I believe, simply miss the point.[194] Again and again he expresses a faith in the "new ecologically sound technologies that must now be developed."[195] There will be "new processes which, while taking advantage of the best available scientific knowledge and technological skills, are relatively labor intensive rather then demanding intensive use of capital equipment and power."[196] The waste treatment system currently in use needs to be replaced by one that collects urban waste, pipes it to the country, and, after appropriate treatment, incorporates the treated waste into the soil.[197] Like this new technology of waste treatment, other new technologies will be developed that as much as possible mimic—or re-create—natural cycles. As a consequence we could expect:

> replacement of synthetic pesticides, as rapidly as possible, by biological ones; the discouragement of power-consuming industries; the development of land transport that operates with maximum fuel efficiency at low combustion temperatures and with minimal land use; essentially complete containment and reclamation of wastes from combustion processes, smelting, and chemical operations . . . essentially complete recycling of all reusable metal, glass, and paper products; ecologically sound planning to govern land use including urban areas.[198]

Commoner proceeds to discuss the genesis of such new technologies in terms that, for their faith in technology, match the zeal of the most fervent technophile:

> If factories are to operate according to principles of social thrift and ecological soundness, we can expect engineers to become impatient with narrowly conceived, single-purpose productivity- (and profit-) enhancing technologies and to invent new ones that are more appropriate to these new social goals. If such new technologies, which would necessarily cut across the narrow lines of present scientific disciplines, are in demand, we might expect scientists to overcome their reductionist bias and to develop new areas of knowledge which more closely than present ones match the structure of the real world and more readily illuminate actual human problems. As they become thus transformed, science and technology would in turn hasten the transformation of the system of production. Thus, once begun, ecological recovery would become an expanding, self-accelerating process.[199]

The "expanding, self-accelerating process" of ecological recovery is driven by an expanding technological base that can become safely self-accelerating once it has been placed on the proper social and scientific foundation.

In the economic realm, the rationalized production system to which Commoner looks forward implies that capitalism's reliance on the market leaves too much out of our conscious control. He laments that the "huge, enormously complex U.S. production system has been built not only without a plan, but also without a guidebook that explains, or even merely describes, its existing intricacies." We have "no comprehensive picture of its design."[200] A production system of which we could have a complete picture, which would not have been developed according to market forces, would clearly have to be consciously developed according to a plan laid out in advance. The criticism he makes of "plan fulfillment" in existing socialist regimes is a criticism of bad or unecological planning, not of planning per se.[201] His hypertrophied sense of rational order even extends itself to "aesthetic" judgments; he is offended by the "Huge numbers of chaotically varied plastic objects" that have been produced.[202]

In Commoner's ideal, politics too undergoes a peculiar rationalization, reminiscent of Orwell's complaint against those socialists who so wanted to let science and technology ease the conditions of human life as to seem to desire to turn humans into "the brain in the bottle."[203] The only criterion seriously discussed in *The Poverty of Power* is efficiency (not, for example, equality, community, fraternity—let alone freedom or pluralism); Commoner's highest priority is the creation of "a rational, thermodynamically sound energy system,"[204] where "sound" means efficient. From an interview conducted by Lawrence Weschler for *Rolling Stone* just prior to his being nominated as Citizens' party candidate for president, one would not know that there was *any* serious public issue except energy policy. Indeed, *Rolling Stone* apparently felt constrained to add a "side bar," explaining what the Citizens' party otherwise stood for.[205] And when he confronted socialist Michael Harrington under the auspices of a Bill Moyers program, he could not agree with Harrington that Ted Kennedy was worth supporting because, as he is reported to have said by *The Nation*, Kennedy's basic assumptions about energy were the same as Carter's and Reagan's.[206]

Commoner, having thought more than Carson about the problems of capitalism she only alluded to, proves to be no enemy of the "rigorously planned" society after all, nor to the centralization that follows from it. This result should not necessarily come as a surprise. When Commoner says that "ecological considerations must guide economic and political ones," he is asserting, in classic totalitarian fashion, that society can be arranged around a single guiding idea. His technological utopianism only exacerbates this tendency, for it teaches that whatever humans can conceive, they can do. The world is open to our efforts to reconstruct and perfect it.

But what happens to nature in this process of transformation? It is a paradoxical result of Commoner's more thoughtful confrontation with Carson's premises and conclusions that nature seems to recede further and further into the background of his concerns. Nature tells us the formal constraints under which we must operate; if nature recycles, so should we. But those constraints become the springboard from which we launch ourselves into a totally new world where the satisfaction of human purposes is paramount. It is true that Commoner wants to deny the premise, so crucial to modernity and particularly to socialism, that we are engaged in a "battle with nature."[207] But he accepts what is really simply the other side of the same coin, that technological development is a route by which "fundamental limitations of human existence" can be overcome.[208]

These generous hopes for technological perfection make it possible to frame environmental problems in terms both of great urgency and of great breadth. If our own action or inaction is the only thing holding back a better world, why have we not already acted—whether it be to clean up our rivers or save the ozone layer? If technology can provide a better life for everybody, then it makes sense to focus on problems that are global in scope, such as global warming, if only to provide the greatest good for the greatest number. Our scientific and technical abilities combined with our hopes and fears about what might be done with them create the context that explains our policy assumptions.

Yet as the perceptive French political theorist Bertrand de Jouvenel has pointed out, this way of thinking about a perfect world
poses a problem. The mind, he notes, "enamored of simplicity,"
seeks to project schemes of perfection into the distant past or far
future, so as to avoid the "annoying complexities of a familiar reality." But these schemes having been created come to serve as "a
rational model against which the disorderly architecture of today
can be measured, and thereby condemned."[209] The more seriously
one takes such lovely rational schemes, the more reason there is to
be dissatisfied with whatever now exists. The future can always, in
every way, be imagined to be better than the present; in light of
that possibility, the present looks bad indeed. That things can
always be better is the reason why, beginning with *Silent Spring*, so
many environmental arguments have been so speculative, involving
large uncertainties, subtle effects, and long periods of time. If these
problems arouse any sentiment beyond my own fear that I may be
a victim, their meaning must come from a vision that we have the
power and the obligation to do whatever we can to make a world
in which such things will not happen. The apocalyptic fears of global ecocatastrophe that we project into the future are but the other
side of the hopes expressed by the visions of writers such as Rachel
Carson and Barry Commoner.

Given the often lamented strictures of scientific specialization, it
is understandable why Commoner and Carson should, when dealing with matters of politics, ethics, or economics in their popularizing efforts, have recourse to what might kindly be called
simplifications. But it remains ironic, given the way they approach
the environment. While careful to encourage us to see complexity
and diversity in natural phenomena, they approach human affairs
wearing ideological blinders, as if any sight of the various entangle-
ments of human living together would divert them from the goal
they have set out to reach.

The consequence for a public educated by such works is yet
more serious. The eloquent clarity with which these popularizers
have presented case after case of complicated ecological disaster
has developed the public taste for such tales to a high degree. They
become the intellectual equivalent of a gothic romance, with a
large cast of characters, involuted relationships, and a lurking men-

ace. But the public's ability to appreciate the delicate balances and interrelationships of political and social structures has undergone a corresponding debasement, evident in rampant sloganeering, shameless emotionalism, and mindless panic and pessimism whenever "what is wrong with our society" comes under discussion. In this realm, only the crudest morality tales satisfy. Carson and Commoner have alerted us to matters that may well demand our attention. But they have done so at the cost of our ability to give that attention in a thoughtful way.

Other popularizers have in a sense been forced to confront the moral issues behind their reforming impulse in a more direct way. In an essentially pragmatic society like ours, perhaps we should not be surprised if those who advocate technological reform miss the ethical dimension. But the popularizers of population limitation, to whom we now turn, at least recognize that when dealing with human reproduction they are treading on ground well paved with a variety of mores and moral norms. Let us see if they can truly show us how to explore "new ethics for survival."

We Happy Few

All other things being equal, the government under which . . . the citizens populate and multiply the most is infallibly the best. One under which a people grows smaller and dwindles away is the worst. Calculators, it is up to you now. Count, measure, compare.

Jean-Jacques Rousseau, *On the Social Contract* (1762)[1]

To say that the world has cancer, and that the cancer cell is man, has neither experimental proof nor the validation of predictive accuracy; but I see no reason that instantly forbids such a speculation.

Alan Gregg, "A Medical Aspect of the Population Problem" (1955)[2]

PEOPLE, PEOPLE, PEOPLE

Paul Ehrlich once pulled Johnny Carson's chestnuts out of the fire. In a 1970 appearance on the Carson show, he was brought on early for the sake of hustling a monosyllabic guest offstage. For forty-five minutes, Ehrlich held forth on overpopulation's link to environmental destruction, prompting Johnny during the commercial breaks about what questions to ask next. "I got paid the highest compliment after the show, when I was walking behind Johnny and Ed McMahon up the stairs, and I heard Johnny say, 'Boy, Paul really saved the show.' " That impression could only have been strengthened when the show received more than five thousand letters about Ehrlich's appearance.[3] From then on, Ehrlich—once described as "witty, sometimes sarcastic"[4]—has been a regular on the talk-show circuit. If you want somebody with impeccable credentials to say something memorable and outrageous about population and the environmental crisis, you call Paul Ehrlich.

Ehrlich is practically the textbook case of a popularizer. He has been teaching at Stanford University, where he is now the Bing Professor of Population Studies, since 1959. His interest in the sciences, and his concern about population growth, are of long standing. He was already studying butterflies, the locus of his Ph.D. and subsequent professional research, in high school in New Jersey. After getting his B.A. in zoology at the University of Pennsylvania, he did graduate work in entomology at the University of Kansas, receiving his doctorate in 1957. Meanwhile, he had married Des Moines-born Anne Howland in 1954, whom he met while she was attending the University of Kansas. Upon arrival at Stanford, she became a research assistant and is currently a senior research associate in biological sciences. He and Anne together and separately have published scores of articles and eight books on environmental topics; Paul has authored, coauthored, or edited some 14 other books. Meanwhile, Anne has been a consultant to the executive branch Council on Environmental Quality and served on the executive committee of the environmental group Friends of the Earth.

Paul keeps up his entomological studies with publications in places like *The American Naturalist* and *Oecologia*, but his articles also appear in a range of journals from *Ramparts* to *McCalls*. He has coauthored regular columns in *Saturday Review* and *Mother Earth News*, and been a correspondent for NBC News. He is the recipient of a World Wildlife Association medal and in 1990 shared the $240,000 Crafoord Prize in Population Biology and the Conservation of Biological Diversity with Edward O. Wilson. The Crafoord prize, like the Nobel prizes, is administered by the Royal Swedish Academy of Sciences and was established to cover disciplines for which there are no Nobel awards. In 1990 Ehrlich also won a MacArthur Fellowship, one of the so-called "genius grants."

In the early 1960s, Ehrlich confined himself to publishing books on evolution and butterflies. His career as a public figure began in a small way when he started giving lectures about population problems during the mid-1960s. A trip to India was, by Ehrlich's own testimony, a turning point. Having long understood the population explosion "intellectually," he gained new emotional insight into it one hot night when returning with his family to their hotel in Delhi:

> The streets seemed alive with people. People eating, people washing, people sleeping. People visiting, arguing, and screaming. People thrusting their hands through the taxi window, begging. People defecating and urinating. People clinging to buses. People herding animals. People, people, people, people . . . Would we ever get to our hotel? All three of us were, frankly, frightened.[5]

David Brower, then executive director of the Sierra Club, heard what Ehrlich had to say and put him in touch with Ballantine Books. The result was *The Population Bomb*, published in 1968 jointly by Ballantine and the Sierra Club. It has been described as "what may be the all-time ecological best seller."[6] Over two million copies have been printed, with a twentieth printing in 1989.

The Population Bomb had a slow fuse. When it was first published, it met with a fair degree of inattention: a tiny if favorable review in the daily *New York Times*, brief favorable reviews in a few nature-oriented magazines, and mention in various library and/or publishing-oriented periodicals. It was after the Carson show that *The Population Bomb* really exploded.[7] Its fortunes rose along with those of Zero Population Growth, a Washington-based public charity of which Ehrlich was a founder and remains honorary president. ZPG disseminates information about and organizes efforts on behalf of population control.

Little attention was initially paid to *The Population Bomb* because "the population problem" (it had even been called a population bomb before Ehrlich used the phrase in his title[8]) was so well established when he first entered the fray. The early reviews are telling for how little they say about Ehrlich's argument. They assume their readers will already be familiar with his main points: that population is beginning to outgrow the resources that support it, so that too many people are chasing dwindling food and material supplies. As a consequence the environment will be ever more exploited and degraded as the need to feed more mouths increases. Under these circumstances, we have a choice: deliberate population limitation or letting famine, disease, war, and civil instability reduce population for us.

The assumption that Ehrlich's argument would be familiar seems to have been a safe one; throughout the sixties, it appears that *everybody* was concerned about overpopulation. Since the Kennedy administration, there had been U.S. government support for birth control programs in developing countries, perhaps following up on Dwight Eisenhower's judgment that "the population explosion" is "one of the world's most critical problems."[9] In the Johnson administration, such aid was increased, consistent with the President's announcement in his 1967 State of the Union address that "next to the pursuit of peace, the really greatest challenge to the human family is the race between the food supply and population increase. That race . . . is being lost."[10] This official recognition of the magnitude of the problem came one year *before* Ehrlich began *The Population Bomb* with the portentous words, "The battle to feed all of humanity is over." *Reader's Digest* ran two stories in 1969, one by Ehrlich and one by Congressman Morris Udall.[11] Margaret Mead did an essay for *Redbook*,[12] and the economist J. J. Spengler published his pessimism in *Parents Magazine*.[13] *Life*'s "welcome to the 1970s" issue had a photo essay on overpopulation with the remarkable title "Problem of People Pollution."[14]

What did Ehrlich add to this barrage of attention? A review of

The Population Bomb in *Natural History* caught the distinctive character of Ehrlich's contribution. Starting from the premise that "we all know there is a population explosion," the notice goes on to explain why it would still be a mistake to overlook Ehrlich's book. Its message is "that there is no refuge. Brilliantly and at white heat, Dr. Ehrlich knifes through much of the nonsense that has been written by optimists and explains that, no matter what is done, the future will be bad—for everyone." The book does not attempt to convince intellectually by "mind-dulling statistics" but makes the reader understand the issue *"emotionally."* Scientists don't usually go around "roaring like Old Testament prophets," but when "the world is in worse trouble than we thought" it is fit to do so. Still, despite the fact that there is no refuge and that no matter what is done the future will be bad, the book presents "a great deal" that the "private citizen" can do about the situation.[13] *Natural History* might have had in mind the sample letters about the population problem that Ehrlich provided for writing to clergy, the pope, TV networks, and politicians.

Here is described a masterful work of popularization. *Natural History* rightly credited the book with bringing the reader to feel Ehrlich's Delhi fears without the necessity of going to Delhi. It manages to suggest both that there was "no refuge" from such fearful conditions and that much can be done to avoid them. In other words, the book encourages hopes even as it arouses fears.

SOMETHING OLD, SOMETHING BORROWED, SOMETHING NEW

It is a truism to call Ehrlich's thought Malthusian or neo-Malthusian, a school of thought tracing its roots to the work of the English philosopher and economist Thomas R. Malthus, who in 1798 wrote—and subsequently produced several revised editions of—a controversial and influential essay attempting to prove that there was a natural tendency for population to grow at a rate that would outstrip available resources.[16] That Ehrlich can so readily be fit into an existing intellectual category is one of the factors that gives his ideas respectability.

But at least one obvious difference makes this categorization suspect: Malthus was no advocate of contraception. Yet birth control is a second well-established cause that lends Ehrlich credibility. He likes to present himself as communicating a largely unheeded message on this topic.[17] The ingrained human impulse to reproduction,[18] and the equally biologically grounded tendency to focus on immediate problems,[19] conspire to cover up the need for birth control to control population. Add various cultural prohibitions and you begin to understand why "*All* of us naturally lean toward the taboo against dealing with population growth."[20]

There is something odd about this insistence on shattering taboos. It is true that for some decades around the turn of the century, powerful legal restrictions made public discussion of birth control difficult. But before that time, and certainly since the late teens and early twenties, there has been lively advocacy of the practice. Radical activist Emma Goldman presented 120 lectures on birth control to 25,000 paid admissions in 1910. Although harassed by the police, she was not imprisoned for this activity before 1916.[21] Margaret Sanger opened her first clinic in 1916, and although it was closed by the police after 10 days, the momentum by that time was on her side of the issue.[22] Clarance Gamble of Procter and Gamble was supporting the distribution of condoms in rural North Carolina in 1937.[23] In 1953, Katharine McCormick began the financial support of Dr. Gregory Goodwin Pincus that would lead to the marketing of the birth control pill.[24] In 1965 the Supreme Court voided state restrictions on the sale and use of contraceptives, although in most states such laws were already dead letters anyway. Even before *Roe* v. *Wade* in 1973, states were liberalizing their abortion laws. Such measures, and doubtless many others, produced the result expected and desired by Ehrlich—a dramatic drop in the estimated U.S. population growth rate between 1960 and 1990.[25] On the global scene, something even more remarkable has occurred: "The early 1970s marked an historic turning point. For the first time in human history, the growth rate began to decline, and this trend has continued."[26]

Arguments on behalf of birth control have over the years been many and varied, but they shared something in common: their first concern was the quality of life of people (perhaps not all people), here and now. As a result, they were overtly political in nature. Birth control has been advocated on the grounds of strengthening family life, or liberating women, or as part of a program for radical revolution, or simply because more and better sex was thought to be a good in itself.[27] It has also been frequently linked with nativist and classist arguments, a concern that birth control needed to be available for the poor or foreign-born, lest they "outbreed" the right kind of people. As one author put it, the sight of the fecund squalor of immigrant life could "shock" Anglo-Saxon stock into infertility and "race suicide."[28] It is but a small step from such arguments to the eugenic advocates of birth control. At one time those advocating the breeding of better human beings—a "progressive" movement whose scope and influence in the United States has been rather downplayed in light of Nazism[29]—looked askance at birth control, precisely because it seemed in reality to be practiced not by the poor and unfit but mostly by those of wealth and education who should be having more, not fewer, children. Furthermore, in an ironic reversal of our expectations, the eugenicists saw themselves as serious men of science; they had no wish to be associated with such a marginal character as Margaret Sanger. But as time went by they came around.[30]

These older positions have not vanished, as we will see. But in the wake of World War II, at least some of them were discredited, while others might have seemed moot. In 1948, a new path was laid out. William Vogt—who was to become one of Planned Parenthood's directors—published *Road to Survival*, a catalog of how humans were destroying the earth and how it could be saved by conservation and birth control.[31] He upped the ante for population control significantly. Our problems are more than merely ours, they are the earth's as well. And because we depend on the earth, earth's problems begin to look like they should have priority. Such assumptions *could*, and in Vogt did, still eventuate in plans for population control and increased food production, along with other kinds of immediate aid to the poor or suffering. Ehrlich—who read Vogt and like authors as he grew up—broke this link between population control and humanitarian aid. He masterfully connected the human suffering that had long been a concern of birth controllers with environmental degradation. In the process, he deemphasized immediate human suffering in the name of preventing greater disasters at a later date and raised doubts that voluntary family planning could avert the dangers of overpopulation.

Just as aspirin masks a fever, so aid to end immediate suffering covers over the deeper environmental malaise and thus makes matters worse in the longer term. "[T]he penalty for frantic attempts to feed burgeoning populations in the next decade may be a lowering of the carrying capacity of the entire planet to a level far below that of 1968." As a result, "we are rapidly destroying our planet as a habitat for *Homo sapiens*."[32] The human suffering that is before our eyes takes on a different aspect, if to alleviate it requires that we put the future of humankind as a whole in jeopardy and risk greater disasters down the road. Ehrlich was not alone in making such assertions, nor was he the first. But he proved extremely good at it.

This change in emphasis also accounts for Ehrlich's outright rejection of the birth control and family planning movement that prepared the way for him. As he put it in a 1970 interview with *Playboy*, "Despite the fact that family planning has existed in many countries for well over 60 years, we still have rapid population growth. We've tried family planning and we know it doesn't work."[33] A core principle of the birth control movement had been that families, or more precisely, women, should be able to have as many children as they wanted. Ehrlich, as we will see, rejects this kind of free choice in favor of out and out coercion, or of the vast changes in society that one might expect would be necessary to alter so intimate a matter as the way we think about having children.

LOSING BY WINNING

The environmental crisis teaches us that the world *already* has too many people. Any significant addition to our numbers simply increases the chances for a global catastrophe that will reduce our numbers for us, if we fail to do it ourselves.[34] We face a clash between evolution and ingenuity. "Reproduction is the key to winning the evolutionary game," so those with a greater urge and ability to reproduce will win out over those with less.[35] Throughout much of the time human beings have been around, this urge coexisted with high death rates, so that the growth of the human population was quite slow.

Our ability to adapt to a wide variety of environments, and to adapt environments to our needs, has increasingly moderated the death rate. The agricultural revolution provided greater security, made it easier to raise more children, as well as gave impetus for larger families. Around 1800 improved standards of living led to an acceleration of population growth.[36] The increasing sophistication of medical science, particularly when exported to underdeveloped countries, was simply "the straw that broke the camel's back" in its ability to provide "instant death control."[37]

The ingrained impulse to breed, along with death control, raises the specter of an uncontrolled exponential growth, and "exponential growth contains the potential for big surprises."[38] The more people there are, the more children they can produce. More children today mean even more tomorrow, so we are faced with ever shorter "doubling times" for the population if the same rate of growth keeps up. (The Ehrlichs have lately admitted in an endnote that true exponential population growth is only rarely seen today, as the rate of growth has been changing [i.e., declining].[39]) As the rapidity of growth increases, the problem of exceeding earth's "carrying capacity" becomes ever more urgent. Carrying capacity is the term Ehrlich borrows from the ecology of nonhuman populations to give a purely scientific justification for the need to limit population.

The basic idea seems reasonable enough. The ability of any organism to be supported by its environment is limited by the carrying capacity of that environment. It is determined not just by available resources but also by how pervasive predators or competitors are. Place an exponentially increasing population in a finite world and sooner or later it will "overshoot" carrying capacity; there will no longer be sufficient resources to support it. At this point, the environment will be increasingly degraded and perhaps destroyed. No longer having the necessary means of support, the population will decline drastically. This scenario is normally called "overshoot and collapse."

For Ehrlich, famine, disease, and conflict are the likely "natural" means by which excessive population will be eliminated as we exceed earth's carrying capacity, just as in nonhuman populations we would see starvation, sickness, and increasing competition under similar circumstances. Hence, his desire to limit population by our own choices reflects, as he sees it, a humanitarian impulse to spare us such suffering. Ehrlich does not know what the global carrying capacity is—it was a topic recommended for research in *Population Bomb*, and not much progress seems to have been made 23 years later. But he does claim to know that environmental degradation shows we are already exceeding earth's carrying capacity.[40]

While the idea of "carrying capacity" sounds precise and scientifically analytical, there is less here than meets the eye. When applied to human populations the concept is not well defined.[41] Ehrlich can reach his conclusion only by abstracting from all kinds of differences between human and nonhuman populations, differences that would be crucial to any meaningful application of the concept of carrying capacity to human beings. Most nonhuman populations do not have the ability greatly to increase carrying capacity beyond what nature provides them, but both ancient and modern technologies give human beings just this opportunity. Nonhuman populations do not engage in trade to supply each other's needs. Periodic population booms and busts have long been thought to be characteristic of at least some nonhuman populations, but Ehrlich wants to avoid this natural cycle for human beings. But most significant is that nonhuman populations do not have the ability to decide what carrying capacity *should* be. The carrying capacity of a particular forest for deer is not determined by the ability of the deer to cultivate their food, or by a debate among them as to whether they would be better off if there were fewer of them.

In fact, for all the talk of carrying capacity, Ehrlich knows full well that in the last analysis, the question of whether there are too many of us is not settled by a scientific calculation. It involves "value judgments about how crowded we should be."[42] What kind of world should we want?

WINNING BY LOSING

In the *Population Bomb*, Ehrlich suggested that the value judgment guiding how many people we want in the world should be a matter of choice: we want a world where an individual may choose to live in crowded conditions or as a hermit.[43] This formula may sound "balanced," but since 10 people can be "crowded" if they want to live in a small enough space (indeed, 3 can be a crowd), such a standard would tend to give the control of population size to those who are most sensitive to the intrusions of the world on their affairs.

In the more recent *Population Explosion*, the theme of choice is developed in a different way. Population control makes it at least possible to live a life that is "more relaxed, more enjoyable," longer, less crowded, less frantic, safer, more peaceful.[44] Who today wouldn't want such a life? The achievement of such frankly mundane pleasures seems, at first glance, anything but utopian. But is it as prosaic as it looks? The Ehrlichs know full well just how extraordinary such goals are. Population control is the "ultimate test of whether human society is even remotely 'perfectible.'"[45] It requires a global "system, the major features of which were somehow mutually enforced by social pressures and other sanctions."[46] Does such a system sound "like a Utopian pipe dream"? There is, they claim, "nothing whatever in 'human nature' to make unattainable most of the features of what many of us would consider to be a Utopia . . . But the road to Utopia, we believe, can be traveled only in small steps, and there can be neither Utopia nor survival without population control."[47]

Utopia and survival—the carrot and the stick. The Ehrlichs admit that population control would leave intact all the problems that they link to overpopulation, and others.[48] But a world with fewer people will have fewer hard choices because there will be more to go around. The problems of scarcity will be alleviated, perhaps eliminated. We will have the pleasure of moderating the undesired consequences of our own choices, because there will be fewer such consequences.[49] The good sought is the maximization of lifestyle choices and the minimization of their bad results.

Nowhere is this clearer than in Ehrlich's discussion of sexual morality, a core issue when population limitation is the goal. The much trumpeted "right to limit our families"[50] does not have to be enunciated because we undergo forced breeding; rather, it means the right to engage in sexual intercourse without risk or consequence. Anything else harks back to a traditional sexual repressiveness that makes it impossible for us to enjoy sex while raising fewer, but supposedly healthier and happier, children.[51]

In the end, we in the United States have experienced much of the relaxation of sexual mores that Ehrlich called for in 1968. Divorce is no-fault, abortion is legal, venereal disease (with the possible exception of AIDS) is just another ailment, and far from being repressed, sexual behavior in general is increasingly public.[52] At the same time, we are raising fewer children. But that they are, as Ehrlich expected they would be, healthier, happier, and more valued by their parents is far from obvious; accounts of a Planned Parenthood ad campaign suggest how easy it is to equate "children" with "burden."[53] The ills Ehrlich attributed to repression have not disappeared, and liberation has been found to have its own costs. Nor is it clear why anything else should have happened, since some of those supposedly repressive institutions were there to protect people from the consequences of relaxed sexual mores (e.g., the problem of children having children).

The confounding of Ehrlich's expectations in this respect stems from a fateful ambiguity in his understanding of our place in the natural world that population limitation is designed to protect. The same problem also suggests the most profound reason why it is superficial to call him Malthusian. Malthus did not use the natural tendency toward overpopulation he described as an excuse for the development of utopian schemes of human perfectibility. Indeed, he used that tendency to critique such schemes. He argued that on balance, better conditions of life tend to produce overpopulation, which in turn creates the worsening conditions that reduce population. Such a cycle he understood as the natural result of the human drive to breed. Ehrlich accepts that it is the natural inclination of population to grow past its resources but argues that this course can and must be subdued to save nature and the natural conditions on which human life depends. So nature must be saved from itself by human artifice. The result of so doing can be a world in which all "should live in ease, happiness, and comparative leisure, and feel no anxiety about providing the means of subsistence for themselves and their families."[54] But this quote, accurately summarizing Ehrlich's expectations, is from Malthus' description of what nature makes *impossible* for human beings. His critique of such utopianism comes from his taking natural constraints much more seriously than those today who are mischaracterized as his followers.

By Ehrlich's own account, overpopulation and its consequences, such as disease and starvation, are perfectly natural, deriving as they do from the natural drive to reproduce—not just to engage in sexual activity. In the past, human beings have been able to reproduce successfully (i.e., in ever greater numbers) owing to their ability to manipulate and modify nature. We are told now that our power has become destructive. But we are nevertheless urged to employ that power *against ourselves* in the ever more precise regulation of our reproduction. For even were we to stabilize population at the desired low level, it would never again be possible for us to reproduce at will. Will the price of the salvation of nonhuman nature control our own nature in ways that will ultimately be as destructive to us as Ehrlich claims we have become to the world around us? Is it really to be expected that there will be no serious costs to the rationing (and rationalizing) of childbearing, or to the divorce of sexual activity from any sense of responsibility to anything beyond the participating individuals? Contrary to what he sometimes says, there *is* something in human nature *as Ehrlich understands it* that stands in the way of utopia, and it is a very powerful block indeed. To overcome it would require sustained and difficult efforts to reshape human nature.

Is it worth it then to seek to have fewer people on earth—not just fewer than we might have if present trends continue, but fewer than now occupy the planet, if this utopia requires reconstructing human beings? Perhaps not. But if the carrot is problematic, the stick of "survival" is substantial. It is when Ehrlich portrays the consequences of a world beyond the "limits of carrying capacity" that he makes the emotionally telling points likely to convince people that population control is worth it.

THE HORROR, THE HORROR

The third Los Angeles killer smog has wiped out 90,000 people. Troops holding the city under martial law are under constant attack by rioters. The President's Environmental Advisory Board has reported a measurable rise in the sea level due to melting of the polar caps. The Board states further that the decline in fisheries in both the Atlantic and Pacific is now irreversible due to pollution and recommends the immediate compulsory restriction of births to one per couple, and compulsory sterilization of all persons with I.Q. scores under 90. It says that, unless the population size in the United States is reduced rapidly, it too will be facing massive famine by the year 2000.[55]

The period 1968–83 was, it should be acknowledged, a remarkable enough 15 years, but reality had nothing on the "possible projections" and "possibilities" that Ehrlich was warning about in 1968. (He stressed that he was not predicting, and that he did not expect his scenarios to "come true as stated, but they describe the kinds of disasters that *will* occur as mankind slips into the famine decades."[56]) U.S. military intervention would be on the rise, he thought, against communism made desperate by its inability to feed its people, or perhaps against communism that had successfully taken over all of Latin America. Repeated famines in Asia, Africa, and South America would cause food riots and swell the ranks of anti-Americanism. The United States would be blamed for biological warfare when the plagues that result from such desperate situations began. Meanwhile, things would not go well at home, with food and water rationing becoming a part of life, and law and order breaking down. Nuclear war would result from rising tensions.[57]

Ehrlich also provided a "cheerful" scenario in 1968. The United States would stop food aid to countries that could not feed themselves. There would be only "moderate" food rationing at home, and the pope would call for birth control. Famines in China and "serious internal problems" in the Soviet Union would remove the threat of superpowers, and hunger would so progressively disorganize the Third World that no nation could be much of a threat to another. After the death of about one-fifth of the world's population from hunger, malnutrition, disease, and the like, global plans would be laid for a recovery that would produce a population of only 1.5 billion by 2100. Ehrlich challenged the reader to create a *more* optimistic scenario than this last one.[58]

The Population Bomb was revised in 1971 and 1978, with the scenarios undergoing major changes. (In the 1978 revision Ehrlich says that "they describe the kinds of events that might occur in the next few decades," a weaker formulation than even his first, already cautious, one.[59]) In one of these new terrorizing vignettes, the United States, driven by 1983 to feed increasing numbers in the face of worsening climate conditions, resorts to ever more dangerous chemical pesticides. Yet food supplies continue to shrink and what there is becomes ever more dangerous to eat. The world community bans trade with the United States as a result of this chemical contamination, bringing the United States to plan a preemptive nuclear strike against somebody. But instead, we are hit first.[60] A second scenario depicts over 1 billion deaths from an outbreak of Lassa fever between 1970 and 1974.[61] The third scenario once again "has more appeal than the others," with 1978 seeing the beginnings of an "arrangement of international controls over population, resources and environment." With the help (once again) of a change of Roman Catholic doctrine, population growth comes under control. The cost is some 700 million people dead of starvation in the 1980s, and 1 billion more such deaths between 1978 and some time before 2055, when the population is projected to be 6 billion.[62]

Ehrlich said all along that he was not predicting, and so he should not be accused of being a bad predictor—which would hardly be a surprise in any case. But scenarios are supposed to illuminate for us the issues and characteristics that are expected to mold the future, even if the precise form it takes cannot be foretold. It is obvious from the changes Ehrlich himself made that his first set of scenarios was spectacularly unsuccessful at catching the essentials of the period it set out to describe. And with the possible exception of the Lassa fever epidemic, since such plagues can break out in any place and at any time, it looks likely that the second set of scenarios is going to be as little illuminating of the basic forces that have characterized the period from 1978 to the present.

Anyone can project his worst fears into the future, and those with greater creativity can create a plausible chain of events from the present to that feared future. If that projection has any analytical purpose, and is not merely an exercise in science fiction writing, we might expect that the failure of the worst to materialize would be treated as a learning experience. We might have expected Ehrlich to give some serious attention to the possibility that he had missed something important in his account of what kind of problems overpopulation would cause and how serious they would be in the short term. Yet in 1990, the Ehrlichs claimed that "the population bomb has detonated."[63] Incredibly, *The Population Bomb* has been vindicated, although they have learned to avoid scenarios. In a rather testy footnote they lament how the stories were wrongly taken as predictions, and hence gave thoughtless critics grounds for dismissing the book because they had not "come true."[64] On the one hand, they note, the stories were there to promote action that would prevent such terrible things from happening. On the other hand, the actions actually taken (largely in the realm of increased food production) have prevented those terrible things only by making the situation worse in the longer term.[65] Now there are more people to face disease and starvation than there would have been had the great die-off of one billion occurred on schedule.

What the Ehrlichs forget to mention here is that in 1968 it appeared to Paul that *nothing* could be done to prevent the "time of famine" from arriving sooner rather than later. The only thing at issue was the degree of severity:

> The battle to feed all of humanity is over. In the 1970's [*sic*] the world will undergo famines—hundreds of millions of people are going to starve to death in spite of any crash programs embarked upon now. At this late date nothing can prevent a substantial increase in the world death rate, although many lives could be saved

through dramatic programs to 'stretch' the carrying capacity of the earth by increasing food production. But these programs will only provide a stay of execution unless they are accompanied by determined and successful efforts at population control. Population control is the conscious regulation of the numbers of human beings to meet the needs, not just of individual families, but of society as a whole.[66]

The 1978 revision of *Population Bomb* qualified these dire statements only to the extent—not a small matter—of extending the hundreds of millions of dead by starvation over the 1980s as well as the 1970s.[67]

Was Ehrlich right when he clearly *was* making a prediction? To judge, we have to be sure we understand what he was saying. A superficial reading might suggest that the passage quoted above is merely self-contradictory. On the one hand, there is the horror: the battle is over, crash programs cannot help, nothing can be done. On the other hand, there is hope: lives can be saved by increased food production, and population control will also help.

A more careful reading can resolve the apparent contradiction. Crash programs will save *some* lives but not enough to prevent an increase in the world death rate. These lives will be saved only temporarily unless population control is undertaken, so that there will not be ever-increasing mouths to feed. The fundamental conditions are scarcity and famine until far fewer people occupy the world. Recall that even under Ehrlich's optimistic scenarios, one billion people needed to die owing to this scarcity in the course of bringing population growth under control.

As of 1990, it can be said with confidence that Ehrlich was entirely wrong on the issue of death rate within the time frame he established. In 1960–65 the estimated crude world death rate (deaths per thousand of population) was 16.4; by 1985–90 it was 10. In Africa, South America, and Asia—areas that Ehrlich saw as particularly vulnerable—there were substantial reductions in death rate, comparing the period 1960–65 with 1985–90. In Europe and the USSR the death rate was slightly increased, while in North and Central America and Oceania there was only a modest decline.[68]

It is harder to assess the question of whether "hundreds of millions" have starved to death because of the imprecision of the prediction. In *The Population Explosion, The Population Bomb* is said to be entirely vindicated on this point, since "at least 200 million people" died since 1968 "of hunger and hunger related diseases."[69] (For the sake of comparison, in 1989 about 51 million people in the world died of all causes.[70]) If this chastening figure is accurate, does it confirm the 1968 warning? It is not entirely a quibble to point out that 200 million is the minimum figure that would qualify as "hundreds of millions," nor to suggest that the figure requires that deaths by starvation—literally not having enough food to stay alive—be supplemented by deaths by "hunger related diseases," a much harder number to quantify accurately. But in one obvious sense the number does not square with Ehrlich's earlier expectations. In 1968 it seemed "inevitable that death through starvation will be at least one factor in the coming increase in the death rate."[71] Since there has been no such increase, the actual extent of famine, however terrible, cannot be as great as Ehrlich predicted.

In other respects as well, the future did not turn out as Ehrlich expected it would. *The Population Explosion* acknowledges in an endnote that the pesticide-induced cancer upsurge "many of us feared" has not materialized.[72] Contrary to expectations, grain production in Asia has kept ahead of population increase.[73] Latin America is plagued by "inefficient use of resources,"[74] not the outright lack of resources that would cause famine to "sweep" across a region. "[O]nly in Africa have there been widespread famines in the past two decades,"[75] where Ehrlich expected to see them nearly worldwide, and even in Africa the Ehrlichs seem willing to consider the possibility that the cause is not simply that enough food could not be grown, but rather that political factors interfere with the sound agricultural policies that could lead to increased food production.[76]

If things are not as bad as Ehrlich expected they would be by now, perhaps he can take credit as one who popularized the issue of population growth so that it got some of the attention it needed. As a result, the trends that worried him did not continue unabated. But Ehrlich would rightly reject this credit.[77] Little that has been done to prevent the worst is what Ehrlich thought could or should be done. For example, the "green revolution" of high-yield crops and energy-intensive farming, not population reduction, has brought about a world food surplus in many recent years. Ehrlich saw that the green revolution had "the highest potential for reducing the scale of the coming famine."[78] But as far back as 1968 he was skeptical about it, and he grew more so by 1978.[79] He has argued that the claims made for it are inflated[80]; and he sees it as more part of the problem than part of the solution, because of its high rates of irrigation, pesticide, and fertilizer usage.[81] Furthermore, family planning efforts have continued in many parts of the world, instead of the program of outright population reduction that Ehrlich wanted to see. As a result, far from being satisfied that the terrible things he feared have not yet come to pass, Ehrlich believes that "the population bomb has detonated."

Yet many quiet qualifications are made. Far from the battle to feed humanity being over, we are now said to face "a long period of coping with high levels of overpopulation."[82] Rather than being concerned about the prospect of vast numbers of deaths from acute starvation, he now focuses on "premature deaths from hunger and disease."[83] Where once the underdeveloped world was "rapidly running out of food,"[84] in part because Ehrlich viewed the United States as the only food exporter likely to be willing to sell even inadequate quantities in the future,[85] now the United States, Canada, the EC, Australia, New Zealand, Argentina, and Thailand are admitted to be "reliable" food exporters.[86] Where he has long tried to forge a link between overpopulation and disease, *Population Explosion* admits that the connection between population size and public health "is often relatively weak."[87] This does not stop the Ehrlichs from hinting at a link between overpopulation and AIDS.[88]

A doctor might say, "You have a terminal illness with only six months to live, even if we treat you." If, ten years later, the patient is still alive, without even having undergone the full course of treatment, and the doctor has not changed his mind, we might wonder about the doctor's competence. Yet Ehrlich is similarly obstinate.

Food supply and death rates are not the only issues on which

Ehrlich has been profoundly mistaken. In 1980 he predicted massive raw material shortages. The economist Julian Simon, a persistent critic of Ehrlich, proposed a bet revolving around the price of certain metals in 1990. Ehrlich expected the (inflation adjusted) prices to go up, owing to increasing scarcity, while Simon was betting on declining prices. In the event, Simon won.[89] But Ehrlich dismissed the significance of his loss. "Julian Simon is like the guy who jumps off the Empire State building and says how great things are going so far as he passes the 10th floor."[90]

Ehrlich exploits an important truth here. Things *could* indeed always get worse; there are no guarantees for the future. Ehrlich's arguments depend on the fear that this uncertainty can cause, particularly among those who are relatively well off. He exploits those same anxieties that make us touch wood or ward off the evil eye when something good happens. People may not remain fearful of evils they have found to be completely fanciful, but then again, it is always possible to think up new evils. In the late 1960s, civil disorder and war were very much on everyone's mind, and they were the centerpieces of Ehrlich's scenarios. By the late 1970s, it was necessary to introduce strange and terrible diseases to make the same point.

What are we to do to avoid any or all of whatever evils are fashionable at the moment? Whatever else we do—and Ehrlich admits other measures are necessary—population must be reduced. If it is not, the increase in our numbers "Will always get us in the end."[91] But how to reduce the world's population (i.e., achieve negative growth) "as soon as possible"?[92] There is less clarity about the answer to this basic question than one might hope for.

In the 1970s, the global rate of population increase began to slow, although it will continue to grow for some time. If we stick to the present growth rate, world population will double in 39 years. Should the rate continue to decline, doubling time could be extended to about 100 years, with global population finally stabilizing at around 10 billion people.[93]

A doubling of global population would be a terrible thing if the world is indeed already overpopulated.[94] On the other hand, if current trends continue, we would have 100 years to deal with their consequences which seems to leave some room to maneuver.

Sometimes it appears as if the Ehrlichs are willing to use this time. To "end the population explosion *humanely*" it is necessary only to begin a "gradual population *decline*."[95] But for the most part the argument is that we already face circumstances that are terribly inhumane, and things are likely to get worse. Ehrlich has often written as if the end of civilization as we know it is just around the corner, because overpopulation will so degrade earthly ecosystems as to make life extremely difficult at best. In a famous 1969 article in *Ramparts*, he placed the death of the oceans and the likely end of civilization—in 1979.[96] Any solution to our dilemma would therefore have to do two things: reduce population to less than its current numbers, and do so quickly enough to head off a collision with ongoing ecosystem degradation.

The problem with achieving these two goals is that it is difficult to reduce population quickly, as the Ehrlichs know full well.[97] Even by halving present birthrates in the United States or China, for example, it would take over 100 years for these countries to reach the target populations Ehrlich has set for them. To speed the process significantly and reach the targets in about 75 years, it is necessary not only to have more dramatic cuts in the birthrate but to allow death rates to rise as well.[98]

Let us try to be clear about what the policy measures behind these estimates would look like. At present in the United States, with the ready availability of contraception and generally relaxed social pressures, many families—perhaps most—are about the size that parents want them to be. Under these circumstances, nearly halving the birthrate for at least one generation means that many people will not be able to have the children they would otherwise want. To accomplish this task would clearly require some strongly enforced system of incentives and/or disincentives, along perhaps with a massive reeducation campaign that would attempt to get people to want fewer—or no—children. Whether such policies would tend to make children more loved, or rather make them appear burdensome and problematic, is anyone's guess. What seems entirely clear is that for any such policy to be pursued consistently for over 100 years would require fundamental changes in politics as we have hitherto known it in the United States.

The quicker course of birthrate decrease and death rate increase is no less radical; mandatory birth control would be the least of it. Limiting money for hospitals, eliminating all heroic measures related to birth or death, letting vaccination programs lapse, restricting money for medical research—some or all would seem to be in the cards if we are to allow the death rate to rise. As has happened in the case of malaria, the world might accept an increase in the incidence of other diseases once thought "under control." After all, Ehrlich is no friend of what he calls the "health syndicate."[99] Serious population reduction, in the face of pressing ecological danger, is likely to be a formidable task. Ehrlich never gives extended attention in his popular works to the time that reaching his goals would take. Therefore, he never has to justify the extraordinary political and financial capital it would take to impose these measures, as compared with other ways of dealing with perceived environmental problems.

CONTRACEPTION, COMMAND, AND CONTROL

So one might think that Ehrlich must endorse some pretty stringent measures of population control. Yet even in the urgently apocalyptic days of *The Population Bomb*, Ehrlich devoted more attention to apparently milder rather than more stringent methods. Compulsion was only to be tried if "voluntary" methods failed. In a crucially important lapse of memory, he forgot to specify how much time voluntary methods were to be given to work. But he did provide a variety of possible programs. On the domestic front, he focused on a tax code that would discourage large families and encourage small ones, sex education and changing attitudes about sex, a new Catholic position on birth control, promotion of rights to abortion and contraception, development of an antigrowth mentality in economics, new pesticides, recycling, and alternative energy sources such as hydropower and nuclear power.[100] All of these "voluntary" measures would clearly take time to work—far longer than the century scale results of more radical measures—and yet already in 1968 we had no time.

As it turns out, however, such "voluntary" programs were to be developed and overseen by a Department of Population and Environment, "a powerful government agency."[101] While in some contexts Ehrlich remembers that there is, among other governmental bodies, a Congress of the United States, he wants the DPE to be able "to take *whatever steps are necessary* to establish a reasonable population size" in the United States and to end environmental deterioration.[102] Since optimal population size involves a complex combination of natural constraints, political and moral values, and economic and technological capacities, the DPE clearly has the potential to *be* the government of the United States. To pick only a small but telling example, Ehrlich has consistently believed that books, stories, or TV programs that feature large families should be at least discouraged and at best prohibited to young children.[103] Would the task of censorship fall to the DPE?

Or consider a much larger issue: compulsory mass sterilization. Ehrlich investigates the possibility of adding a contraceptive to the water supply and making the antidote available only selectively. His main objection to this plan was that no such contraceptive was available. He also thought it very unlikely that such an additive would ever be accepted.[104] Nevertheless, among the research efforts of the DPE was to be the development of precisely such a contraceptive.[105]

When he is not speaking about the United States, coercion only hinted at becomes explicit. In *The Population Bomb* Ehrlich endorses what he himself calls "draconian" methods. Compulsory sterilization of Indian males with three or more children would have been "coercion in a good cause."[106] Population growth is like a cancer, and like a cancer it must be cut out. "The operation will demand many apparently brutal and heartless decisions. The pain may be intense. But the disease is so far advanced that only with radical surgery does the patient have a chance of survival."[107]

Therefore, on the international scene, *The Population Bomb* endorsed aid triage, since "our giant food surpluses are gone."[108] Only nations (or actually, special areas within nations) that show some ability to pull themselves out of their problems (i.e., that exercise "coercion in a good cause") would get food aid. Basket cases, or those not willing to cooperate on the right terms, would be left to their own devices (i.e., to the starvation and disease that would cause rapid and massive population declines), the necessary security having been provided to the special areas to keep the wrong sort of people out.[109] Those who showed they wanted to be helped would be given some food aid, but more important, they would be pushed down the path of proper development. They would be educated by portable TVs, selling them on birth control and new agricultural methods with all the skill of Madison Avenue.[110] Miserly paternalism—a particularly Dickensian combination—was the order of the day.

"Triage" is no longer an issue in *The Population Explosion*, nor are the Americans in gray flannel suits to be called upon. Far from highly selective aid, the Ehrlichs now speak of a massive international effort of financial and technical assistance, financed by the wealthy nations.[111] Without having followed Paul's advice, we can now afford a level of global generosity that once seemed impossible. The Ehrlichs see such aid as a possible basis for a world government.[112]

At home, because population growth has slowed somewhat in the United States, 23 years after *The Population Bomb* predicted imminent disaster, the Ehrlichs still express the pious hope that draconian measures can be avoided.[113] Yet perhaps stung by the charge that Paul had reserved tougher measures for those who were furthest away, the Ehrlichs are at pains to suggest how the real population problem is not in the underdeveloped world but in the developed world, because each individual in the wealthy nations has much greater environmental impact than a corresponding poor person.[114]

For all that, it is enough that parents "stop at two" to accelerate the decline in U.S. population that will come because, along with other wealthy nations, our birthrate is already near replacement level. This effort requires more effective contraceptives and more effective use of contraceptives. Sex education is still of great importance. So is political correctness; don't expect a baby present from the Ehrlichs beyond number two.[115] Such mild measures seem odd, given the wasted time and our supposed vastly disproportionate global environmental impact. Are the Ehrlichs relying on our ability to reduce environmental impacts through technology at a much faster rate than we will likely be able to reduce population? (A 1991 book, *Healing the Planet*, puts a good deal of stress on such factors.[116])

In fact, the individual actions they call for are merely indicative of a change of thinking about children and family life that the Ehrlichs call "cultural evolution," the way in which information is passed on "from person to person and from generation to generation."[117] The Ehrlichs would like to see this process "harnessed and directed" to the proper ends.[118] Paul has coauthored a whole book on the topic.[119] Whatever the subtleties of that more interesting presentation, in *The Population Explosion* "propaganda" would have been as good a term as "directed cultural evolution." The Ehrlichs are thoroughgoing social engineers. Everything from the six o'clock news to elementary education should link increasing population with declining quality of life to encourage population reduction.[120]

With the necessity for propaganda campaigns in mind, we can better understand the Ehrlichs' admiration for the Chinese model of birth control, the "most successful population control program in the world," although in fact it has not met its goals.[121] The Ehrlichs seem to waver about just what made it successful. Was it that it was "indigenous," part of a program "to bring basic health-care to the entire population," involved extensive peer pressure and government openness, and was "carried out in a nation where the government has put substantial effort into providing equal rights and education for women"?[122] Or, as the obvious ironies of this last point suggest, was the key to its success that "their rigidly organized society allowed the government to implement steps that might well be impossible in a democracy"?[123]

Lest we too quickly conclude, "so much the worse for democracy," the Ehrlichs point out that the one child per family program "had many elements of coercion that are offensive to those of us who believe reproductive decisions should basically remain in the control of the individual."[124] But just who are the "us" here? The Ehrlichs at least are not unambiguously in the offended class, given that *at best* they believe that such choices are safely left to individuals only *after* those individuals have been extensively reeducated. Their readiness to explain away the apparent offense is likewise telling. Such coercion, they say, was made necessary because the regime waited so long to do anything about its population problem.[125] Of course, they are constantly pointing out that we have all waited too long. Furthermore, to make China's coercive policies seem democratic, they note that forced sterilizations might be seen simply as the punishment for breaking the rules "the society had determined."[126] As good as Paul has shown himself to be in writing imaginary vignettes about future horribles, we are told no stories about what it is like for a real Chinese woman to undergo forced abortion or sterilization.

Ehrlich conveys the impression that the sooner we act, the less draconian the measures we need to use. Yet even *more* stringent measures of control than the Chinese have employed would still mean a dangerously long time before a still too high, but stable, population level would be reached. If Ehrlich, acting not as a scientist but as the crudest kind of propagandist, has simply overstated the urgency of his case for the sake of effect, then perhaps he would be satisfied by the kind of slow progress toward population reduction that could be achieved by incremental changes in policies and attitudes.

But another possibility provides a great deal more coherence to his work over the years. Beautiful hopes about a world where we do not face hard choices combine with dreadful fears of the end of civilization to move us toward a utopian totalitarianism that is all too familiar. The apparently "modest" measures Ehrlich recommends when followed up lead to ever-increasing regulation of our most private affairs. It is hardly surprising that the "Chinese model" should look so attractive to the Ehrlichs. Only a totalitarian regime such as China could hope to successfully introduce the measures necessary to regulate and control sexual and procreative behavior. Only such a regime could hope to stifle the dissent and alternative points of view that would otherwise compromise the success of the massive reeducation campaign that would make a "voluntary" program of population reduction possible. Why not choose that means, given the terrible consequences we can *imagine* without it? We might spare people the long, drawn out suffering of death by starvation. After all, "radical surgery" means blood. When famine, pandemic disease, or nuclear war is the likely alternative "solution" that will reduce population for us if we do not do it ourselves,[127] what is a little "coercion in a good cause"?[128]

"Coercion in a good cause" is no new claim; it has justified numerous atrocities. On the other hand, it is not always a false promise. To judge, we have to know the good we are being promised and the scope and intensity of the coercion required to reach it. Furthermore, the two must be proportional. A police officer on every streetcorner is not the way to prevent tricycle theft. For Ehrlich, the means fall somewhere between massive propaganda campaigns and draconian measures, in either case extending the power of the state into our most intimate choices. Those who are not convinced by the lurid fears or by utopian hopes will judge that he fails the proportionality test.

But perhaps Ehrlich has relied too much on expediency, and thus left himself open to the moral scruples that make us question just when the end justifies the means. Perhaps there is a case to be made that such coercion is the ethical thing to do under the circumstances. Such is the case that Garrett Hardin would like to make.

THE FIRST TIME IS TRAGEDY

A June 1992 cover story for *U.S. News and World Report* highlighted "The Rape of the Oceans."[129] Declining catches by the U.S. fishing fleet, along with reduced quality of the fish being caught, are due, the article argued, above all to overfishing. Ever more efficient fishing fleets, and ever growing demand for seafood, mean that so many fish are being caught that their reproductive rates cannot keep up. As a result, fishermen must work ever harder for declining yields. Searching for previous analogies to this problem, the article notes that free access to federal grazing land had "nearly destroyed" those rangelands. "Could this classic tragedy-of-the-commons be repeated in America's oceans?"[130]

That the phrase "tragedy of the commons" can be used without explanation, indeed that it is the conceptual framework for the whole news report, is likely due to the work of one of environmentalism's most remarkable popularizers, Garrett Hardin. Hardin was born in Dallas in 1915 and received his bachelor of science degree from the University of Chicago. He went on to get his doctorate in biology from Stanford in 1941 and in 1946 became an assistant professor of bacteriology at the University of California, Santa Barbara, where he is now emeritus professor of human ecology.

His research in the early 1940s involved using algae as a food source, but in the course of that work he became convinced that efforts to feed massive numbers of people would only make the problem of overpopulation worse. Already in the 1950s he was writing for a lay audience about evolution, eugenics, and population, and developing ideas that would be central to his subsequent work. In the 1960s, well before it was fashionable, he was lecturing and writing on behalf of abortion.

His growing reputation in scientific circles made him president of the Pacific Division of the American Association for the Advancement of Science in the late sixties. It was the address he presented on retiring from that position, revised and published in *Science* as "The Tragedy of the Commons" (1968), that brought him his present public fame.[131] The essay has been "reprinted in more than sixty anthologies within the fields of political science, sociology, ecology, population studies, biology, conservation, law and economics."[132] It, along with Hardin's other work, has been the topic of Ph.D. dissertations in theology and politics. A whole literature on "commons problems" has developed.

Hardin might have made his greatest splash with one 6,000-word essay, but he has produced a flood of writings on the theme of overpopulation and morality: over 200 articles, essays, and reviews, with some dozen books authored or edited. His blunt style and almost Voltairian iconoclasm have made him one of the most controversial thinkers within the environmental movement; the adjective "obscene" is linked with his thought.[133] Yet he also, not unreasonably, has been called "one of the intellectual leaders of our time."[134]

Hardin's work displays a remarkable coherence. "Tragedy" is entirely of a piece with earlier writings on genetics, eugenics, evolution, competition. Concepts he developed after the tragedy of the commons, such as the infamous "lifeboat ethics," are restatements of the same themes. Hardin's continuing influence is due in part to his skill in presenting the same points in such a way as to appeal to a variety of audiences, and in part to the tendency of his many readers not to look too closely at the assumptions behind arguments they find appealing. To see how these two parts fit together, we begin with a look at the tragedy of the commons.

If a resource "open to all" is employed to the unregulated, individual profit of its users, Hardin asserts, the degradation or destruction of that resource will inevitably result, if the users are rational maximizers of their particular interests. Let us take the example of ocean fishing. Most of the ocean is unowned (i.e., a commons), and for the most part fishing is unregulated. Given the opportunity for a bigger catch, fishermen must take it to remain competitive with their fellows, because that is the way each will maximize his own return. Fish being a renewable but still finite resource, as catches enlarge the resource base will begin to decline. Even so, it remains in the interest of each individual fisherman to continue to increase the size of his catch, for he appropriates the whole benefit of that increase to himself, while the harm done to the resource as a whole is divided among all fishermen.

> Each man is locked into a system that compels him to increase his
> . . . [yield] without limit—in a world that is limited. Ruin is the des-
> tination toward which all men rush, each pursuing his own best
> interest in a society that believes in the freedom of the commons.
> Freedom in a commons brings ruin to all.[135]

While Hardin applies the analysis of commons behavior to resource policy and pollution problems, the purpose of the original essay was above all to deal with the implications of the tragedy of the commons for the measures necessary to regulate population growth. Were it the case, he writes, that those who had children were completely responsible for their maintenance and welfare, reproductive behavior would not be a matter of "public concern," because the children of those who had more than they could take care of would simply die of neglect. But in a welfare state, and in a world where the control of family size by individual families is taken to be a matter of right, the situation is not so simple. The mechanism that would limit family size is impaired when the responsibility for taking care of children is no longer borne only by those who bring them into the world.[136] When the success of modern medicine at "death control" is added to this situation, the stage is set for a dramatic and destructive tendency toward overpopulation.

Does the "logic" of the commons apply as readily to having children as to using natural resources? To bring them as much in accord as possible, Hardin speaks as if people increase their numbers deliberately to maximize the resources available to them, just as the fisherman deliberately seeks to increase yield. Today there is little reason to believe that a larger family or population will guarantee a larger share of the world's resources. But we also know that many regard this fact as a premier example of injustice. We have all heard how the United States, with only a small portion of the world's population, consumes a "disproportionate" share of its resources, as if consumption should be directly proportional to population size. Hardin is really concerned about a hypothetical, but not implausible, situation in which a nation, or the world, makes policy assuming both the right of families to control their own size and the belief that resources should be distributed according to the communist principle "to each according to his need."[137] The result would be too many children.

In extending the analysis of "Tragedy," Hardin points out how impoverished nations' demands for a "new economic order" mean creating a global welfare state, in which their poverty, a function of overpopulation, would be subsidized by wealthier nations. Such welfare measures, he says, are attempts to create a "commons" of wealth and resources, allowing the population of poor countries to continue to expand rapidly even if they are intrinsically incapable of taking care of their own people at even lower levels of population.[138]

How is this problem to be solved? To seek to avoid the "tragedy" by asking for the *voluntary* cooperation of the users to limit exploitation of the commons is to put a premium on noncooperation. Returning to the example of ocean fishing, we see it might not seem too difficult to convince fishermen that they should limit their catch to the maximum *sustainable* yield, replacing short-term with long-term self-interest. But Hardin's argument is that it would not be enough to convince some, or even many, of this policy. For as soon as even one fisherman continues to act in a rationally egoistic manner, those who restrain themselves will either be at a competitive disadvantage or be forced to abandon their restraint; in either case, resource depletion will continue to the point of resource destruction.

In like manner, the danger Hardin sees with respect to population is that those who do not control the number of children they have will be advantaged over those who do, exacerbating the population problem. This argument reflects one of the most pervasive tenets of Hardin's thought, even though it was not directly articulated in the original "Tragedy" essay: the competitive exclusion principle.

The competitive exclusion principle states that if two populations occupy exactly the same ecological niche in the same geographic territory, the one that breeds even slightly more successfully than the other will eventually displace the slower breeder completely.[139]

The competitive exclusion principle is more than a restatement of the possibility, inherent in any competitive situation, that there will be winners and losers. By speaking of two species that occupy the same ecological niche in the same geographical location—apparently a rather rare occurrence—it defines the circumstances under which breeding rates are the sine qua non of evolutionary success. The principle suggests the evolutionary advantages of diversity; *"ecological differentiation is the necessary condition for coexistence."*[140] If two species with unequal birthrates are to coexist over the long run, they must be different from each other either in the way they live or where they live.

Hardin asserts that the competitive exclusion principle implies the failure of any population limitation policy that depends on voluntary restraint. Or, at least, it does so under certain circumstances. For if we leave decisions about family size to the conscience of individuals, and if there is an inherited component related to family size, and if we treat a given nation or even the whole world as one big ecological niche (i.e., a commons), then over time people with a genetic disposition to large families will displace those who would have smaller families. To appeal to conscience to limit reproduction is to work "toward the elimination of conscience from the race," as those who do not succumb to the appeal displace those who do.[141] We will thus have made an already bad population situation worse.

Hardin argues that it does not matter if there is a genetic component to family size or if large families are a result of "social heredity" (i.e., daughters of mothers with large families choosing to have large families themselves).[142] If hitherto slower breeders would then deliberately increase their own numbers to remain in a competitive position, obviously the population picture would only get worse faster.

Hardin offers two kinds of solutions to the commons problem. In his original essay, he presents the formula "mutual coercion, mutually agreed upon" as the foundation for any democratic means of dealing specifically with overpopulation.[143] In other contexts, he discusses alternative systems of ownership and appropriation to the common ownership/private benefit that is the key to commons destruction.

A "managed commons," for example, holds resources in common but employs them for the public good. Hardin understands socialism to be an attempt to manage the commons.[144] But it has a problem. A way must be found to make the managers sufficiently responsible in their allocation of resources, since those who make decisions do not necessarily face the direct consequences of their mistakes. If I farm my land badly, I lose out without any third-party intervention; if I promulgate the wrong agricultural plan, the consequences will be quite attenuated by the time they get to me. Hence some third party must apportion blame where appropriate. This question of "who will guard the guardians" is a continually vexing one for Hardin.[145]

Private ownership with private benefit seems to offer a direct inducement to responsible use of resources if the costs of misuse fall directly on the owner. Since private owners will seek to avoid such costs, they will employ their resources responsibly. This is the argument that "free market environmentalists" have taken up as their own.[146] But Hardin also suggests that "utterly free competition" is problematic since free markets aim at continuous economic growth, which he believes to be neither possible nor desirable.[147] Furthermore, private owners can pass on costs of overexploitation to nonowners, hence evading responsibility.

How do private ownership and a managed commons translate into population policies? Hardin advocates a kind of privatization when he asserts that rich nations have no moral obligation to provide aid to poor ones to support their excess populations. To assume such an obligation is to commonize wealth and end up hurting those one intended to help. Propping up nations that are systemically unable to provide for their own people promotes depleted resources, dependency, and further irresponsible policies in those nations. It creates a larger pool of those requiring aid than would exist if nature were allowed to take its course to solve local overpopulation problems (i.e., than if people were left prey to starvation, disease, and conflict as an object lesson in what should not be done).

This point is restated by "lifeboat ethics," which, Hardin notes, is "merely a special application of the logic of the commons."[148] If we think of our nation as a lifeboat where people are doing relatively well, it becomes obvious that we sacrifice our well-being if we let too many from other lifeboats in straitened circumstances aboard. Even if for a time we can support those in need, in the end the once prosperous lifeboat will itself begin to fail, and everyone will be worse off. There can be no moral obligation to help any and all of the needy under such circumstances.

As the example of lifeboat ethics suggests, Hardin's arguments are generally directed to the international arena. While there is no reason to believe the logic would be any different, Hardin does not explicitly argue for "privatization" by the elimination of domestic social welfare programs (i.e., keeping the responsibility of providing for children entirely on individual families as a means to encourage smaller families). The only clue to his silence about the welfare state is a comment that "our legal system of private property plus inheritance is unjust."[149] Instead, he advocates "mutual coercion, mutually agreed upon."

To maintain a welfare state in light of the irresponsibility it encourages, we need a managed commons that would force everybody to regulate family size, just as it uses coercion to make sure that resources are exploited and distributed according to the public benefit. Hardin claims that our fear of coercion is only the fear of a word; if we say it "over and over without apology or embarrassment" the word's "dirtiness can be cleansed away."[150] Indeed, the formula is nothing more than "an operational definition of any law in a democracy."[151] We should be no more surprised at state intervention to limit births than we are at laws and police that prevent bank robbery (i.e., treating a bank as a commons).[152] "The alternative . . . is too horrifying to contemplate."[153]

CHARM AND CARNAGE

How have readers responded to Hardin's tough-minded message? "The Tragedy of the Commons" first appeared in *Science* in December 1968; five responses were subsequently published. Three of them took issue only with Hardin's assertion that there was no "technical solution" to the problem of overpopulation, one going so far as suggesting that girls routinely have a birth control capsule inserted under the skin, allowing it to be removed only under specified circumstances. As against such casual presentation of "drastic methods and new techniques,"[154] one can only admire Hardin's recognition that some moral revaluation is called for to make such measures palatable. Only one author took genuine critical issue with the essay, suggesting that Hardin's "insidious arguments," while presented with "awesome" skill, amounted to a justification of almost any kind of tough treatment against societal dissenters.[155]

But if the readers of *Science* did not find the essay worthy of much attention, a great many others did. By late 1971, when Hardin was writing the preface to *Exploring New Ethics for Survival/The Voyage of the Spaceship Beagle*, he could note that the essay had been reprinted in about "two dozen anthologies in the fields of biology, ecology, political science, sociology, law, and economics." Yet while the essay had received "much notice," it had only produced "guarded comment." "I sometimes feel as if I were living in the eye of a hurricane, waiting."[156]

Exploring New Ethics attempted to combine an elaboration of the original "Tragedy" essay, which Hardin noted was "too compact for the general reader,"[157] with a science fiction novella that was illustrative of the principles under discussion. The novella tells the story of a voyage to Alpha Centauri, begun in the wake of a violent antiecology, proeconomic growth revolution in the United States. Whatever its scientific trappings, the project is undertaken simply because capitalist economies require large amounts of "institutionalized waste" lest they self-destruct.[158] Hardin's judgment of the character of American democracy is likewise encapsulated in his use of the phrase "the Pee-pull" for "the people."[159]

The spaceship is divided into two parts; a hidden group of observers made immortal by secret advances in medical science watch the goings on of a larger population of ordinary people, called Quotions, whom the guardians must leave to their own devices. The Quotions, committed as they are to freedom, voluntarism, and brotherhood, nearly destroy themselves with overpopulation and pollution. A huge population boom is followed by a great crash. The surviving Quotions are reduced by circumstances and their excessive breeding to little more than a crowded herd of animals.

In the meantime, the spaceship has returned to earth orbit, and the guardians find that there is only enough power left for them either to land a shuttle themselves or to stay on and die with the now animalized Quotions. A debate follows over whether to kill the Quotions quickly by gassing them before the guardians abandon ship. The guardian who proposed to do so is murdered by one of his fellows who is shocked by such a horrid suggestion. The remainder return to earth, which, we have reason to believe, is itself nearly destroyed by the same forces that have destroyed the Quotions. The Quotions are left to a slow and painful death.

It is a tribute to the frequently noticed wit and charm of Hardin's writing that he could make even a story that centers on riot, destruction, and mass murder witty and charming.[160] While understanding that the "sometimes heavy handed parable"[161] of the space trip was closely connected with the themes of the nonfiction part of the book, critics were content by and large not to investigate how what one noted as its rather unsatisfactory conclusion might reflect seriously on the message Hardin was attempting to get across.[162] Only a few suggested that by making survival the "fundamental value for ethics," Hardin might be preparing the way for desensitizing us to the real moral issues behind the hard choices that he claims we are facing.[163] On the whole, reviewers were happier to avoid thinking about mass murder as a solution to the population problem, and looked to other of Hardin's proposals for population limitation, such as a system of several husbands for one wife, or creating a market in baby vouchers, or limiting female births to one per woman.[164]

Hardin need not have worried that the book would receive a blizzard of criticism. The book "should be read by every concerned citizen,"[165] it makes "exciting—and controversial—reading."[166] From this point of view, even a critical review in *Choice* contained a kind of backhanded compliment: "Recommended for browsing collections, but not as a serious work in ethics."[167] Hardin had managed to popularize himself.

Indeed, praise for the book came from some unexpected quarters. It is an understatement to say that Hardin is not a fan of Catholic doctrine, but the book was praised as "witty and controversial" by the Jesuit magazine *America*, which went on to agree with Hardin that the fundamental issue was the moral one; if people do not limit their own offspring, then "coercion may come as the only alternative."[168]

Perhaps even Jesuits are susceptible to what one reviewer called Hardin's Twain-like style. "He begins deceptively simply, almost folksy . . . and about the time you are wondering why he is dealing in such elementary platitudes, you are in over your head and striking out frantically to keep afloat."[169] That sense of being drawn just beyond one's depth may have made many of the reviews confident that, however controversial the material might be, the scientific foundations for Hardin's analysis were decisive and unimpeachable—even if "scary"[170] or "frightening."[171] Yet it was an extremely enthusiastic review in *Science* that imagined with glee the "squawks" that would be produced by a biologist who *departed* from his field and dared encroach on the "sacred arena" of economics and policy.[172]

With Hardin, as with all our popularizers so far, the relationship between his scientific and policy discussions is not so clear as it seems at first glance. But in Hardin's case, we have someone much more self-conscious about the essentially ethical nature of his enterprise. The problem is that in the end, we are being asked to revamp politics and society to make the world safe for little more than selfishness.

PRUNING THE GROWTH

According to Hardin, "[d]eliberate population control is the greatest need facing every nation today."[173] What are the dangers we face if this need is not met? The poverty of India is indicative of the "cultural sink" and "downward spiral" that might, if the "doomsayers" are correct, become the fate of the whole world.[174] The effects of overpopulation are so pervasive that one is almost always talking about them when something bad happens. For example, population pressure is the cause of deaths by drowning that occur when storms inundate people living on newly made delta land.[175] While Hardin warns us against the "panchestron," or explain all,[176] he has something very like it in overpopulation; he even admits that environmentalists see overpopulation "everywhere."[177]

Hardin's starting point is no different from Ehrlich's. "All organisms naturally and necessarily reproduce too much for their own good"[178]; too much because "[t]he world is finite."[179] Its finitude is its carrying capacity. While always careful to deny that indefinite population growth is possible, Hardin presents frightening pictures of exponential increase. At a 2% per annum growth rate starting from the present world population, it would be only 615 years before there were literally "standing room only" on the earth's land surfaces.[180] Of course, this sort of thing cannot actually happen, Hardin notes. Indeed, it appears that exponential increase is not at all "natural" if by that word we refer to the usual events in nature, rather than hypothetical possibilities that make contrary-to-fact assumptions. Such "hypothetical conclusions are intended as a *reductio ad absurdum*" of the position that there is *no* population problem, to shake the complacent and try to "compel choice," not as predictions.[181] A truly impossible absurdity may frighten, but why should it compel choice?

In the real world, resource availability, predation, and other forms of competition limit population growth. In the absence of major environmental dislocations, these limits keep a population close to a "set point" that is roughly equal to the carrying capacity for that organism. This situation Hardin labels a "homeostatic plateau."[182]

Do the same factors control the size of human populations? Hardin admits that the question "Is man a part of nature?" does not have an easy answer.[183] But he is strongly inclined to believe that human population growth is not headed toward a homeostatic plateau unless we make deliberate efforts, because the mechanisms that would naturally keep population at this level are missing. "For two centuries we have had marvelous success in increasing the carrying capacity of the environment,"[184] owing significantly to the "growth of science and technology."[185] (By his narrow time frame Hardin plays down such basic factors as agriculture and artificial dwellings in the human ability to increase carrying capacity through expanding available resources.) He is most impressed with the increase in carrying capacity caused by control of human predation (i.e., factors causing sickness and disease). It is because this "Pasteurian" world of "freedom from disease" has not been balanced by the "Sangerian" world of birth control that humans are headed toward a disaster in which nature will step in to control population by famine, disease, and the like.[186]

Now, if we look at nonhuman organisms, it would hardly seem to matter to a given organism whether it was killed by a predator in the "normal" course of maintaining a homeostatic equilibrium or killed by disease aggravated by starvation owing to a population boom that overshoots carrying capacity. Nor, in many instances, does it matter to the population of organisms as a whole. Both deaths are equally natural, both serve to keep down or bring down the population. But it matters very much to Hardin which kind of cycle human beings are to participate in. When he presents "starvation, mass disease, or universal warfare and civil disorder" as the results of human overshoot, he assumes it matters to his audience as well.[187] But these preferences are not dictated by nature's methods of population control.

The terrors of death and destruction—if mere survival is at stake—are not the whole story. Carrying capacity comes implicitly to be equated with what Hardin calls "survival under emotionally satisfactory conditions."[188] While "emotionally satisfactory" is nowhere systematically defined, in various contexts Hardin mentions "a comfortable, or even gracious, standard of living,"[189] and the "arts of peace—science, music, painting, sports and other arts of living" as elements of a good life.[190] Again, one reason he favors a low over a high population is the diversity of "lifestyles" that the lower numbers make possible; people could "enjoy, if they wish, Cadillacs, symphony orchestras, wooded wilderness—and meat with their meals." But high population growth "permits only one kind of life, namely the ascetic, which is then no longer an option but an inescapable fate."[191] These definitions make explicit the implicit ideas about the human good that Hardin has imported into carrying capacity.

Hardin asserts that survival under emotionally satisfactory conditions requires social and political arrangements that will produce the homeostatic plateau. For human beings, this equilibrium is defined as the "middle region in which a laissez-faire attitude toward control of the environment works perfectly."[192] We want to arrange our affairs so that they require as little arrangement as possible. But what usually happens naturally for other organisms must be constructed for human beings. The first requirement for "enduring stability" of "a political and economic unit" is "*zero* percent growth."[193] After that, we must consider what "political restraints" are necessary to "keep a laissez-faire system from destroying itself in a limited world."[194]

The determination of the maximum amount of freedom consistent with social stability is a worthy project; few would claim the issue has been definitively settled. But Hardin has not placed the problem in a context that allows fruitful consideration. The natural, nonhuman ecosystems that Hardin draws on for his model of political life do not (so far as we know) have to accommodate themselves to the desire for freedom that Hardin himself sees as a claim that must in some way be satisfied in the human world. They do not provide a ready framework for dealing with beings who can articulate the difference between "survival" and "survival under emotionally satisfactory conditions," and make this difference the subject of joint action or debate.

What is at stake in this employment of carrying capacity is the extent to which Hardin himself is willing, as he claims we must be, to revise our ethical horizon in such a way as to make it "consonant with basic scientific facts."[195] If we look to natural science for guidance in formulating the population problem, we may find that emotionally satisfactory conditions already overvalue humanity looked at from a purely biological perspective. If we start from the purely biological perspective, we have to add the "important premise" that "the continued survival of mankind is desirable. This can certainly not be proven from any point of view that is demonstrably 'objective,' but most men will be willing to accept it."[196] Hardin's inability to find a stronger argument here explains his attraction to Tertullian's comment that natural disasters are nature's means of pruning back "the luxuriant growth of the human race."[197] Yet like Ehrlich, ultimately he is unwilling to leave population control to nature. If we seek to maintain stability of emotionally satisfactory conditions, we are looking first to our wishes, desires, and values to define what the problem of overpopulation is, and not to what science teaches or what nature does about carrying capacity.

WASTE AND UTOPIA

Hardin has another way of arguing that natural science can tell us something about the quality of life we should want, and that is the necessity of competition:

> Man, freed of the population-controlling factors of predators and disease organisms, must—willy-nilly, like it or not—control his own numbers by competition with his own kind. By taking thought he

can elect the kind of competition he employs; but he cannot escape all kinds. This is not to imply that the election is a trivial matter. Surely there are few who would not prefer the endemic celibacy of the Irish to the ritual blood sacrifices of the Aztecs.[198]

Humankind cannot escape competition because of natural selection. Genes compete with one another for their "effect on success in leaving progeny."[199] But if the key to natural selection is breeding success, internalized limits on population growth will be difficult and unnatural.

The extent to which Hardin believes human childbearing behavior is determined by this genetic imperative is, however, unclear. To maintain the general relevance of selection to the human world, Hardin speaks of "social selection" (i.e., selection that comes about on the basis of laws, customs, mores, etc.).[200] Human beings have become what they are through the interaction of hereditary and environmental factors. Laws, norms, and customs must, on the one hand, be compatible with the possibilities inherent in the genetic determinates of human behavior, but they will also help mold those determinates over time.

We already saw some of the implications of these arguments at work in the tragedy of the commons and competitive exclusion, where we discussed the possibility that those who have large families could "outbreed" and bring the extinction of those who would have small families. Yet the time frame required for the competitive exclusion principle to do its work suggests why one would have to limit carefully any conclusions drawn from it about human behavior. In one place Hardin suggests that it would take over 250 years for a group whose members have 2 children to be displaced by a group whose members have 12.[201] In another he quotes C. G. Darwin to the effect that in "hundreds of generations . . . the variety *Homo contracipiens* would become extinct and would be replaced by the variety *Homo progenitivas*."[202] Depending on how many hundreds of generations we are talking about, the time period in question could reach the beginnings of human history.

If there is an urgent need to deal with overpopulation, the slow course of social or natural selection is not liable to make much difference. If we put aside urgent concerns, we have to wonder about the likelihood of any group's pursuing the same policy for "hundreds" of generations. In the contemporary world, even religious dictates have a hard time lasting this long. Is the competitive exclusion principle any more likely to operate in an unobstructed form than the geometric population growth that forms one of its assumptions? Even Hardin seems to have his doubts.[203] Once again, the consideration of imaginary horribles is unlikely to lead to useful policy options.

That may be fine with Hardin. The real purpose of discussing competition may be to get us to think about eugenics and the extrinsic natural forces like disease that control our powerful drive to have progeny. We need to understand the necessity of waste.

Contrary to what one might think, given the propensity of individuals toward self-preservation, nature is not an economizer of lives. The competition of natural selection works to control the "superabundant vitality of nature"[204] by wasting the lives of those individuals whose genetic makeup puts them at some relative disadvantage. The appearance of the balance of nature is the result of the wastage, over eons, of all those parts that did not fit into the developing natural "design."[205]

To attempt to do away with natural waste "by preserving all of the mutants and breeding equally of all genetic types ultimately brings about the extinction of the entire species," as genetic changes that make a species less competitive become entrenched in the gene pool.[206] Hence to do away with waste is to "threaten a very foundation stone of evolution and progress."[207] It is dangerously utopian to believe that all waste can be eliminated and a "completely planned heaven" substituted for it.[208] But while suspicious of complete planning, Hardin celebrates the "foresight, design," and "progress" that result from unplanned, natural wastage.[209] Waste seems to be a way of having one's cake and . . . wasting it.

What happens when human beings limit the waste of lives that results from natural selection, to save lives, for example, that would otherwise be taken by disease? What happens when this death control is not balanced by birth control? What would it mean for us to be guided by the lessons of natural waste?

Hardin distinguishes between disease for which "the hereditary component is negligible—say, for smallpox," and those with a large hereditary component (e.g., hemophilia).[210] In the first case, elimination of waste has been an "unalloyed blessing."[211] But in the second case, Hardin suggests that the interests of society and posterity are not served when lives are saved and disease-producing genes are passed on to another generation: "Evolutionists look with horror at pictures of ten-year-old children equipped with pacemakers or artificial kidneys."[212] Modern medicine makes "negative eugenics," or the attempt to eliminate harmful genes, difficult when we save or prolong lives in the face of diseases that would otherwise be fatal early enough, or sufficiently debilitating, to prevent reproduction and hence the passing on of the genetic defect. The necessity of waste apparently provides the context in which Hardin does argue that we should be willing to let nature take its course. Has he presented a clear account of those circumstances?

In the case of disease, there is less to Hardin's distinction than meets the eye. The elimination of diseases with a supposedly negligible hereditary component cannot be an "unalloyed blessing," since it does away with a natural mechanism of population control; such "death control" without birth control is a source of overpopulation. There is an argument to be made on Hardin's premises that nature should be left to take its course for *all* disease. But Hardin does not advocate this course. Instead, he advocates the deliberate "wastage" of abortion and contraception to compensate for the limit we have put on the spontaneous waste caused by disease.

Hardin's extended arguments in favor of legalized abortion[213] do not attempt to justify this preference for contraception and abortion over allowing the waste of lives that comes about on the basis of supposedly nonhereditary disease. After all, he is not arguing against anyone who would accept the "pro-disease" position that is an unstated but logical consequence of combining concern for population growth and praise of waste. If we have to have waste and "balance the books" of population growth, it might seem mere "common sense" to prefer saving the lives of those already born at the expense of those not born, just as it appears that common sense would prefer celibacy over blood sacrifice as a means of population control. Aztec common sense thought otherwise. "Common sense" is confined by certain moral assumptions that would have to be articulated and defended—moral assumptions that are called attention to by but not grounded in the supposed biological need for waste. Perhaps we should prefer to save the innocent over the sinning, or prefer to allow a death rather than take a life. Perhaps we should give new life a chance, rather than sustain an existing life. And so on. Each of these possibilities implies a different kind of obligation. Is any one of them more "consonant" with science than another?

The need for waste alone does not tell us exactly how human beings, unlike beings strictly confined to natural necessity, are to make choices about waste and create "designs" (but not plans, for plans are "detailed [and] rather rigid") that mimic the spontaneous action of nature.[214] What is required to make the argument is some account of the obligations we owe to different persons under different circumstances, whether it be to provide them with medical care, allow them to have children, and so on. The wolf does not ask the sick young caribou whether it would rather die of old age. But we are going to have to make some hard choices, and once we call for a justification of them, we have entered a totally different world from the unplanned, progressive heaven of natural waste that, when applied to human beings, is the highly utopian basis of Hardin's anti-utopian arguments.

TIME MACHINE PHILANTHROPY

The guidance concerning our obligations to our fellows that is lacking in the discussion of waste is provided by "discriminating altruisms."[215] Hardin begins from the position that competition generally does not favor behavior that places the welfare of another over the welfare of oneself. Presenting a continuum of altruistic behaviors, ranging from an individualism that cares for others "mostly on a one-to-one basis" to universalism, Hardin argues that the narrower the form of altruism, the more likely it is to be practiced.[216]

While Hardin says biology shows that altruism cannot "displace the natural egoism of a species,"[217] he acknowledges an altruistic side to human behavior. Thus the question of when or how much people act from altruistic motives is complicated and fraught with ambiguity.[218] But it is precisely these uncertainties that, in his view, justify the following "Cardinal Rule of Policy": *"Never ask a person to act against his own self-interest."*[219] At best, we can only expect people to be discouraged from behaving in demonstrably harmful, egoistic ways.[220]

Despite this acknowledgment that *egoism* needs to be limited, Hardin gives more attention to debunking *altruistic* claims: "[S]urvival under emotionally satisfactory conditions is possible only if we set limits to the practice of altruism."[221] To this end, Hardin discusses the dangers of promiscuous altruism, or universalism. Universalism and its corresponding political hope of "One World" is, "in the strictest sense, impossible of achievement," it is "impossible in principle."[222] By One World, Hardin means a universal commons of material resources, or indeed any good. One World, Hardin rightly claims, actually makes altruism impossible. When everything is shared, then the condition that calls for altruism, which is a giving up of one's own, no longer exists. Likewise, Hardin argues, the extension of the idea of brotherhood to include all humanity is the destruction of that idea, since brotherhood is an exclusive relationship.[223]

Beyond these undoubted conceptual difficulties, the irreducible competitiveness of humans means that One World would universalize competition rather than peace. All lesser forms of altruism recognize some measure of egoism by defining groups among which one behaves altruistically. But universalism denies the legitimacy of such groups. It requires that "distance—in space, in time, and in culture" make no difference among human beings.[224] Far from leading to world peace, competition would intensify when there is no longer a limited "we" among whom peaceful relations are the norm. Such peaceful internal relations are based on the need of limited groups to withstand the external pressures of other groups. In One World, the whole would be "vulnerable to destruction by the smallest minority of nonconformers" and their nonconforming descendants.[225] Either the nonconformers would be unopposed, in which case they would be victorious, or they would be opposed, in which case there would no longer be One World.

Hence Hardin claims to eschew global solutions and criticizes those who place our only hope for survival on such solutions. We should "consciously seek to retain a world of more or less separate, more or less antagonistic units called (most generally) tribes. They may be synonymous with nations as we now know them, or they may be some new political inventions." Hardin judges that such a world, in which each individual identifies "himself with several tribes of different degrees of inclusiveness sounds very much like the world we now live in." It would not be wise, he concludes, "to try to escape this condition."[226]

The conservative sound of this and many like formulations is misleading. Hardin is aware that "the best is the enemy of the good,"[227] but he relies more than he seems to know on utopian political invention. Coexistence, for example, is still more honored as a principle than practiced in the "world we now live in." Hardin himself unwittingly indicates why: "Put bluntly, every community must be free to go to hell in its own way, so long as its action does not endanger the continued existence of other communities."[228] Without global arrangements for conflict resolution, such freedom is not a recipe for coexistence, but conflict, as groups disagree about what constitutes a separate community and whether the actions of one threaten others. It is very well to say that we should outlaw atomic bombs and international warfare,[229] and redirect patriotic competition into peaceful paths.[230] But these goals, if they mean anything at all, point back to One World. For all his criticism of it, Hardin also admits that "there must be some sense in which our world must be One World."[231] To put it another way, the arrangements Hardin describes are perhaps seen in liberal societies if they are seen anywhere, with their relative tolerance of diversity, and encouragement of cross-cutting identifications and affiliations. To have such arrangements globally is the hope of just the kind of liberal internationalism that Hardin's criticisms of One World undercut.

The urgency of limiting conflict in Hardin's world will be the greater since discriminating altruism is an attempt to *justify* particularism by liberating self-interest from universalistic claims of compassion, right, or brotherhood. It is no surprise that Hardin is forced back to universalistic conclusions; there must be "a few moral principles that are accepted by all, if all are to survive," even if these principles are only "such as will assure the continuing existence of the smaller units."[232] Yet it may or may not appear evident to one small group why its existence requires the existence of another. History is testimony to the infrequency with which this conclusion is drawn. How much more frequently will it be drawn if, as Hardin hopes, people learn to moderate or in some cases abandon ties of brotherhood and compassion that extend beyond a small group?

Hardin may well be right that care for everyone is care for no one. But neither recognition of that truth, nor his belief that he has not described a system that will solve all the world's problems at once, is enough to save him from utopianism.[233] The inner tensions in his description of how the world should work already point in that direction, and we see the problems multiply when we begin to talk about the choices individuals are to make.

The difficulty of avoiding universalistic forms of altruism, given Hardin's goals, is evident also in the relationship between altruism and the positive and negative eugenics that were suggested by the need for waste. Finally, the need to limit egoism comes into focus. For the question of eugenics is a question of altruism: is there any reason why I should forgo having and raising children as I please, for the sake of a larger good?

The first hurdle Hardin must clear to answer this question is a widespread opinion that people have a right to make such choices for themselves. Hardin is very suspicious of such talk. Universal human rights, an "absolutist concept,"[234] are a "rhetorical deception" to mask competitive situations[235] and egotistical demands.[236] Rights are little more than the needs of some projected into obligations imposed on others.[237] While in their claim to be universal they lead to "ethical imperialism,"[238] they are based on a "highly individualistic view" that is "not adequate for a world of more than four billion human beings."[239] Any claim to a right must be "evaluated in the total system of rights operating in a world that is limited," so that we know "the effect of each right on the suppliers as well as on the demanders."[240] Some rights pass the test, apparently; although Hardin notes quite correctly that "Claiming rights is a major oratorical sport of our time,"[241] he is happy in seeming seriousness to advocate the right of "the lilies, the trees, and all the other glories of nature" to standing in court cases.[242]

But even without a right to support childbearing, why restrain what Hardin himself regards as a powerful natural tendency? Hardin's attempt to solve the problem of egoism in a manner consistent with discriminating altruism is to suggest that we have an obligation to take "care of the interests of posterity."[243] Hardin admits he has difficulty finding a rational foundation for this obligation,[244] and indeed it is a curious answer. In the case of eugenics, we will be asking some people not to have children not because their children will be miserable (medical help may allow them to lead normal lives) but for the sake of the health of the species. This is precisely the kind of universalism that is, from the perspective of discriminating altruism, most suspect. As part of his critique of universalism, Hardin is critical of the "telescopic philanthropy" that cares more for distant and unknown persons than those close by.[245] But the same argument could be made against advocating a universal concern for those who do not exist (i.e., future generations), as against those in the here and now.

If a concern for posterity is not necessarily the best ground on which to seek to overcome egoism and promote eugenics, it may seem that it provides a better ground for population limitation. Here, the case is clear: concern for our posterity means sparing them the misery of an overpopulated world. Better not to bring children into the world than to bring them into a crowded one. This argument can be made only by those who are already here. Hardin provides no evidence that there is a pervasive tendency among those born into miserable circumstances to wish seriously that they had not been born at all. In expressing our concern for posterity by curtailing the number of those for whom we are concerned, we are acting already as "guardians" under circumstances where those who might have an interest in guarding us do not even exist. This is not exactly a formula for responsible political or moral behavior.

Even if we accept the moral logic that expression of concern for posterity means reducing posterity, it is necessary to call attention to the premise that—absent population reduction—the future will be miserable. In other words, the moral worth of our restraint depends on our ability to predict our social, political, and economic future, an enterprise in which humans generally have exhibited relatively little success so far. The necessity to ground our moral judgments in such predictions flows from the "promethean ethics" that Hardin puts forward as his best attempt to legitimize the concern for posterity, or indeed justify any moral choice. The central question promethean ethics would have us ask when faced with a moral dilemma is "And then what?" In this respect, promethean ethics is the same as the situational or relativistic ethics to which Hardin gives high praise.[246] Situational ethics starts from the observation that the same act can have different consequences, depending on the circumstances under which the act is performed. It concludes that the only way to judge any act, then, is in accordance with its consequences under the circumstances.

But when faced with a choice of having children or not or, more to the point, of accepting coercive programs to limit the number or kind of children I can have, what exactly does asking "And then what?" tell me? At what level am I to consider the consequences: for me, or my family, or my nation, or the world? Am I to look at consequences in one year, or ten, or one hundred? How do I balance my pain today for having few or no children, against the good that might accrue from this act to society as a whole some fifty or more years from now? Hardin's turn to situational ethics merely recapitulates the commons problem and the problem of discriminating altruisms. It does not provide a way to solve those dilemmas. Indeed, with its stress on the moral significance of changeable and contingent circumstances, it opens the door to an extreme of moral egoism. My situation is never so similar to that of others that I cannot find in it the basis for a moral distinction. Situationalism justifies making me the final, perhaps only, legitimate judge of my actions. While in practice any moral principle may be distorted according to the whim or wish of the actor, situationalism provides a theoretical justification for the liberation, rather than the restriction, of an actor's will or passions.

So far, then, Hardin has been unable to find a justification for what he himself regards as the necessary limitation of egoism that population or eugenic policies require, raising more than a suspicion that all he can offer us is coercion in what he happens to regard as a good cause. When you add this to his attack on rights and advocacy of situationalism, you get a politically terrifying result.

The first thing to go is the rule of law. "Law, to be stable, must be based on ethics," Hardin says,[247] but when the ethics is situational, the result can never be stability. In the very same book, Hardin criticizes those who attempt to understand law in terms of principles.[248] Rights as general principles are defective guides to lawmaking and make it more difficult for law to address the variety of circumstances, and changing circumstances, that must be faced. What we need is case-by-case administrative decision making (or perhaps a population *so* low that people could be allowed to do pretty much as they please, a state of affairs not known to human history).[249]

Hardin acknowledges the danger of tyranny inherent in rule by administrative decision in his repeated exhortations that we must solve the problem of "who will guard the guardians." But solutions to such a problem do not come merely because we wish them. Hardin has only increased the severity of the guardian problem by his apparent advocacy of an unrestrained majoritarianism. When Hardin says that "mutual coercion, mutually agreed upon" is a democratic principle, he is right.[250] Pure or direct democracies present the danger of the tyranny of the majority implicit in that formula. Is not this majority that same "Pee-pull" for whom his contempt is otherwise so evident? Yet Hardin is suspicious of the fact that representative democracy allows the will of the majority to be thwarted.[251]

As we trace through the course of Hardin's argument, it becomes less and less clear who the guardians are, who exactly is to guard them, and what they are to guard against. In his government of men and not laws, where higher principles are eschewed in favor of situational judgments, what recourse in principle or practice will there be against the will of whoever Hardin believes should have the power to achieve the goals he sets out? And make no mistake, we are talking about great goals and substantial power, even if we could somehow be convinced that the realm of the guardians would be confined "only" to population control and eugenics. The tasks that Hardin lays on the "guardians" are awesome, for all that he speaks out against "millennial thinking" and for accommodation with an imperfect world.[252] The guardians will have to avert imminent crisis and at the same time secure the well-being of humanity into an indefinite future. In doing so they must avoid both rigorous planning, which assumes more knowledge than we have, *and* laissez-faire, which accomplishes too little. They need to find the proper "cooperation" with natural forces that Hardin calls "designing."[253] Then we will have a designed human world that echoes the undesigned self-regulating mechanisms that characterize natural ecosystems.

> To understand the world and to control it, one must have faith that understanding is possible, that solutions can be found, that control is attainable. The more creative spirits in science are engaged in a continuous internecine war with the less creative, who cherish their impotence.
>
> Is not this same spiritual disjunction found in the realm of law and politics? Are there not lawyers and political scientists who so cherish impotence that they merely collect tales of the malfunction of administrative systems, making no effort to analyze the reason for the malfunction in order to prevent it in the future? Since an ever larger proportion of our legal directives must be filtered through administrative systems, we had jolly well better set about making these systems more flexible, more intelligent, and less corruptible. Inventiveness is called for.[254]

If we act as "we had jolly well better," then it will be possible to create the "new kind of communities that are neither nation nor caste nor anything that has yet been conceived of."[255] Hardin, who has remarked, "It's no good saying that mankind *must* reform immediately,"[256] correctly identifies the basis of this hope for the as yet unconceived: faith. This hard-boiled rationalist is asking us to have faith in the ability of science to understand and control the world and faith in the charitable dispositions of those "guardians" to whom this power of control will be granted.

Far from teaching us about the need for limits, Hardin has defined the population problem in such open-ended terms that it becomes nearly impossible to solve by political and moral measures that are any less open-ended themselves. With any and all possibilities open, "depending on the circumstances," the problem is less to *justify* coercion in the particular case of family size than to explain how coercion is to be *limited* at all. If the new human communities, the ultimate justification of our actions, have "not yet been conceived of," in the name of what will morality exercise restraint on our behavior?

It is faith in and hope for some better future learned from the successes of modern natural science—for who would have dreamed yesterday of today's accomplishments?—that makes Hardin a searcher for limits who is unwilling to admit any moral absolute that might limit human choice and action. Even such a fundamental as "Thou shalt not kill" is explicitly rejected as an absolute prohibition.[257] While any reasonable ethic may have to struggle with the justification of exceptions to this rule, Hardin finds himself in a position where he has to argue why overt mass murder is *not* the preferred response to population pressure. His reasons are thin: "*There is no need to kill.* We have better and more humane ways of achieving the same end."[258] But "better" is a situational term, as the Quotions never do quite find out. There may be circumstances in which guardians think other methods are "situationally" preferable in order to follow the rule that will replace "Thou shalt not kill": "Thou shalt not suffer the carrying capacity to be exceeded."[259]

Hardin has the debunker's incisive ability to see the problematic conclusions that might be drawn from the premises of arguments that he disagrees with. He seeks to force his readers to reexamine those premises or draw their consistent conclusions. But situational ethics frees him from the same hard look at his own premises. It represents a kind of cosmic fudge factor that he can bring to bear whenever he does not want to acknowledge the "and then whats?" that his assumptions suggest. After all, one must "perforce" adopt some "moral directives . . . to give stability to daily life."[260]

No one could claim that mindless, heartless, and limitless breeding—which is how Hardin generally pictures the miracle of children—should be the goal of human life. Yet to control reproduction, Hardin and Ehrlich constantly find themselves explaining—in a not very convincing way—why they have not brought us over the brink of indecency. The life-style freedom that both seem so to look forward to, if it can be achieved at all, is to be purchased by an unprecedented breadth and depth of coercion over one of the most powerful and intimate aspects of human life. How it could ever be lifted without a return of the "whole dirty business" is left as a mystery of scientific progress; perhaps in the fashion to which the totalitarian regimes of our century aspired, we can remake human beings so that their existing evolutionary imperatives are eliminated. For all Hardin's and Ehrlich's talk of limits, this kind of hope is the liberating cry of utopian extremism.

Perhaps, however, there is a better way of thinking about limits. After all, there is something to the environmentalist case: wanting to take a stand against excessive materialism and consumerism, and for the moderation of desire and envy; against scientific and technological hubris, and for prudence and foresight; against reckless consumption, and for obligations to humankind present and future. Perhaps looking narrowly at population is not the best way of getting to such reasonable goals, because it puts too much pressure on one highly charged aspect of our lives. Why not try to combine technological innovation and the teaching of limits into one great environmental synthesis? We turn now to such efforts.

CHAPTER THREE

Small-Knowing Souls

To return to the Lacedaemonians. Their discipline continued still after they were full grown men. No one was allowed to live after his own fancy; but the city was a sort of camp, in which every man had his share of provisions and business set out, and looked upon himself not so much born to serve his own ends as the interest of his country.

Plutarch, "Lycurgus"[1]

It would seem that, if despotism were to be established amongst the democratic nations of our days, it might assume a different character . . . [I]t is well content that the people should rejoice, provided they think of nothing but rejoicing. For their happiness such a government willingly labors, but it chooses to be the sole agent and the only arbiter of that happiness; it provides for their security, foresees and supplies their necessities, facilitates their pleasures, manages their principal concerns, directs their industry, regulates the descent of property, and subdivides their inheritances; what remains, but to spare them all the care of thinking and all the trouble of living?

Alexis de Tocqueville, *Democracy in America*[2]

THE END IS NIGH

On February 27, 1972, the world woke up to find that within 100 years would come "an uncontrollable and disastrous collapse of society."[3] The prediction was no back-page filler about some fanatical religious sect. Featured on the front page by no less than the *New York Times*, the news came out of the Massachusetts Institute of Technology; the research discussed was funded by the Volkswagen Foundation for a prestigious—if mysterious-sounding—group of industrialists, businesspeople, and academics called the Club of Rome.

While arguments about the imminent demise of everything seem to have perennial appeal, *The Limits to Growth* seemed to be something new: an objective result reached by the use of a computer.[4] The study's authors—Donella and Dennis Meadows, Jørgen Randers and William Behrens III, all from MIT—had refined and developed a global "model" first developed by Jay Forrester (also of MIT) that purported to describe how worldwide population growth, pollution, industrial output, and resource exploitation were interrelated. This "systems analysis" used mathematical equations to describe these relationships, then set the computer to work projecting current trends into the future.

The results seemed mere common sense, once you thought about it. The growth of population and the accelerating use of "non-renewable" natural resources (like oil) caused by an expanding global economy would sooner or later mean that the resources that provide materials and energy for modern civilization would simply be used up. When the material basis for our civilization disappears, so will civilization. As resources vanish, industrial output will collapse, pollution will soar, food supply will dwindle, and the death rate will go up.[5]

Maybe the projections underestimated the resources available? Assume twice as many, the study concluded, and the same thing happens.[6] Assume unlimited resources, pollution controls, and more food production, and the same thing happens.[7] Assume perfect but voluntary birth control, and the same thing happens.[8] After all, the earth is finite, a small, fragile globe alone in space. There is only so much oil, so much tin, so much gold out there. Once it gets "used up," we're stuck. And obviously, if more and more people are using it faster as the level of global economic and technological development rises, it's going to be used up faster.

The only solution that prevented global disaster, according to *Limits*, was to create a "global equilibrium" (i.e., to end population and economic growth). Births per year must be made to equal deaths per year, resource consumption per capita reduced to one-fourth its 1970 level, a shift made from the production of goods to the provision of services, pollution reduced to one-fourth its 1970 value, food production increased, and goods made more durable—all by 1975.[9] Although *Limits* admitted that it did not expect such policies to be initiated so rapidly, it also purported to show that the longer they were delayed, or the less stringent they were, the more unlikely it was that disaster could be avoided.[10]

The MIT team gave next to no indication of just how such drastic changes were to be brought about or what the resulting world would look like. "No one can predict what sort of institutions mankind might develop under these new conditions," they admitted, and they offered no "guarantee that the new society would be much better or even much different from that which exists today." But they did think it possible that, released from the problems of growth, we might have "more energy and ingenuity available for solving other problems," and thus create a society that would be more innovative, equal, and just than the existing system.[11] Equality might result from abandoning the false promise that growth will produce more for everybody.[12] Activities that do not require "large flows of irreplaceable resources or produce severe environmental degradation," such as "education, art, music, religion, basic scientific research, athletics and social interaction" could flourish.[13] How were these activities, traditionally paid for through the surpluses created by growth, to be funded? The fixed output of society could be produced through ever more efficient means, thus leading to surpluses of both time and money—unless a given country wishes to take up the slack with population growth.[14]

Limits claimed to be "an attempt to create freedom for society, not to impose a straitjacket."[15] But a "Commentary" section added to the book and signed by the Executive Committee of the Club of Rome was more direct about what it would take to produce such results: "[I]f mankind is to embark on a new course, concerted international measures and joint long-term planning will be necessary on a scale and scope without precedent."[16]

SELLING THE BAD NEWS

The computer model on which *Limits* was based was widely recognized to be primitive, and the data that it employed incomplete and defective.[17] Nevertheless, the conclusions caught on, and publication of the book is still widely regarded as a watershed. How did it achieve, and maintain, this status? Part of the answer is to be found in the remarkable story of how *Limits* was brought to the public's attention, and part has to do with the debate that followed its publication. The way *Limits* went about its popularizing project reveals a good deal about what has come to be a typical pattern of debate about environmental issues. It suggests what happens when, as Commoner suggested, scientists are freed from the obligation of trying individually to produce objective results. *Limits* proves to be a textbook example of doing science by press release.

The first news of *Limits* was not the result of some science or economics editor finding an interesting story in a professional journal. Rather it was the carefully arranged product of a public relations campaign, the culmination of a series of events going back to the founding of the Club of Rome by Aurelio Pecci in 1968. This Italian industrialist, who had held leading positions at Fiat and Olivetti, brought together "a group of scientists and intellectuals alarmed at what they considered ominous trends in the world."[18] Even before the club sponsored any research, its members were united by a common belief in "a breakdown of society that they felt was intrinsic in the uncontrolled growth of technology and population."[19] In 1970, the club met with Jay Forrester, already famous for his computer modeling and systems analysis of industrial processes, who was working on a global model published in 1971 under the title *World Dynamics*.[20] He outlined for them the study that was to become *Limits to Growth* and turned the project over to the Meadowses and their team.

Meanwhile, as Pecci later described it, club members had been seeking out political leaders in the East and West to warn them of the coming dangers. "Our message was received with sympathy and understanding, but no action followed," he would later comment. "What we needed was a stronger tool of communication to move men on the planet out of their ingrained habits."[21]

Limits was to be that "stronger tool," hence the care with which its appearance was orchestrated. Even before the book was published, a symposium was arranged by the Woodrow Wilson International Center for Scholars for the day it would appear in stores. The meeting, funded by Xerox, was held at the Smithsonian Institution. The public relations firm of Calvin Kyle Associates had distributed "zingy press releases and background material" embargoed until February 27, a Sunday, so as to promote maximum readership of the articles that would appear.[22]

The plan worked in just the way it was intended. As a review in *America* was to put it later, "*The Limits to Growth* is not just a book, it is an event."[23] The only thing wrong with this statement is that it may overestimate the significance of the book and underestimate that of the event. The initial news coverage was not at all confined to the "national" press; I well remember the excitement with which I cut out the story from a Cleveland paper, headlined "Study Sees Disaster by Year 2100," and eagerly started searching for the book. And as this headline indicates, the stories reflected almost entirely the urgent tone that *Limits* itself sounded. Any criticism mentioned at this early stage could hardly be terribly serious, since none of the critics had yet seen the book. Forrester's work had been published, and criticisms and defenses of his model were already in circulation. Still, the Meadowses' group had as yet published nothing in professional journals, and the actual model they were working from (i.e., the computer program with all its equations) was not to be published until *after Limits* came out.

This was, as a British reviewer later put it, "a curious way for scientists to behave—especially in a controversial subject-area which they believe to be of earth-shattering importance."[24] It is a little like holding a press conference to announce that the moon will collide with the earth in 100 years, and noting in passing that the calculations are not yet available that show how all our previous understanding of orbital dynamics—that seem to make this event impossible—are wrong.[25]

Meanwhile, the Wilson Center was bombarded with phone calls from "ambassadors, industrialists, high government officials, congressmen, and a flock of distinguished scientists" who, having seen the Sunday papers, wanted to attend the symposium.[26] The morning session, at which Dennis Meadows summarized the results and a panel discussed implications of the study for social policy, was covered by TV. After all, would the Smithsonian host a reception and seminar about the book if it were not serious? Would then Secretary of Health, Education, and Welfare Elliot Richardson attend such an event, and praise the effort as "too thoughtful and significant" to ignore, if there was not something to it?[27] And his praise was relatively restrained. Once the cameras had gone during the afternoon session, objections began to emerge. But criticism was difficult, given the way the study had been released—or rather, not released.

Curiously enough, given the dry and academic tone of *Limits*, the passion that eventually greeted it comes close to that generated by Carson. In March, for example, the *Times* published two two-part op-ed pieces on the report, one by Anthony Lewis and one by Leonard Silk. Lewis essentially endorsed the findings, worrying only that the right kind of conclusions be drawn from them (e.g., the need for the redistribution of the world's wealth).[28] Silk, on the other hand, was critical of the study's faulty assumptions and scanty data. Yet for all that, he argued, "It would be madness to ignore the warning of Dr. Dennis L. Meadows." Indeed, he agreed with the major thrust of the study that "this industrial society is getting dangerously crowded, complex and putrid" and that the situation calls for a radical change in values and the way things work, changes we must now begin to think seriously about.[29] With critics like this, who needs advocates? In early April, on the other hand, the lead Sunday *Times* book review was a highly, and far more thoroughly, critical account not just of *Limits* but of Forrester's *World Dynamics* and *Urban Dynamics* as well. *Limits* was called "[l]ess than pseudoscience and little more than polemical fiction," a "rediscovery of the oldest maxim of computer science: Garbage In,

Garbage Out."[30] While the model allowed pollution or consumption to increase exponentially, it did not allow the scientific or technical growth that might help ameliorate such problems likewise to increase; arbitrary limits were placed on them that force a collapse sooner or later.[31]

Lester Brown writing in *Saturday Review* defended the study against such charges; no one had ever addressed the question of limits to growth "in such an empirical and systematic fashion."[32] Yet, a review in *Journal of Politics* disputes the extent of empiricism; the book tells us about "the quirky behavior of a complicated set of equations" but "gives no assurance at all that the model says anything about the world."[33] Even a largely favorable review in *Living Wilderness* regretted that no comparison was made between "real world data and the model," which is one of the reasons it "cannot be considered a scientific book." Still, it is a "readable treatise" that makes "important reading."[34]

Gunnar Myrdal handled the book in a similar way during a speech he gave at a UN Conference on the environment. He noted that although a computer simulation "may impress the innocent general public," it "has little, if any, scientific validity" and represents "quasi-learnedness."[35] Myrdal also spoke of the scanty data, and argued further that the level of aggregation used in the study, treating all data in terms of global quantities, produced misleading results. Yet while for the "serious student" the study is faulty, "it will probably have the useful effect of popularizing the ecologists' broad warnings of the necessity of giving up our expectations to continue on the road of unrestrained growth."[36] Kenneth Boulding writing in *The New Republic* had the opposite concern; there is "so much to turn people off in this volume" that it may lead to denial of the serious issues it raises. Furthermore, he saw a danger that a "mystique of computerized prophecy" would produce a "sectarian movement" that would thereby deny the question of limits the attention it deserved.[37]

Perhaps because so much effort was expended on criticism of the computer program, not a great deal of attention was paid to the political program—vague as it was—outlined in the report and in the Club of Rome's appendix. True to form, *The Nation* questioned why redistributionist policies were not given more attention; and lest predictions of the collapse of capitalism seem a good thing, it made sure its readers knew the book had been criticized in Moscow.[38] But it was left to *Bookworld* to wonder seriously about the politics of the report. Despite the fact that "[o]ne more warning about the folly of unlimited growth is always welcome," the reviewer did wonder whether the "prospect of a rigorously planned society" held out by *Limits* might not make "even doomsday seem more bearable." Did Orwell, he wondered, foresee what would be necessary to the equilibrium state? "The Anti-Sex League (for population control), perpetual war (for rigid allocation of resources), the Ministry of Truth (for stifling consumerist dissent) all fit neatly with the solution proposed by the Club of Rome." Those who might think that a benign form of these same controls is equally or more possible should remember that "people do not run governments out of benevolence; they govern out of love of power."[39]

Intense controversy—even if not always predicated on a complete or profound understanding of the work in question—rarely hurts the purposes of the popularizer. But what accounts for the fact that so many who rejected the book's methods tried as hard as they did to salvage the conclusions drawn from those methods? Causes peculiar to the early 1970s may have played a role. The idea of limits doubtless appealed to many for the reason it appealed to me: still powerful remnants of the 1960s cultural revolution kept us on the lookout for yet more reasons to reject bourgeois capitalism. On the other side, perhaps it appealed to those bourgeois capitalists who, from a desire to protect their own economic position, thought that "no growth" might mean their stability and safety.

But more seriously, *Limits* came at a crucial time for American environmentalism. The first Earth Day in 1970 had introduced large numbers to a new issue and higher expectations for government action. With the passage of the National Environmental Policy Act in 1969 and the subsequent creation of the Environmental Protection Agency in 1970, environmentalism had achieved two important objectives. It had advocated assessments of "environmental impact" as a routine part of government policy-making, and this the NEPA seemed to provide. Further, it had in the EPA an organ of government that, at least in theory, was capable of environmental oversight and research.

Yet with the battle for public opinion and bureaucratic representation thus far won, a different struggle was on the horizon. For the more scientists were convinced that they should turn their attention to environmental problems, the more complicated those problems seemed, and the less it appeared that science had the kind of information needed to deal with them. Normally, such ignorance would be viewed as an opportunity for more research. But now, it presented a difficulty. If there were urgent environmental problems out there, then the delay that further research into them would necessitate was surely not a good thing. And, of course, a nagging question also followed from this relative ignorance: if we don't understand the environment very well, how can we be sure just what is and is not a threat to it?

Increasingly, the answer to both these questions was that if we are not sure that a given environmental situation is a problem, best to make the "conservative" assumption that the danger is real, since delay could create a worse situation (remember, everything is connected to everything else). The result was a vast proliferation of the environmental doomsdays that Carson had used so effectively. An apotheosis was reached with Gordon Rattray Taylor's *The Doomsday Book*, accurately described by its cover copy as "A terrifying roll call of man's sins against the earth as she plunges toward a future of sterility and filth."[40] The book chronicles literally dozens of ways for life on earth to be destroyed, some of them mutually contradictory (like the imminent return of an ice age and global warming). Yet when everything becomes a disaster in the making, a certain numbness begins to set in, or a certain skepticism. The "environmental" view, which allows us to see the complex and cascading effects of everything we do, was beginning to backfire.

The idea of limits to growth was perfect for short-circuiting all this uncertainty and fragmentation. Rhetorically, it matters little that the model used in *Limits* was primitive and inadequate, or that everybody admitted that its basic data were scanty.[41] To unify all the apocalyptic possibilities required only that people accept the intuitively plausible notion that uncontrolled growth in a finite world is not possible.

The serious technical discussion of *Limits* that eventually took place within the specialized fields of the academy was too late, and too academic, to make much headway against such a simple starting point. Economists and natural scientists in particular produced long, detailed, and highly technical critiques of the model and the conclusions drawn from it.[42] But the fact that the criticisms of the experts would be so abstruse and delayed was precisely what the Club of Rome counted on, when they embarked on their publicity campaign. Carroll Wilson, a club member and then professor of management at MIT, noted that "so few will read the technical report and so many will read the book that it doesn't really matter" that the book was published in advance of the technical reports on which it was based.[43] The remarkable cynicism of this statement does not lessen its truth. It certainly didn't matter from the point of view of making a splash. But of course it *did* matter, precisely to the extent that it precluded early and serious expert scrutiny that might then have been made accessible to the public, and cast more doubt on the techniques and conclusions of the work.

It is unreasonable to claim that, in all issues of public policy, expert opinion (i.e., the opinion of those with highly specialized knowledge somehow relevant to the question at hand) should govern debate and discussion. But it does have to have some place, and that place needs to be consistent with the relatively slow and cautious way in which such knowledge develops, for two reasons. On the one hand, those in the best position to evaluate the claims being put forward have to have time to do their work. On the other hand, it is just as necessary that there be an opportunity to present the results in such a way that the nonspecialist can appreciate their significance. When science is done by press release, those with expertise can simply take advantage of the gap between their knowledge and that of the public to further their own agendas. The debate that results is rarely more illuminating to outsiders than children shouting "says so," "says not."

CALL IN REWRITE!

Perhaps the best indication that there really was something seriously wrong with *Limits* is that the Club of Rome produced a second report in 1974, titled *Mankind at the Turning Point*.[44] This one was coauthored by Mihajlo Mesarovic, a professor of systems research at Case-Western Reserve University, and Eduard Pestel, an engineering professor at Hanover University in Germany. The need for the new report was based not only on the technical flaws of the *Limits* model. Whatever the hand wringing that greeted *Limits*, "no-growth" simply was not in the cards. To call for such radical, global changes in such a short time was really a counsel of despair.[45] And despite implications of massive redistributionist policies, it seemed all too likely that "no-growth" would simply condemn large portions of the world to continued poverty.[46] Could the analysis be made more rigorous and the policy implications more palatable while retaining the same urgency and simplicity?

The Club of Rome apparently thought it could. *Turning Point* rejected utterly the computer model used in *Limits*—but it did not reject computer modeling. It rejected the conclusion that there would be a global catastrophe—but it did promise regional catastrophes unless redistributionist policies were pursued. It rejected the proposition that a global restructuring was required yesterday—but it did claim that any delay would cost *"human suffering and lives."*[47] It claimed to reject the "no-growth" prescription of *Limits*—but it spoke plainly for planned and managed growth that would look very much like the equilibrium society of *Limits* as time went by. Thus *Turning Point* represents a rhetorical triumph to the extent that it walks this fine line. The only thing it didn't manage to do was make the immediate splash that *Limits* made. As a result it is less known today but probably of more enduring interest, given its close connection with the current focus on "sustainable development."

The authors of *Turning Point* agree with other critics that the model used in *Limits* was biased toward collapse. Treating the world as one system and attempting to aggregate all inputs (e.g., *world* birthrate, *world* resource reserves, etc.) "led to the formulation of problems not based in reality and therefore to prescriptions for solving these problems, which are erroneous."[48] The problems are not based in reality because there were only two choices to the *Limits* model—either the whole system collapses, or not. Yet in fact the world is not that well integrated; resources are not evenly distributed, birth and death rates vary, and so on. Parts of the system can collapse without having the whole thing come down. Everything may be connected to everything else, but the connection can be more or less close or powerful. The collapse of a part will be felt in proportion to its magnitude and the intimacy of its connection with other parts.[49] A famine in Ethiopia does not reverberate as strongly in the global system as one in Japan would.

The model used in *Turning Point*, therefore, broke the world down into various regions and also allowed the modelers to intervene along the way to adopt policies relevant to the changing conditions the model produced.[50] As a result, it appeared that global collapse beginning around the middle of the next century was not necessarily in the cards. Instead, we could expect "catastrophes or collapse" on a *regional* level "possibly long before the middle of the next century."[51]

Such a statement sounds very much like a prediction. But *Turning Point* was cautious on this point. The study claims to be analyzing "scenarios" (i.e., examining possible futures that might arise on the basis of various assumptions). "In principle, in such an analysis, we are not trying to predict the future—an effort of rather doubtful value when one is concerned with very long time horizons—but to assess alternative future developments."[52] Yet at the same time, if a variety of scenarios all seem to point in the same direction, "it can be considered as inevitable that these attributes will be observed in the future."[53]

The authors of *Turning Point* thought they had such a case in the region they called South Asia, which included among other nations India, Afghanistan, and Pakistan. The model suggested that there would be increasingly serious food shortages there even under very "optimistic" assumptions about slowing population growth and increasing food production. The "only way to avert unprecedented disaster in South Asia" was "emergence of a new global economic order" that would plan the best use of labor and capital, balance global economic development, provide an effective population policy, and diversify industry worldwide. "*Omission of any one measure will surely lead to disaster.*"[54] Absent such changes, we would now be seeing a steadily rising rate of childhood mortality due to malnutrition and starvation in South Asia.

We have no new international economic order of the sort that *Turning Point* advocated, and whatever the policy "mix" that was pursued 1974 to the present, it has not included all of the elements that *Turning Point* said would be necessary to avert disaster. Yet in all of the countries the report classified as South Asia, there have been improvements, often substantial, in infant mortality, comparing the period 1965–70 with 1985–90.[55] Of course, past results do not guarantee future performance. But in this case the confluence of scenarios allowed the authors of *Turning Point* to make a prediction—and they have so far got it wrong.

Famine in South Asia is not the only reason why *Turning Point* thought we needed a new global order, nor does their political program stand or fall on that one result. But their failure does allow us to look more dispassionately at their plans for global reconstruction, to see what good it might achieve other than solving problems that, apparently, do not exist. The new global order is characterized by "organic growth," *Turning Point*'s answer to the no-growth prescription of *Limits*. What is organic growth and how does it differ from no-growth? In answering this question, *Turning Point* paints a picture that is as overtly totalitarian as anything to be found in the environmental literature.

A CUNNING PLAN

Turning Point argued, sensibly enough, that the debate between "growth" and "no-growth" missed the important issue of the kind of growth we want. It contrasted two kinds of growth "found in Nature": "undifferentiated growth" and organic growth.[56] Undifferentiated growth is the exponential increase we saw was of such concern to Ehrlich and Hardin. It is such "[g]rowth for growth's sake in the sense of ever increasing numbers and larger size" that characterizes the contemporary world.[57] It has already assumed "truly cancerous qualities in some parts of the world."[58] Yet in other parts the problem of poverty is precisely lack of growth—for example, in the ability to produce goods and services.

Undifferentiated growth cannot go on indefinitely. Just as the growth of undifferentiated cancer cells will kill the body in which they grow, sheer numbers will sooner or later overwhelm and destroy the conditions that made the growth possible in the first place. Here again we meet "overshoot and collapse"; it is the situation that current patterns of growth threaten, according to the projections of both *Limits* and *Turning Point*. Hence, it is what organic growth should be introduced to prevent.

Organic growth in nature, which is to provide the analogy for global development, occurs where there is differentiation in structure and function among the growing parts of a whole, and where the growth reaches a limit that represents a dynamic equilibrium among these various parts. A tree does not grow by accumulating one kind of cell but by the development of cells that have distinctive purposes and places within the larger structure. If organic growth continues throughout the lifetime of a being, the rate slows as it ages. Perhaps it even reaches a certain absolute limit. Yet that limit does not mean the end of all growth; until death there is an ongoing process of cell renewal and replacement.[59]

What makes the authors of *Turning Point* certain that present growth trends are dangerously undifferentiated rather than organic? The question is not as easy to answer as it might at first seem. They understand that organic growth can have *phases* that suggest exponential tendencies, as anyone knows who has watched a baby grow.[60] Even the present patterns of world growth could turn out to be the exponential phase of a process of organic growth, and not some uncontrollable cancer. The question is, do we have to do *anything* for that to be true? You would look pretty silly creating a huge cage for a baby in fear that its incredible initial growth rates would continue until it was a monster.

The fact that organic growth can "look" exponential at times suggests that the difference between it and undifferentiated growth is less the often touted rate of growth than the extent of "differentiation"; that is, do the growing parts exhibit differences in structure and functions that form them together into a whole?

Turning Point does not give a fully clear answer to this question. They call present patterns of growth "*unbalanced and undifferentiat-*

ed,"[61] yet they also note how the "world community" has been transformed into a world "system" (i.e., it exhibits already significant differentiation in the complex interdependence among the various productive and consuming activities people engage in).[62] Perhaps there is the *potential* for a great deal of differentiation, but it needs to be actualized. Hence, we are at a "turning point." We can develop this aspect of the global system further, or not. In other words, what remains is the question of the extent to which these (actually or potentially differentiated) parts form an organic whole. Here we finally arrive at the key fact about today's world that, independent of rates of growth or extent of differentiation, makes the authors of *Turning Point* certain that what we have is *not* organic growth:

> In Nature organic growth proceeds according to a "master plan," a "blueprint." According to this master plan diversification among cells is determined by the requirements of the various organs; the size and shape of the organs and, therefore, their growth processes are determined by their function, which in turn depends on the needs of the whole organism.[63]
> Such a "master plan" is missing from the processes of growth and development of the world system . . . The master plan has yet to evolve through the exercise of options by the people who constitute the world system.[64]

But it must therefore be *made* to evolve. As the authors put it, the present situation *"demands that all actions on major issues anywhere in the world be taken in a global context."*[65]

Despite the halfhearted attempt to moderate their message by putting words like "master plan" and "blueprint" into quotation marks, there is no getting around the fact that the model of organic growth they are employing is, quite literally, totalitarian. Theirs is not the crude totalitarianism of uniformity but something more sophisticated.[66] The character and functioning of admittedly different parts is still subordinated to the needs of the whole, without which the parts could not function normally, or even survive. The one thing needful turns out to be the deliberate imposition of such a master plan on human affairs.

The fact that *Turning Point* says very little about just how such extensive planning is to be done, and who is to do it, is hardly a reassuring indication that they are willing to own up to the nature of the change they are calling for. No serious institutional structures are discussed, yet clearly to manage and integrate global affairs with a completeness analogous to that exhibited in natural beings would be an extraordinary accomplishment. One might think that a race of philosopher kings would be necessary to achieve such results, or at least a committee of systems analysts.

While the institutions necessary to achieve such complete integration are left largely in abeyance, there is a good deal of talk about the changing values necessary to create and support it. *Turning Point* presents a "new global ethic implicit" in the results of the analysis.[67] "Implicit" is meant quite seriously; *Turning Point* argues that it has provided a moral grounding for cooperation—its primary value—that has hitherto been lacking. As a result of their modeling efforts cooperation is shown to be "no longer a schoolroom word suggesting an ethical but elusive mode of behavior . . . [but] a scientifically supportable, politically viable, and absolutely essential mode of behavior for the organic growth of the world system."[68]

Such a statement is not only an example of scientific hubris, but it forgets that the authors themselves have argued that a great degree of interdependence (i.e., cooperation) is *already* characteristic of the world system. It is hardly a new ethic. But the cooperation they are pushing has some specific new elements: a "world consciousness" that makes membership in "the world community" one's primary allegiance, an ethic of "saving and conserving" that will accord with the "oncoming age of scarcity," an attitude that seeks not the conquest of nature but harmony with it, an unwillingness to trade benefits to coming generations for benefits to the present generation.[69]

Here is the main point of contact between *Turning Point* and the latest environmental wisdom, sustainable development. For if there is a coherent meaning behind this phrase, it is to be found in the values articulated by *Turning Point*. Simply put, sustainable development seeks to improve the condition both of humanity and nature by finding paths to development that are not environmentally harmful (i.e., can be sustained over the long haul).[70] But the ready acceptance of such ideas today should not blind us to *Turning Point*'s difficulty in maintaining them consistently. For despite the call for a world consciousness in which a famine in Africa should matter as much to Germans as a famine in Bavaria,[71] *Turning Point* also calls for diversity of culture and "a feeling for one's own place under the sun."[72] Saving and conserving must be our ethic, but a large part of the world must be able to consume more. Mankind is to live in harmony with nature, except it must take it upon itself carefully to plan and regulate human lives either to make up for the lack of a natural "master plan" or to avoid the "natural" process of overshoot and collapse. Future generations should be given greater attention, but the harm coming to this generation demands immediate action. Organic growth will spare us the hard trade-offs that no-growth seemed to promise, but organic growth sooner or later levels out.

There may be very good reasons for trying to reach some kind of accommodation between the conflicting tendencies of local and global or present and future that *Turning Point* lays out. But they remain unresolved conflicts in the report, since the authors fail to perceive them. Given that the huge changes they call for contain such internal tensions, their thinking has clearly developed in a utopian direction, and the call for a "master plan" that will guide the world is the familiar language of totalitarianism. Still, the fact that their argument culminates in an attempt to discuss the kind of good they seek in the new world order is revealing. It makes clear how, despite any failures of prediction that authors have experienced, what is really at stake is less *predictions* about the future than *prescriptions*. We should hardly be surprised when people who predict the future get it wrong. But the appeal of the prophetic side of these works is the key to understanding them, once we remember that prophecy is not merely about what will happen but about what we should be doing.

Besides, however much in retrospect we can see that the modern prophets have been wrong in particular, they are likely to be right in general. They foretell great social upheavals and the necessity of new ways of life. But a society such as ours, in which technological innovation, material consumption, and psychological self-development play such a major part, not only accepts that the future will be radically different from today; it requires it. One hundred years, and still no replacement for the internal combustion engine? Who can be shocked at the projection that meat may have to play a smaller role in our diet, when there is a food technology industry that manages on its own to produce veggie-burgers and artificial fat substitutes? Why is it implausible that "we will destroy the earth" when, for its faith in our power to change our own condition, that message is merely the bad news version of "today is the first day of the rest of my life"? The prophets push an open door.

Thus, it may be that if the ecodoomsayers told us 20 years ago that today oil would be getting scarce, they were wrong. But such an error will appear as a mere detail if there is every reason to think that oil will not have the same place in our world 50 years from now as it has today. What is really at issue is not what will happen, but what we want to happen. Doubtless many constraints exist in the world that make it difficult or even impossible to achieve all that we would desire, hope, or expect. But we will never find or test these limits until we have some idea of what kind of life we are trying to achieve. This question cannot even be addressed, let alone answered, by the best models of economists or systems theorists. It is in the classic sense a philosophical question. And it is as such that one of the greatest exponents of limits within the green crusade—E. F. Schumacher—claimed to have an answer to it. The promise that indefinite growth in a finite world is possible, Schumacher once remarked, has long been attacked; but *Limits* simply "exploded" it. And with a certain edge whose source will become clear, he added, "Now mankind listens because one could say that the computer has spoken, not just the human voice."[73]

WILL THE REAL E. F. SCHUMACHER . . .

Born in 1911 in Bonn and trained as an economist, Schumacher emigrated to Great Britain in 1937 only to find himself two years later interned as a farm worker in Northamptonshire. Released after three years, he worked for the London *Times*, briefly helped with the preparation of the Beveridge social security plan, and worked for the United States Strategic Bombing Survey. In 1946 he became part of the British Control Commission and in 1950 settled into the civil service work he would do for the next 20 years at the British National Coal Board.

In 1966 he founded the Intermediate Technology Development Group, "a small private body, half charity, half pressure group,"[74] as a means to develop, and to encourage industry to develop, new technologies suitable for the special needs and conditions of the "developing" world. When he died only 11 years later, he had from these beginnings founded what came to be known as the "intermediate technology," "appropriate technology," or "alternative technology" movement. His is a record of extraordinary influence exercised in a brief span of time.

Part of that influence was exercised through three books: *Small Is Beautiful* (1973),[75] *A Guide for the Perplexed* (1977),[76] and the posthumous collection of lectures mostly given on a tour of the United States, *Good Work* (1979). His prestige in the United States can be judged from the fact that, while in 1973 *Small Is Beautiful* went almost unnoticed in this country, by 1976 *Science* magazine could print a triumphant article, titled "Congress Buys *Small Is Beautiful*," about the various legislative initiatives then under way to create agencies to forward Schumacher's work.[77] These activities included programs under the Agency for International Development, the National Science Foundation, and the Energy Research and Development Administration, as well as the creation of a National Center for Appropriate Technology in Butte, Montana.[78] The well-publicized adherents on communes were not alone; then Gov. Jerry Brown of California was only one of the more vocal disciples of Schumacher among the powerful.

But if the record of Schumacher's influence is striking, so too is the confusion about his work. Some aspects of his thought are so obvious that most commentators could agree on them. That Schumacher was a critic of economists and the "science of economics" was clear, also that he had grave doubts about the desirability of unrestricted economic and technological growth. Further, that he was proposing the development of something called "intermediate technology" was widely noticed. But what was the basis for his criticisms of economics and technology? Just where were his solutions to the world's problems designed to lead us? On such questions, consensus broke down.

On the critique of economics, one reviewer could say that Schumacher "reports findings which transcend that discipline and show up its limitations,"[79] while another claimed that he was just developing "one aspect of the theory of comparative costs."[80] Yet perhaps economics as such was not even that important to Schumacher. One reviewer noted that he "practiced Buddhism" and spoke of what some might see as the "inscrutable Buddhist style" of *A Guide for the Perplexed*,[81] while for another, Schumacher was a "syncretistic" neo-Thomist.[82] Meanwhile, *Christian Century* could wonder whether Schumacher was moved primarily by religion or by a more fundamental "socialist humanism."[83]

The *New Republic* tried to finesse such problems about Schumacher's starting point by ignoring the "metaphysics" and finding the strength of *Small Is Beautiful* in "long experience"; Schumacher was "practical, sensible and eloquent."[84] But the *Times Literary Supplement* went so far as to suggest that the truly important practical themes of the book—economic, technical, and ecological—"seem almost irrelevant" in comparison with the book's speaking "so emphatically about our need to 'seek first the Kingdom.' "[85] Apparently others missed that message in *Small Is Beautiful*, for it was also suggested that only in the *Guide* did Schumacher "come clean" about the degree to which religion is the answer to our problems.[86]

If the foundation for Schumacher's thinking is unclear, so apparently are his solutions to the problems he described. Take, for example, the meaning of intermediate technology. *Science* suggested broadly that Schumacher was "Cutting Technology Down to Size" and arguing that "the cure for all the ills caused by technology is [not] more of the same technology."[87] But what characterizes "the same" technology that we are to avoid? A *Newsweek* article, deliberately or not, pointed up some of the difficulties of defining when technology is properly cut down to size. In a story about a 43-day, 12-state tour of the United States—presumably not a walking tour, nor one in which Schumacher spoke without benefit of microphones and electric lights—it said that one of Schumacher's "few concessions to technology" is an electric wheelbarrow. "But that, says Schumacher, is appropriate technology for an elderly man with a bad back."[88]

Was changing the kind of technology we produce even Schumacher's primary concern? *Environment* thought that the stakes were much higher; Schumacher was "a changer of cultural paradigms" who saw in "the proliferating paradoxes of our industrial cultures . . . signs of the exhaustion of their logic: of utilitarianism, materialism, technological determinism, and their anthropocentric blindness to ecological realities."[89] Compare that with the suggestion that Schumacher "seems to shy away from" recognizing that the changes he proposed would require "the transcendence of the international capitalist system . . . and the cultural values which are both the product and underpinning of this system."[90]

Given this level of confusion, we should not, then, be surprised that, after Schumacher's death, *Environment* would aver that "the triumph of his ideas was in the *overdeveloped* world,"[91] unless we had taken to heart the 1973 judgment that Schumacher's "distinctive contribution" had to do with the role of technology in the *developing* world.[92]

Perhaps it is the case that Schumacher changed his mind over time, or that there was a turn in the direction of his thinking. Yet there is disagreement here too. When the *Guide* was published after *Small Is Beautiful*, the *Economist* noted that Schumacher, "[l]ike other priests" of the "cult" of ecology, had shifted ground and turned to philosophy (not, it seems, religion at all).[93] Still, a philosopher could note that "*Small Is Beautiful* is, among other things, a philosophical book." In a remarkable effort, he even derived much of the teaching of the *Guide* from *Small Is Beautiful*, without having seen the *Guide*.[94]

Schumacher's work clearly meant many things to many people. That may help explain his success as a popularizer. But a closer examination shows that behind the slogans about technology there is indeed a quest for spiritual reform that would be likely to produce profound and troubling changes in the way we lead our lives.

TOOLS WITH A HUMAN FACE

The phrase "small is beautiful" is often taken to be the best distillation of Schumacher's teaching, and it is often assumed that the saying applied particularly as a description of "intermediate technology." There is some truth to both of these propositions. Schumacher criticizes modern technology because it develops "by its own laws and principles," which contain no "self-limiting principle—in terms, for instance, of size, speed or violence."[95] Thus, modern technology is best symbolized by the "satanic mills" of nuclear power plants that, along with nuclear weapons, bring us to the brink of self-destruction.[96] While any technology has as its "primary task" the lightening of "the burden of work man has to carry in order to stay alive and develop his potential," modern technology has been "most successful in reducing or even eliminating . . . skilful [*sic*], productive work of human hands, in touch with real materials of one kind or another."[97]

Schumacher's alternative, "intermediate technology," is supposed to be very different. Schumacher favors technologies that are "small" in the sense that they are labor-intensive (although not all labor-intensive technology is thereby "intermediate"), require minimal initial capital outlay, and have the capacity to operate independently, so as to promote decentralization. Intermediate technology makes "use of the best of modern knowledge and experience." At the same time, it is "conducive to decentralization, compatible with the laws of ecology, gentle in its use of scarce resources, and designed to serve the human person instead of making him the servant of machines."[98] Instead of mass production, intermediate technology is *production by the masses*," which uses "clever brains and skillful hands, and *supports them with first class tools*."[99] In the Third World, intermediate technology seeks to improve productivity far above the level of the "indigenous technology," while at the same time using methods much cheaper than the "highly capital-intensive technology of modern industry."[100] Hence the name "intermediate" technology, as it falls between the extremes of modern industry and traditional practices.

For example, Schumacher says, given a large earth-moving job in an underdeveloped area, one can import expensive machinery or set up local production of shovels, wheelbarrows, and so on. He advocates the latter option, because it creates the possibility of higher employment, both from doing the job itself and from the supporting industries. More employment will bring higher demand for consumer goods, which, as much as possible, should be produced locally, hence creating even greater employment.[101]

Or again, Schumacher tells of a visit to Sri Lanka, where a large number of small sugarcane farms were served by one centralized sugar refinery. Was there not, he was asked, such a thing as a minirefinery, so that the costs of transport to the one plant could be saved? (Never mind that the refined sugar would still have to be transported to market.) Schumacher was able to point them to a "mini-plant" that had been developed in India so that "Thank God . . . now the little people of Sri Lanka and other places have a chance of making a living."[102]

Intermediate technology does not imply "going back" to primitive technologies, let alone abandonment of technology altogether. Schumacher argues that the accumulation of scientific knowledge in fact makes it possible today to do some things in a "small" way that could not have been done in that fashion without such "progress."[103]

Now, there is a lively debate as to whether the intermediate technologies that have been developed in the wake of Schumacher's work have the virtues that he ascribed to them; indeed, there is some question as to whether they work at all.[104] But that important issue aside, it is not even as easy as one might think to distinguish between intermediate and modern technology. For one thing, Schumacher makes clear that part of his emphasis on smallness is rhetorical: "If there were a prevailing idolatry of smallness, irrespective of subject or purpose, one would have to try and exercise influence in the opposite direction."[105] Different scales are appropriate to different kinds of enterprises. "I don't suppose that one could produce Boeing aircraft on a small scale,"[106] but he does not seem moved therefore to reject airplanes as a "satanic" technology.

Or consider the following technology; is it intermediate or modern?

It will be large enough for the family but small enough for the individual to run and care for. It will be constructed of the best materials, by the best men to be hired, after the simplest designs that engineering can devise. But it will be so low in price that no man will be unable to own one—and enjoy with his family the blessing of hours of pleasure in God's great open spaces. . . . When . . . [it] becomes as common in Europe and Asia as it is in the United States the nations will understand each other. Rulers won't be able to make war. They won't be able to because the people won't let them.[107]

This inspiring intermediate technology is that bane of the modern environmentalist, the automobile, as described by Henry Ford. Schumacher realizes that once the automobile had qualities to which intermediate technology might aspire.[108] Modern technology, like intermediate technology, can promote decentralization, as in the case of the car. Like modern technology, intermediate technology seeks to increase productivity and to satisfy a demand for consumer goods. It requires us to use our best knowledge to create first-class tools (i.e., more technology). The most noteworthy difference between modern and intermediate technology is Schumacher's animus against labor-saving machinery, about which more below.

We might expect, then, that Schumacher would provide us with a sustained examination of various intermediate technologies to show how they are superior to modern technology in their ability to utilize our labor productively. Most of Schumacher's attention, however, is not centered around describing the merits of this or that technology. Instead, Schumacher's analysis is directed at the assumptions behind the forms of economic *organization* that produce the wrong kind of technology. Emphasizing the context in which a technology develops rather than the technological devices suggests one reason why the phrase "intermediate technology" was quickly replaced by "appropriate technology."[109] The natural question when faced with this phrase is, "Appropriate to *what*?" But that question is not so difficult to answer.[110] Schumacher looks to the development of technology appropriate to undermining capitalist economic systems.[111]

On Mistakes in Metaphysics

Schumacher attacks capitalism in the guise of a critique of the "science of economics" generally. Even granting, as any good follower of Marx would, that there are shared premises between capitalist and socialist economics, it is clear his focus on individualism, free markets, and voluntary exchange means that Schumacher intends his arguments primarily against capitalism. He begins by questioning whether economic problems are reducible to statistics or the findings of a "value-free" science. Schumacher, reasonably enough, is quite certain they are not. Rather, he rightly argues that economic issues are at root questions about the way we should live as individuals, as well as how we should organize our common life. Schumacher attempts to expose and critique the notion of the good for humans that rests at the heart of capitalism and, not so incidentally, of political liberalism as well.[112]

Capitalism and liberalism have not only failed to achieve what they promised, but those promises were flawed from the start. Capitalism claimed that the "'problem of production' has been solved," so that humanity could finally provide ever-increasing plenty for all.[113] Solve the problem of scarcity, the argument went, and we can develop a "system" where "everybody behaves well, no matter how much wickedness there may be in him or her."[114] Gandhi, Schumacher notes, "used to talk disparagingly of 'dreaming of systems so perfect that no one will need to be good.' " Yet that is what "our marvelous powers of science and technology" promise to do. "Why ask for virtues, which man may never acquire, when scientific rationality and technical competence are all that is needed?"[115]

Yet, Schumacher argues, scarcity remains a fact of life, precisely because of the "solution" to the problem of production that has been pursued by capitalism. For capitalism is premised on the liberation of selfishness; as Keynes argued, we must "'pretend to ourselves and to every one that fair is foul and foul is fair; for foul is useful and fair is not. Avarice and usury and precaution must be our gods for a little longer still.' "[116] Not only does Schumacher believe we should be shocked at such a teaching—and would be, if anybody knew anything about ethics anymore[117]—but he also points out that it is self-defeating. While capitalism has maintained that, properly organized (e.g., in free markets and voluntary exchanges), the liberation of selfishness will produce the maximum public good, Schumacher believes this liberation can produce nothing but unsatisfied desires. There is no evidence that the sought for, ever-increasing material prosperity, even if it *could* be achieved, would produce happiness or peace—indeed, quite the opposite. The cultivation of "vices such as greed and envy" will necessarily produce "a collapse of intelligence." Under these circumstances, societies "may indeed achieve astonishing things but they become increasingly incapable of solving the most elementary problems of everyday existence."[118]

The modern "solution" to the problem of production has paid insufficient attention to the question of how much wealth is enough. It is at best unrealistic, and at worst ecologically suicidal, to think that the whole world could enjoy the standard of living of the United States or western Europe. While Schumacher believes that *Limits* used a howitzer to swat a fly, he is in complete agreement with its conclusion.[119]

The failure to understand the problem of production correctly—that is to say, the misunderstanding both of what is possible to achieve and of what is desirable—is the result of a "metaphysical position of the crudest materialism," i.e., one "for which money costs and money incomes are the ultimate criteria and determinants of human action, *and the living world has no significance beyond that of a quarry for exploitation.*"[120] Schumacher fully exploits the many meanings of materialism, using it to refer to an overwhelming concern with the production and consumption of goods, the judgment that these aspects of life are the most telling indicators of the quality of life, and the assumptions behind modern science (i.e., the notion that nature is made up of matter in motion and is malleable to human ends). Scientism, modern rationalism, or "the loss of the *vertical dimension*" have a similar constellation of meanings for him.[121] He traces materialism back to Descartes, whose "primary interest" was making us *masters and possessors of nature.*"[122] Despite acknowledging the existence of this overarching purpose, Schumacher also maintains that materialistically based modern science and the technology based on it "cannot produce ideas by which we could live" because they deny any intrinsic natural order or hierarchy.[123]

Schumacher is correct that modern science, technology, and capitalist economics share assumptions about the way the world works. But he adds the argument that this "*'modern experiment' has failed*."[124] Its principles destroy the moral fiber of human beings, its practice in capitalism and technology threatens to destroy the natural world. Therefore it is necessary to discover the elements of "an alternative system which might fit the new situation."[125]

Most of Schumacher's readers find the definitive expression of the alternative system in what Schumacher called "Buddhist economics." Under this rubric Schumacher lays out how a conception of the world different from the materialistic one will produce very different goals and means to achieve them. Where capitalist economics assumes that it is rational to seek the least amount of work that will produce the most, Buddhist economics calls us to seek creative work. Where capitalism assumes that most people will be satisfied by the comfortable self-preservation that comes from the acquisition of property, Buddhist economics points us to higher callings. Where capitalism simply consumes, Buddhist economics guides us to use what can be renewed and play a part in its renewal.[126] As each has a different picture of nature and human nature, each has a different understanding of what makes for success and a good life.

Buddhist economics is central to the confusion surrounding Schumacher, because it has been thought to be an expression of his personal commitment to Buddhism. But asked once whether "Buddhist economics" were not in fact deeply informed by Catholic thought, "Schumacher grinned. 'Of course. But if I had called the chapter "Christian Economics," nobody would have paid any attention!' "[127] Buddhist economics is a thought experiment in overcoming materialism, demonstrating that the "science of economics" contains debatable assumptions about the human good. The choice of Buddhism was "purely incidental."[128]

But in fact, neither Christian nor Buddhist economics is the complete picture of Schumacher's "alternative system which might fit the new situation."[129] We need to deal systematically with the organization of production and ownership of the means of production. Since modern technology and capitalism are built on a defective understanding of our place in the world and the human good, Schumacher will have to provide us not only with a picture of the "system or machinery" necessary to replace capitalism, but of the "metaphysical foundation" that system rests on.[130] We will take up each in turn.

FUNCTION AND FREEDOM

Although Schumacher does not believe that any "system or machinery" will of itself make people good, he does accept that some are more conducive to being good than others.[131] The important role played by the political and economic theory called functionalism in his discussion of this point has not been widely appreciated, despite the fact that the chapters that take up this topic are among the few specifically written for *Small Is Beautiful*.[132]

Schumacher openly borrows most of his discussion of functionalism and industrial organization from the British social theorist R. H. Tawney (1880–1962). To understand the foundations for Schumacher's functionalism, we may turn to Tawney's *The Acquisitive Society*, where he defines a function as "an activity which embodies and expresses the idea of social purpose." In other words, a function is an activity done not "merely for personal gain" or gratification but to "discharge" a responsibility "to some higher authority."[133]

Starting here, Tawney takes direct aim at liberalism and capitalism by attacking property rights and suggesting that the allocation of property instead be made dependent on the work done with it. As things are now, "[o]wnership and use are normally divorced. The greater part of modern property . . . is normally valued precisely because it relieves the owner from any obligation to perform a positive or constructive function." Such property may exist for the sake of further acquisition, or for power, or for exploitation, Tawney notes, but it is not "actively used by its owner for the conduct of his profession or the upkeep of his household."[134]

Such "passive" property leads to work that is exploitative, dangerous, and drudgelike, while active property goes along with work that is creative. The transformation of industrial labor into professional work requiring "energy and thought and the creative spirit" means that we must make distinctions involving the kinds of ownership appropriate to various enterprises.[135]

Private ownership is appropriate to a craftsman owning his tools but not to shareholders owning factories. Similarly, collectivism or nationalization are neither always appropriate nor always inappropriate. Such judgments are to be made according to what service is to be accomplished for the public good.[136] Private ownership might for a time have been the best means of industrial organization, but it has lost its claim to be able to provide what people want in an efficient and just manner.[137] Furthermore, a rights-based society, with its stress on individual freedom and excessive suspicion of obligation, is unacceptable. A professional orientation needs to take its place. Those who do a job should have direct control over the property that is necessary to do it, and they should commit themselves to certain public obligations and to the means by which fulfillment of such obligations can be monitored.[138]

Having overcome a dogmatic adherence to the legitimacy of private ownership, a new organization of industrial production becomes possible. To establish the principle of functionalism is to create a society marked by proper limits, unity of purpose, and distributive justice. The result seems indistinguishable from "organic growth":

> The famous lines in which Piccarda explains to Dante the order of Paradise are a description of a complex and multiform society which is united by overmastering devotion to a common end. By that end all stations are assigned and all activities are valued. The parts derive their quality from their place in the system, and are so permeated by the unity which they express that they themselves are glad to be forgotten, as the ribs of an arch carry the eye from the floor from which they spring to the vault in which they meet and interlace.
>
> Such a combination of unity and diversity is possible only to a society which subordinates its activities to the principle of purpose.

For what that principle offers is not merely a standard for determining the relations of different classes and groups of producers, but a scale of moral values.[139]

The "moral values" Tawney seems to have in mind flow from the subordination of private interest, though Tawney does not draw out their content systematically. For functionalism's highest purpose, Tawney quotes Bacon: "the work of man ought to be carried on 'for the glory of God and the relief of men's estate.' "[140]

While submission to the divine will may produce peace of the spirit, or the organization of inanimate objects may produce the beauty of the cathedral, a society in which human beings organize themselves with similar thoroughness and devotion to a single end would be totalitarian. And what is this end? There is a significant tension in Tawney's thinking on the question of unity and diversity, or order and freedom. Although Tawney is eloquently aware that the provision of material necessities is in no way the sole or highest purpose of human life and indeed suggests that functionalism sets the economic realm in its proper, lowly place, he assumes, with Bacon and modern "materialism" generally, that the higher things are built or best built only on these secure material foundations; to solve the economic problem is to solve the essential human problem.

Hence, the ultimate importance of "the glory of God" (i.e., of spiritual goods) is in doubt: "The instinct of mankind warns it against accepting at their face value spiritual demands which cannot justify themselves by practical achievements."[141] Tawney does not seek to challenge this instinct and the priority it implies. The rationality of the functional society resides in its being a totalitarian organization for efficient productivity.

Schumacher follows Tawney in his reorganization of the economy and production. Individual enterprises, whole industries, and large segments of the economy are to be structured so as to make them more "human," more productive, and (not so incidentally) more profitable. The key to this reorganization is rethinking ownership. And finally, as with Tawney, we see in Schumacher a tension between the requirements of order and freedom that is largely resolved in favor of order.

"[A]ll real human problems arise from the *antinomy* of order and freedom," Schumacher says, that is to say, from the conflict of two principles that "appear to be founded equally in reason."[142] At first, it appears as if Schumacher is concerned with strengthening the "freedom" side of the freedom-order dichotomy. "[F]reedom *versus* totalitarianism" is "the major consideration from the metaphysical point of view taken in this book."[143] He indicates that he is wary of central planning and all other centralizations of power. By breaking up larger organizations, he says he is seeking to maintain freedom for the individual. He is critical of socialists whose single-minded devotion to nationalization leads them to want to "out-capitalise the capitalists," thus offering (like capitalism) nothing "that is worthy of the sweat of free-born men."[144]

Yet Schumacher also makes a deliberate attempt to blur the distinction between order and freedom. He acknowledges that, speaking *abstractly*, there is a tension between the triplets "freedom, market economy, private ownership" and "totalitarianism, planning, collectivized ownership,"[145] but he asserts that these various options may in *practice* be mixed and matched in any permutation (e.g., freedom, planning, and collectivized ownership or totalitarianism, market economy, and private ownership). He "leaves it to the reader's diligence" to find historical cases of such hybrids.[146] This task, if successful, would serve to make us aware of the dangers of "conceptual frameworks" that are not "derived from reality."[147] The human "reality" has a special character for Schumacher; it is "full of antinomies and bigger than logic."[148]

In light of this argument, Schumacher's assertion that "freedom *versus* totalitarianism" is a central theme in *Small Is Beautiful* takes on a clearer meaning. Totalitarianism is "founded equally in reason" with freedom. We would therefore need somehow to reconcile the two in practice. We know that Schumacher had a weakness for at least one great totalitarian: Mao Tse-Tung. Mao, Schumacher says, is an example of someone who derived his conceptual frameworks from reality. He provided the "best formulation of the necessary interplay of theory and practice" that Schumacher knows of: "Go to the practical people," turn their experience into "principles and theories," and then return to them to put these principles into practice "to solve their problems and achieve freedom and happiness."[149] Schumacher is full of praise for such achievements of freedom and happiness as forcing university students to return to the countryside to work in compensation for their educations, one of the more notorious practices of the Cultural Revolution.[150] We are entitled to wonder just what kind of freedom Schumacher is interested in preserving—even what kind of order he wants to maintain—in light of such fulsome praise.

ORGANIZE, ORGANIZE, ORGANIZE

When we turn to more concrete discussions, the totalitarian cause seems to fade for a time into the background. Schumacher appears to want to take a nondogmatic view of the question of public versus private ownership; each has its place. But private ownership operates under a cloud. In an essentially positive discussion of socialism, Schumacher notes that the question of kinds of ownership is just a question of means. Much more important are the ends pursued. But that is precisely the problem with private ownership; the ends it can pursue are "severely limited." Private ownership is "compelled to be profit seeking and *tends* to take a narrow and selfish view of things." Public ownership, on the other hand, "gives *complete* freedom in the choice of objectives and can therefore be used for any purpose that may be chosen." Its goals "are undetermined and need to be consciously chosen."[151]

The purposes to which property is to be put should determine whether it is public or private; there is no presumption of a right to private property. Schumacher quotes Tawney saying that property rights are to be maintained only on "the performance of service."[152] He allows that property owners, up to a point, can decide what services are to be performed, and whether they are being performed adequately. But who these owners *are* varies with the size of the enterprise in question. As we have seen, he does not expect that all production can take place on a small scale. Small may be beautiful, but it is not necessarily most interesting to Schumacher. He is content that small enterprises be left under the old system of private ownership; only medium- and large-scale organizations raise creative questions of reconstitution.[153]

For medium-sized firms (up to about 350 employees[154]) Schumacher commends the example of the Scott Bader Commonwealth, a plastics and polymers firm operated under a system of collectivized ownership. The "Commonwealth" of workers and (previous) family owners operates under a constitution that regulates size, payscale, and business practices, including stipulations about doing no war-related work and giving half of the profits to charitable purposes. Schumacher claims that the commonwealth has been not only a financial success but also an example of how to "combine real democracy with efficient management" and achieve "the Christian way of life" in business.[155] Instead of giving an account of how the Commonwealth manages this feat, Schumacher quotes approvingly a family member who offers instead a "tour of our forty-five-acre, ancient Manor House Estate" to see how it is all done.[156]

Large-scale firms present most clearly the problem we saw raised by Tawney: how to reconcile order and freedom. Schumacher seeks to show how in this case rational organization can mesh managerial (order) and entrepreneurial (freedom) skills. Indeed, it is here that Schumacher attempts an account of how economic life may be organized generally—yet another indication that large is here to stay.

Large-scale enterprises need to be broken down into smaller, semi-independent units *"within* large organisation."[157] Schumacher cites his employer, the British National Coal Board, as a successful example of a large yet decentralized structure, with specialized, smaller "quasi-firms" for various types of mining, supply, and distribution. At its best, the coal board operates neither by merely exhorting the coal industry nor by directives that go from the top down. Instead, as Schumacher describes it, they employ "the Principle of the Middle Axiom," whereby standards are set from above but procedures are in place by which those standards may be waived, should the "lower formations" be able to make a case for so doing.[158]

Schumacher likens this kind of organization to a man holding helium balloons; each balloon has its own lift, but they are gathered together by someone who "stands beneath them," nevertheless "holding all the strings firmly."[159] Who, in Schumacher's scheme of things, should be "holding the strings" so firmly, preventing each balloon from going off on its own?

Ownership and organization of large-scale firms involve a scheme of functional representation, where, outside of the realm of government and bureaucracy, "all legitimate interests can find expression and exercise influence."[160] Schumacher outlines a "truly 'mixed economy' " in which "Social Councils" "integrate large scale business enterprises as closely as possible with their social surroundings."[161] These local councils would own a 50 percent share of local industries. They would be formed "along broadly fixed lines without political electioneering and without the assistance of any governmental authority." The councils would be constituted as follows:

> one-quarter of the council members to be nominated by the local trade unions; one-quarter, by the local employer's organisations; one-quarter, by local professional associations; and one-quarter to be drawn from local residents in a manner similar to that employed for the selection of persons for jury service.[162]

The choosing of council members according to occupational class is a way of making sure that the various functional elements in the community are represented, although surely it limits the scope of what constitutes a "legitimate interest."

These councils become a government within the government. Under normal circumstances, Schumacher says, they are to operate without the interference of local government; the "Social Council would have legally defined but otherwise unrestricted rights and powers of action."[163] They will have a significant "power of the purse" in their ability to dispose of, for public purposes, their 50 percent of the profits of the firms that they regulate (there would then be no corporate income tax). Usually they are not to interfere with the actual management of these firms, and normally the publicly owned shares would not even be voted. Nor are the firms to be managed by civil servants. But if the social council decides that management practices are contrary to the public good, they would apply to a special court in order to have their voting rights activated.[164]

We seem to be a long way from the totalitarian element in Tawney's functionalism. Indeed, it is not entirely clear how the system that Schumacher describes is any more likely than capitalism to be conducive to good behavior, or guided by his or any other "consciously chosen" vision of the public good.

Let us start once again at the level of "small" enterprises. Given Schumacher's treatment of the flaws of private ownership, it is unclear why private property is allowed at all, even if we concede the important fact that private property and all that goes with it exist only at the sufferance of the higher powers that define what a "small" enterprise is. Are small enterprises private to encourage production to stay small, that is, out of a recognition of the attractiveness of private property, as we might expect from the emphasis on independence and the decentralizing tendencies of "intermediate technology"? Or are they suffered to remain private because when all is said and done they are not expected to play much part in economic life, as we would expect from the criticism that private property is conducive to selfishness?

Similar ambiguities characterize the treatment of medium and large enterprises. Following the Scott Bader model, Schumacher transforms the medium-sized business into a community in which all participate and benefit. That may teach lessons about getting along together that would carry over into the wider world, but it could also produce a corporate culture all the more inclined to see the world as "us" against "them." In this connection, it is ironic that, whatever good it might achieve in the world, Bader is hardly an example of a company producing "intermediate" technology. As a creator of high-technology plastics and polymers, it is deeply involved in the world of oil dependency and "large" technologies like the aerospace industry. Its activities are ultimately predicated on mass production as well, as, for example, their production of materials for microwave cooking. Had Bader been a large firm, would one of Schumacher's social councils have wanted to have its voting rights activated to prevent Bader's attempt to undermine local, natural-cloth dying technology in Pakistan in order to increase the market for their synthetic products?[165]

We see the consequences of Schumacher's refusing to dream of a system so perfect that people do not need to be good: he has created one in which it is eminently possible for them to be—by his own standards—bad. The irony here is that we know that capitalism does not make it impossible for people to be selfless, public-spirited, and charitable. It might be that the system Schumacher lays out would tend to replace the self-regarding behavior of private organizations and individuals with the self-regarding behavior of public organizations. Whether this change would be a net gain (i.e., whether the new system would accommodate the demands of order and freedom better than capitalism) is hard to decide without knowing the goals of these public organizations.

If we are to find the proper combination of order and freedom in specific institutions, we will need answers to questions like "Freedom from what?" or "Freedom to do what?" or "Orderliness to what end?" We are thus led to the more complete account of the "metaphysical principles" for which Schumacher prepared us with his discussion of Buddhist economics. What exactly is the good behavior this new system or machinery is to encourage, and why is it good? Only with answers to these questions can we make a judgment about the likely character of the promised land to which Schumacher would lead us.

Old Wisdom Made New

The mistaken premises of materialism and its progeny, modern technology and capitalism, are, according to Schumacher, clearly evident from the threat of ecological disaster and an increasingly alienated humanity. But if "the modern experiment has failed," where are we to look for guidance? To change technology alone is not enough; we have to change the understanding upon which technology is developed. Likewise, functionalism as "system or machinery" is not enough; to achieve Schumacher's goals it needs to be completed by an explicit account of the "common end" it seeks.

Schumacher claims in *Small Is Beautiful* that our guiding principle should be "permanence."[166] Permanence means the recognition of quantitative limits to growth; we should not seek ever-expanding material satisfaction. This argument is not simply, and perhaps not even mainly, based on a belief in limited resources in the style of *Limits to Growth*. It comes from a view of things that, while Schumacher in explicating it has frequent recourse to the "Christian tradition," is really in accord with what he calls "all genuine traditions of mankind."[167] Schumacher calls it "wisdom" or "traditional wisdom." We can turn to *A Guide for the Perplexed* for Schumacher's "systematic" presentation of traditional wisdom.

This *Guide* deals with that most serious question—What is the good life?—to which Schumacher must give an answer if the parts of his argument are to hold together. But it approaches its subject in a bewildering way. The book begins with a critique of the dogmatism of modern science and materialism, for their narrow view of what constitutes the human reality: "Our task is to look at the world and see it whole."[168] The Cartesian-inspired philosophy that is the dominant strain of our time has led to the loss of the "vertical dimension," or the belief that there is a rational, meaningful hierarchical organization of the world.

But to bolster his case against modern thought, Schumacher is anything but "hierarchical." In good democratic form, for example, one finds Gurdjieff and Ouspensky side by side with Aquinas, Dante cited along with Edgar Cayce, and, in three only slightly atypical pages, quotations from Plato, Philo, Plotinus, the *Theologia Germanica*, Paracelsus, Swami Ramdas, Azid ibn Muhammad al-Nasafi, and the *Tao Te Ching*.[169] Schumacher's source for all his quotations is *A Treasury of Traditional Wisdom*, a sort of *Bartlett's Familiar Quotations* with a metaphysical twist. He is following in the footsteps of various scholars who, under the banner of "perennial philosophy," assert the essential unity of world religions.

Traditional wisdom speaks of a world organized hierarchically with humans in an important but, as Schumacher repeatedly only hints, by no means dominant position in the hierarchy. The hierarchy is formed of "levels of Being" (mineral, plant, animal, human), with each level upward incorporating but transcending in an "ontological discontinuity" the previous level. Humans possess the matter (mineral), life (plant), and consciousness (animal) of the previous levels. But they are distinguished by self-awareness, that is, by the possibility of enlightenment.[170]

This self-awareness, along with a faith that is "not in conflict with reason, nor . . . a substitute for reason," is the key to our ability properly to live in and understand the world.[171] Schumacher takes some pains to describe the four kinds of knowledge that he sees as necessary for this right living: knowledge of the inner self, knowledge of the inner self of others, knowledge of self as seen by others, knowledge of the outer appearance of others (i.e., sensory knowledge).[172] Each kind of knowledge has its own place in the fourfold hierarchy and in our understanding of that hierarchy. But all four revolve around "the central teaching of the great religions," which "urge man to open himself to the 'pure ego' or 'Self' or 'Emptiness' or 'Divine Power' that dwells within him." Such "self-awareness" means "liberating oneself from the thralldom of the sense and the thinking function."[173] To gain our true selves, and thereby insight into the true character of the whole of which we are a part, we have to transcend the contingent and particular aspects of character that we tend to think of as our "self" and enter into a mystical communion with the whole. Implicit in this account is a sense that reason is, at very best, of limited utility in understanding our true place in the world—a critique we will see radicalized by the deep ecologists in the next chapter.

Having gained enlightenment, we are in the best position to understand and deal with the problems of this world. We see, Schumacher argues, that we face two kinds of problems: convergent and divergent. Convergent problems are susceptible to scientific or technical solution; they deal with the manipulation of matter. Divergent problems involve the antinomies of human life. They cannot be solved in the formulaic way that convergent problems can be; they must be transcended by the introduction of a higher principle.[174] The antinomy between order and freedom, for example, may be transcended by brotherhood, love, or compassion.[175] It is the tension created by the antinomies of divergent problems that can lead us to higher levels of thought and action.

As we ascend these levels, we find that the "true progress of a human being" presents us with three tasks. The first is to learn to find "temporary happiness in receiving directions from outside," that is, from society or tradition. The second task is to begin to become "self-directed" by weighing this outside knowledge and making what is good in it one's own. The third task is doubtless the most difficult: the overcoming of self-direction by the subordination of ego. Having done so, one "has gained freedom or, one might say, one is then God-directed."[176]

It seems a long way from technology and functionalism to this unapologetically mystical position. Yet we have seen how what Schumacher wants to achieve through both intermediate technology and functionalism depends on some such moral teaching. Economic and technological practice will not change unless removed from their materialistic context and placed within the "God-directed" sphere.

But if we pay heed to the tasks of "true progress," why need we be concerned about the economic and technical realm at all? The most Schumacher can say is that materialistic modern technology and capitalism block our access to the truth by misdirecting our attention. This claim is by no means trivial. But books like the *Guide*, created and distributed through all the capacities of profit orientation and "large" technology, can apparently serve to call our attention to the timeless truths of traditional wisdom. Indeed, Schumacher and those modern scholars whom he follows down the paths of "perennial philosophy" seem themselves to have been able to overcome the misdirections of materialism without the need for revolutionary transformations of society as a whole. The very timelessness of traditional wisdom suggests that contingent historical circumstances—call them capitalism, socialism, communism, or fascism—are only of passing interest.[177]

Perhaps the continuing tension between the need of functionalism and intermediate technology for traditional wisdom and the independence of traditional wisdom from technical and economic contexts is an indication that we face one of Schumacher's antinomies and a divergent problem. While the higher calling of "God-direction" may help put our material requirements in their proper place, it could still be true that those same requirements, which make "materialism" an ever present threat, could always be a source of tension with spiritual life. But then, according to Schumacher, what would be the way of transcending this problem?

We might think that to transcend this worldly problem requires ultimately another, different world—a not uncommon teaching of "traditional wisdom." But nowhere does Schumacher suggest that our goal in life is to achieve salvation, the intimation of salvation, or any other "other-worldly" end. Indeed, a transcendent or transmundane realm, while *hinted* at throughout the *Guide*, plays no role whatsoever in Schumacher's description of human ends.

Recalling that the antinomy between order and freedom is to be transcended by new principles—brotherhood, love, or compassion—is likewise of less help than might at first appear. As Bertrand de Jouvenel has pointed out, we know from the existence of monastic communities that people can be organized around such principles. But such communities work because their members are directed to something entirely other than worldly success and comfort. Property is shared in them because such possessions are rejected; competition is rejected because God attends to all equally.[178] Yet Schumacher, with his interest in material improvement and social reorganization, clearly wants the ethos of the monastic community to prevail while keeping in view comfortable self-preservation and like worldly concerns. Thus, even if it is reasonable to believe that the issue of "freedom *versus* totalitarianism" has been transcended in what from the outside appears as the highly totalitarian structure of monastic life, it is not so clear that the same judgment could be made of public and social structures that put the coercive powers of the state behind the same kind of organization.[179]

Rather than turn to another world, Schumacher tries to transcend the tension between his material and spiritual goals through the notion of "productive work." Traditional wisdom, he says, teaches that *work* is the center of life.[180] Hence a major purpose of all of Schumacher's practical proposals is to maximize the amount of time used for "actually producing things," and also to maximize the number of people involved in production. He regards it as a great advantage that his schemes put old people and children to work.[181] The necessity of work closes the door to the leisure that makes possible a life of unnecessary consumption. On the other hand, productive work itself can be "sanctified"; perhaps Schumacher has in mind Gandhi at his spinning wheel.

Yet we might have thought that enlightenment would be a matter of much study and contemplation. Contemplation would seem to require leisure, as is clearly argued, for example, in the "tradi-tional wisdom" of Aristotle. That helps explain why, throughout history, wisdom has been the province of the few, not the many. But there are two reasons why Schumacher believes, with his rationalist enemies, that it is possible to have both productive work and mass enlightenment.

In the first place, if Schumacher's use of the phrase "traditional wisdom" is understood properly, it is easier to understand why leisure and contemplation are not important to him. For although he is respectful of the difficulties of gaining true enlightenment, he still believes he can tell us "all ye know on earth and all ye need to know" in the 140 pages of the *Guide*, if not a single line of poetry. All the necessary wisdom or truth can already be found, in suffi-ciently unambiguous form to be broadly useful, in the "genuine traditions" of mankind. It is enough for something to be false that "no sages or holy men in our or in anybody else's history" believed it.[182] Unthinking deference to the authority of the scientist is replaced by unthinking deference to the authority of sages.

While he speaks of the importance of spiritual "inner work," Schumacher is less interested in this inner process than in its results. The *Guide* seems to suggest that it is enough to exhort peo-ple to "overcome the self" to get them to do it, and then we can all get down to some good work. The very claim that the book allows us to see the world whole demonstrates that Schumacher's inten-tion is not to spark the wonder that will start us down the road of philosophy. He is looking for what in secular terms would be called ideology; he seeks the authoritative inculcation of such sound doc-trine as will best support sound work.

In the second place, the conjunction of spiritual enlightenment and material labor is made possible by Schumacher's tacit accep-tance of key elements of the modern, technological world view that he claims to be rejecting. In a remarkable concluding passage in the *Guide*, Schumacher points to the deep affinity between his own thought and the premises of modern technology:

[A] "turning around," a *metanoia* . . . leads to seeing the world in a new light, namely, as a place where the things modern man continu-ously talks about and has always failed to accomplish *can actually be done*. The generosity of the Earth allows us to feed all mankind; we know enough about ecology to keep Earth a healthy place; there is enough room on the Earth, and there are enough materials, so that everybody can have adequate shelter; we are quite competent enough to produce sufficient supplies of necessities so that no one need live in misery.[183]

This passage does not promise an automated utopia where human beings need only work for the joy of work or merely to "express themselves." But it is remarkable nonetheless. It could be said to moderate the message of modern materialism by speaking only of the prevention of "misery," provision of "adequate shelter," and so on and neither encouraging greed nor promising an ever-improving standard of living for all. But what is regarded as adequate shelter today is not the same as what adequate shelter was 200 years ago. The outhouse today is a symbol of backwardness, not a fact of life. Can traditional wisdom tell us *once and for all* what we should seek, and what to avoid in all the choices that are now available: how long we should live and of what we should die, how many calories we should consume and from what kinds of food, what kinds of homes we should live in? If Schumacher thinks it can, then he has misled us about transcending the antinomy between order and freedom: he clearly wants to impose totalitarian orderliness in precisely the same way as Tawney.

But if Schumacher would not make such a naive (though not uncommon) argument, he falls into the difficulty of nearly eliminating his quarrel with modern technology. First, he would be in agreement with the promise of modern technology that providing food, shelter, and health no longer need be seen as perennial challenges but as "convergent" problems. It is all the more remarkable that the solutions promised by Schumacher are implicitly global.

Second, the productive work we will engage in to meet these goals will be transformed to the extent that his promises are fulfilled; that is, the guarantee of food, shelter, and health removes from our labor at least the "knife's edge" of necessity. We will be freed from the fear that the failure of our personal labor will bring disaster to us, even if in the broader scheme our work remains somehow necessary to the whole. Thus far, at least, we will have, as modern technology has from the start promised, and as Tawney reminded us, relieved our estate—and in comparison with the lives of most human beings in most times, this is quite far indeed.

Third, we should remember that Schumacher is not describing a relatively simple economy but a complex and technologically sophisticated one. Large-scale enterprises are here to stay; they may even be necessary to make first-class tools. Think of the industrial "infra-structure" behind Schumacher's own electric wheelbarrow, or behind a first-class shovel. It is amazing what technological wonders are behind the drafting pen that sketches out the preliminary plan for an alternative technology, or the postal system that gets the plan to those who need it in a timely fashion. In comparison with the technological devices (to speak of "technology" only in the most obvious sense) called for by these "small" things, the absence of "large" nuclear power plants would hardly be a decisive indication that Schumacher had managed to cut technology "down to size."

We come full circle in Schumacher's thought, having returned to his initial emphasis on technology to understand how to reconcile his spiritual message with his "system or machinery." Schumacher's claim to be able to accomplish the promises of the modern project he seemed to have rejected must have a crucial impact on our reading of the place of his picture of true human progress in his broader teaching. His abiding concern for improvement of the material conditions of life, a concern that duplicates the fondest hopes of Descartes or Bacon, is not just the means to the ultimate goal of spiritual renewal, but the goal itself.

The failure of Schumacher's radical conservatism (i.e., of his attempt to return to an older tradition as a decisive alternative to present modes of thought) has crucial implications for how he understands the balance of order and freedom. The "wisdom" he supplies to replace capitalism and materialism implies that agreement of all people on ends, whether spiritual or technological, is both possible and necessary. Given the uniformity of ends, the only realm of diversity left concerns means. But what kind of freedom is confined to means only? It is just the advantage of functionalism, or other "organic" forms of organization, over capitalism that, once there is a clear idea of the whole, it is possible to create the relevant division of society into functions and to decide what functions serve society. In this way, the supposed selfishness, inefficiency, and irrationality that are a consequence of private property are avoided. Thus, questions of means once left to individuals become in this new context susceptible to public control, based on the edifying sayings of the wise and/or the satisfaction for all of a supposed "basic" need.

Traditional wisdom's role in Schumacher's thinking is to bring us back to Tawney's "totalitarian" vision of a society built up with the same orderliness as the spheres of Dante's heaven. But when paradise is in *this* world, purchased with the coin of technological development and based on the overcoming of nature, will the result resemble paradise or the hellish excesses of this century's totalitarianism? The supposed selfishness, irrationality, and inefficiency of the private realm, whose status is so dubious in Schumacher's thinking, are more closely connected with the freedom Schumacher espouses than he would like to admit. His own choices suggest how fragile freedom is likely to be in the face of a clamor for the benefits promised by technological development. Nor is this merely some theoretical observation; we see its truth in the clamor for new government regulation every time there prove to be risks that go along with the benefits of some new technology. Schumacher follows suit. He is not only unable to confront adequately the goals of the modern technological project, but in the guise of premodern "traditional wisdom" he adopts them as his own in such a way as to endanger that in which he claims to believe.

At his best, Schumacher tries to teach that we can hardly be serious about limits until we limit our own desires. A cultivation of spirituality such as he points to might begin to accomplish that end far more effectively than the pious talk about "cooperation" to be found in *Mankind at the Turning Point*. But his other message is that we can "have it all"; grace will apparently lead us to fulfill all the promises of the modern project he spends so much time criticizing. Schumacher's picture of human purposes concedes too much to the secular and materialistic. The contradiction that makes his thinking utopian makes his utopianism curiously mundane. Unlike the Club of Rome, he tries to deal openly with the antinomy between totalitarianism and freedom that necessarily arises from any thoughtful confrontation with the planning mentality that is so strong among these advocates for limits. That he should not ever transcend this antinomy, and merely point us to totalitarianism, is bad enough. But are we in addition really to believe that the accumulated wisdom of East and West really culminates in an electric wheelbarrow?

Schumacher represents an important transition in the popularization of environmental issues. The existence of an environmental crisis is taken for granted, and thus he can focus on the appropriate moral and political response to it. But perhaps in this respect he simply failed to go far enough. If he remains "modern" by virtue of his acceptance of "the things modern man constantly talks about," perhaps he should have become "post-modern," and subjected that talk to a more radical critique. It is thus appropriate to turn now to those who are at this cutting edge—writers who are popularizing the deconstruction of modern civilization.

The Mind O'erthrown

What awaits is not oblivion but rather a future which, from our present vantage point, is best described by the words "postbiological" or even "supernatural." It is a world in which the human race has been swept away by the tide of cultural change, usurped by its own artificial progeny . . . Today, our machines are still simple creations . . . But within the next century they will mature into entities as complex as ourselves, and eventually into something transcending everything we know—in whom we can take pride when they refer to themselves as our descendants.

Hans Moravec, Mind Children¹

Perhaps Sasquatch does exist—as an ideal. Perhaps Sasquatch represents a more mature kind of human, a future primal being. Understood in this way, Sasquatch has a fully realized ecological self. While we, who are children of technocratic civilization, must bring cumbersome technology into the forest to provide shelter and to satisfy our other needs and desires, Sasquatch dwells freely in the forest unencumbered by the burden of complex and complicated technology.

While we are torn with desire for more power over other people and domination over nature, Sasquatch dwells peacefully and unobtrusively with other creatures of the forest. While we are dependent on huge bureaucracies such as schools, governments and military agencies, Sasquatch is independent and autonomous and fully integrated with the forest.

William Devall, Simple in Means, Rich in Ends²

THE NEW CUTTING EDGE

The environmental torch is being passed. The popularizers we have so far studied, while for the most part still active and engaged in public affairs, must be prepared to watch the generation whose outlook they helped to mold pick up the cause and carry it into the future. Surely there is reason for them to feel satisfaction. Perhaps only a very little of what they hoped for has been done, yet for their efforts we are all, in some sense, environmentalists. When there are at least 101 things to do to save the earth, who cannot claim in at least some corner of his life to be acting on behalf of "the environment?"

But like any generational shift, this one is not without its Oedipal side. The sons are not content merely to follow in Dad's footsteps. Indeed, at times some of them sound downright ungrateful. The "reform environmentalism" that they are being bequeathed is "like attempting to rearrange the deck chairs on the Titanic."[3] We need instead a diagnosis and response to our present ills that gets to their root. That can be done only if we look even more closely into the values that form both our sick society and its supposed environmentalist opponents. The root of our ills turns out to extend further than the seminal work of philosophers like Descartes and Bacon, who articulated the modern scientific and technical project for the conquest of nature for human purposes. It reaches beyond the Platonic foundations for "anthropocentrism"— the belief that human purposes are unique in the world and properly authoritative. Deeper yet, monotheism is implicated in our present crisis, and the root may extend all the way to a wrong turn we took when we abandoned the hunter/gatherer life for settled agriculture. In other words, much of the talk of "new environmental values" has hitherto not even scratched the surface, and indeed has hidden the fact that there is less difference between reform environmentalists and their opponents than either would like to believe. Clearly, if the sources of our current ills are this entrenched, it will take extraordinary efforts to dislodge them.

Who are these seemingly ungrateful children? For the present, they attack the old policy of their fathers under the banner of "deep ecology." These deep ecologists are not popularizers in the same sense as Carson and Ehrlich. For one thing, they are not natural scientists; their backgrounds are more often in the humanities and social sciences. For another thing, they are not yet popular. Their writing so far tends to be directed to a different audience; while no doubt any one of them would be happy to have as big a following as Barry Commoner, their works are not yet widely read or reviewed. Some attention is paid to the deep ecology movement as a whole in the popular press; *Rolling Stone* devoted an article to it,[4] and mention of a deep ecology perspective is becoming increasingly common in articles looking at environmental problems. The highest-profile home for their thinking in the United States has been the radical environmental group Earth First!, but that obviously fringe organization is not the best measure of their impact.

Although those who pride themselves on involvement in the "real world" may scoff at the idea, the best way to gauge the influence of deep ecology is by looking within the academy. Already by the late 1980s deep ecology had become a "standard reference point" by which other positions in environmental philosophy were defended or critiqued.[5] Why should those outside of colleges and universities care about this development? It means that deep ecology is being disseminated to the next generation of those who, as citizens or policymakers, will be deciding about environmental issues. The environmental science courses that once could only be found in "teach-ins" are now requirements that students must slog through. Deep ecology is where to go for the radical stuff. Indeed, deep ecology even without being widely acknowledged has, by its influence among intellectuals, already opened new avenues for expression of environmental concern. For example, it is a not so unusual paradox of contemporary religiosity that, despite the hostility of many deep ecologists to biblical religion, deep ecology arguments have paved the way for the burgeoning interest in ecology among mainstream churches and theologians.[6] That their ideas may now sound strange is in and of itself no warrant that they will not gain wide acceptance. It is only for the moment that deep ecology occupies the fringes of the environmental movement taken as a whole.

So we examine the work of deep ecologists in a book about environmental popularizers, even if their work is not yet popular, because their efforts, which focus not on science but on ethics and politics, are at the cutting edge of what the environmental movement is becoming. This development should hardly be a surprise, for by this emphasis deep ecology only makes explicit what has remained too often implicit in environmental thought.

Furthermore, deep ecologists *seek* to be popularizers of a new morality, even if they have not yet found the voice that allows them to be taken seriously by a large public. A great deal of effort is spent trying to bring as many people into the fold as possible, as we will shortly see. Part of their problem is that they have to try to clear away what they regard as the misconceptions fostered by hitherto existing environmentalism, even as they build on the sense of danger and urgency it has engendered. Already, then, a certain complexity of argument is suggested, a problem exacerbated by the tendency of some deep ecologists to pitch their writings in the academic tones to which they are accustomed.

Another problem of deep ecology is analogous to the ease with which Carson's supporters were dismissed as mere "birdwatchers." For there is a side to deep ecology that, from our vantage point today, is likely to appear just plain odd or cranky. Of course, this may not be a disadvantage in all constituencies; nor has like craziness hampered the ultimate success of other initially marginal social movements. For example, Orwell's fear that "fruit-juice drinker, nudist, sandal wearer, sex-maniac, Quaker, 'Nature Cure' quack, pacifist and feminist" socialists would compromise the movement's success in England now seems overblown, however descriptively accurate.[7]

Who are the deep ecologists? The Norwegian philosopher Arne Naess is the father of the movement. Naess was an internationally famous professional philosopher long before he introduced the phrase "deep, long-range ecology movement." He is credited with having begun a revival of Norwegian philosophy upon his accession to the chair in philosophy at the University of Oslo in 1939.[8] Born in 1912, Naess has a reputation as an outdoorsman and mountaineer; in 1950 he was the first to ascend the highest peak in the Hindu Kush range.[9] Noted for his energy both in mental as well as physical activities, he has authored over 28 books and 200 articles in the course of his long career, as well as being founder and editor of the interdisciplinary philosophy journal *Inquiry*. His work as a professional philosopher prior to his turn to deep ecology involved the study of Spinoza, the philosophy of science, logic, ethics, semantics, and contemporary continental philosophy.

But Naess has not confined his activities to the ivory tower and the towering mountains. No stranger to politics, he was involved in "the Norwegian nonviolent resistance movement to Nazi occupation during World War II" and in the postwar peace movement until 1955.[10] The publication of *Silent Spring* brought some change of direction. What seems to have most impressed Naess and a circle of colleagues who met to discuss the work was Carson's evident love of and respect for nature. Naess coined the phrase "deep ecology" in a paper presented at the 1972 World Future Research Conference in Bucharest to describe what he saw as this growing sensibility within the environmental movement.[11] Skeptical of the "technical fix" direction that existing environmental policies were taking and of the focus those policies had on "the health and affluence of people in the developed countries,"[12] Naess claimed to see a dawning recognition of the need for a fundamental reevaluation of man's relationship with nature. As one history of the movement puts it, "a decade later Deep Ecology would become the banner under which radical environmentalism rallied its forces."[13] In this cause, Naess has done his bit in practice as well as theory, having been a participant in a Norwegian protest against a dam and power plant that provoked "the biggest police action in Norway's history."[14]

If Naess is the center of deep ecology, there is also a large and varied periphery. Deep ecology is deliberately eclectic. Shinto, Buddhism, reconstructions of "Mother Goddess" religions, St. Francis, Native American religions, Thoreau, John Muir, and Aldo Leopold are just a few of the wells from which deep ecology sips. Contemporary authors such as novelist and essayist Edward Abbey, Pulitzer prize–winning poet Gary Snyder, skier and t'ai chi teacher Dolores LaChapelle, and anthropologist Paul Shepard have all influenced, and been influenced by, deep ecology. And of course,

Dave Foreman and Earth First! have brought a good deal of notoriety to deep ecology by acts of protest and "ecotage."

But sociologist William Devall and professional philosopher George Sessions have been central to the articulation of deep ecology in the United States. A sympathetic analyst has noted that these two are largely responsible for bringing Naess's work to wide notice among eco-philosophers and convincing many eco-philosophers to identify themselves as deep ecologists.[15]

Born in Kansas City, Devall has a doctorate from the University of Oregon and has taught at Humboldt State University in California since 1968. Although his dissertation was on the governance of the Sierra Club, he professes to have had little interest in environmental issues per se until he arrived at Humboldt State and saw what was happening to the forests in heavily logged Humboldt County. Much of his work has been as an activist and consultant, but he has published two books on deep ecology (one with Sessions), along with numerous articles; is a contributing editor of *The Trumpeter*, a journal devoted to deep ecology; and has guest lectured throughout the United States and in Australia.

George Sessions met Devall in 1968, when they shared an office at Humboldt State. Sessions had just finished his graduate work at the University of Chicago and had a long-standing interest in environmental issues. He joined the Sierra Club when he was 15 and was appointed to their Mountaineering Committee at age 24. In 1969, he moved to Sierra College in California, where he has taught ever since. While his graduate work in philosophy did not have a great deal to do with environmental philosophy—indeed, at that time such a subspecialty hardly existed—by the early 1970s he was thinking about, and publishing articles on, the anthropocentric bias of Western philosophy. At around the same time he had his first contacts with Naess.[16]

Sessions and Devall worked together intensively throughout the 1970s, with Sessions focusing on philosophical issues and, as Sessions has described it, Devall developing what it meant "to put his deep ecology commitment into practice."[17] By 1980 their ideas had begun to catch on, and other writers began to publish on deep ecology.[18]

ECO-EGALITARIANISM

What makes deep ecology deep? According to Naess, "The essence of deep ecology is to ask deeper questions. The adjective 'deep' stresses that we ask why and how, where others do not."[19] Deep ecologists profess some concern that the "deep" distinction seems to have alienated reform environmentalists by implying that their efforts are shallow in the commonly pejorative sense. There is even occasional talk of finding a new, less easily misunderstood label.[20] But the fact remains that deep ecology believes that deep *is* superior to shallow, and that the reform environmentalists are *not* entirely on the right track for not having asked the right questions.

For deep ecology culminates in an "ecosophy," a normative system of thought that produces "policy wisdom" and "prescription."[21] "Shallow," or reform, environmentalism operates within a set of insufficiently questioned assumptions about nature and our relationship to nature. It is concerned mainly with fighting pollution and improving human life.[22] But that means it is really not so different from the forces supposedly arrayed against it. Even Schumacher, as we saw, fails to confront adequately the modern premises that put the conquest of nature so high on our list of things to do.

Environmental degradation stems from these assumptions that modern technology and science make about nature and the relationship between humans and nature. These problems are above all, then, problems of a certain way of thinking and therefore must be addressed on a philosophical plain. The outlines of part of this critique are already familiar to us from Schumacher's argument that the scientific revolution turning nature into mere object for human manipulation needs to be overcome by attention to "perennial philosophy." But deep ecologists have radicalized both elements of this account by, as they would claim, going deeper into the assumptions behind modern science and understanding more carefully the wisdom of the past. The scientific revolution is not our only problem, and perennial philosophy is not enough to solve it. The key to where we have gone wrong is anthropocentrism— "the central concern of deep ecology."[23]

While the precise meaning of anthropocentrism is a topic of disagreement among deep ecologists, and between them and their critics, it can be understood broadly as the view that human beings have an understanding of and place in nature that is somehow privileged. From this point of view, modern science and technology are merely a particularly obvious expression of anthropocentrism. In fact, anthropocentrism is practically coeval with Western philosophy. Deep ecology provides one more example of the present vogue for blaming the world's ills, be they racism, sexism, or exploitation of nature, on serious thought.

To make this case, Sessions (for example) presents a pale imitation of the thinking of Martin Heidegger. Socrates is the first culprit, by turning philosophy to a concern primarily with human questions like "What is justice?" or "Can virtue be taught?" and away from the pre-Socratic contemplation of the cosmos.[24] Judaism and Christianity further privileged the human place in the universe, and the Enlightenment merely secularized that position with its stress on progress.[25] In the modern world, the "absolute subjectivism" of philosophy stands completely revealed as the "will to power" exhibited not just by technology but by pragmatism and analytic philosophy.[26] Its bankruptcy calls forth the need for a new paradigm for thought that, according to Sessions, is available in the "tenuous thread" of a "minority tradition" that survives in thinkers like the pre-Socratics, neo-Platonic mystics, Spinoza, Santayana, and Robinson Jeffers.[27]

Anthropocentrism must be replaced by the new paradigm of "biocentrism" or "ecocentrism."[28] Ecocentric is regarded by some to be a preferable term to biocentric, because biocentric may seem to focus too much on *living* things, whereas ecocentric is "Earth-centered" and as such allows us to say things like "Let the river live!"[29] "Ecocentrism means rejecting the position that some life forms (such as humans) have greater inherent worth than other life forms."[30] It likewise means a rejection of any notion of a "great chain of being" or hierarchical organization of the cosmos that is usually taken to be one of the insights of "perennial philosophy."

Naess has called ecocentrism *"biospherical egalitarianism—in principle,"*[31] or equality of the *"unfolding of life."*[32] There is *"the uni-*

versal right to live and blossom."[33] The qualification "in principle" indicates that Naess knows full well that the blossoming of some requires harm to others; such a right taken absolutely would be completely inimical to life. The criticism that deep ecology would put the life of a mosquito on a par with the life of a human being is only partly on target.[34] Better to ask how much protection of *any* individual life this right to live and blossom provides.

A way to reconcile the necessity for harm with the right to live and blossom is suggested by Paul Shepard. "Ecologically, death leads to life, not in a hazy obscure way but in the eating of the prey."[35] Naess agrees:

> [I]t is against my intuition of unity to say "I can kill you because I am more valuable" but not against the intuition to say "I will kill you because I am hungry". In the latter case, there would be an implicit regret . . . In short, I find obviously right, but often difficult to justify, different sorts of behaviour with different sorts of living beings. But this does not imply that we classify some as intrinsically more valuable than others.[36]

Yet as regards human beings, this line of thought has troubling results—results that are only slightly less disturbing for the knowledge that Naess has long been an advocate of nonviolence. "The ecological viewpoint presupposes acceptance of the fact that big fish eat small, but not necessarily that large men throttle small."[37] To say "not necessarily" is not a strong condemnation. But Naess is against attempting to justify violations of the right to live and blossom on the basis that some beings have greater intrinsic value than others, either because they are ensouled, or rational, or self-conscious, or higher on an evolutionary scale. While he means this refusal to limit justified human violence against nature, it cuts both ways—neither would these same qualities be grounds for a special respect by humans for human life. Even if Naess has not been able to resist the opportunity for a lighthearted remark about fish and men, the logic of his position suggests that if big men are not justified in throttling small, it may be because for the most part big men are not that hungry. Whatever might be said against cannibalism, it is not evidently unnatural, nor necessarily inegalitarian. The *"realis-*

tic egalitarian attitude" requires not that no harm be done, but that (for example) the hunter apologize to the bear for the necessity of killing him.[38]

The right to live and blossom turns out to be a right to eat and be eaten, suggesting that greater respect for both living and nonliving nature depends on how much, and in what spirit, we are, quite literally, consumers. Such an ethic, if rigidly adhered to, might indeed promote less human intervention in nature—depending, so to speak, on one's tastes. The value we are likely to place on an individual life must confront the fact that nature, as Hardin also noted, is not itself a great respecter of the individual life. So deep ecology's egalitarianism must promote a respect for life different from that protection for the individual's well-being that we might initially be inclined to give. As a result, we may or may not be prompted to save the life of a mosquito over the life of a human. What is certainly clear is that any *individual* mosquito life, or any *individual* human life, is for deep ecology equally unimportant in the scheme of things.

WHOLES AND PARTS

The deep ecologists attempt to change our perspective on the value of individual life by a challenge to the very possibility of individualism and a definitive separateness among beings. The central concept here is "Self-realization."[39] "Self" is not to be understood narrowly, as an isolated ego. The burden of much of Naess's work is to show how Self must be understood in all its manifold connectedness to Other, or as a certain perspective on the totality of what is. Self-realization means knowing that "[t]he identity of the individual, 'that I am something', is developed through interaction with a broad manifold, organic and inorganic. There is no completely isolatable I, no isolatable social unity. To distance oneself from nature and the 'natural' is to distance oneself from a part of that which the 'I' is built up of."[40]

As Naess presents his "ecosophy," he discusses the proposition that "The higher the level of Self-realization attained by anyone, the broader and deeper the identification with others."[41] This hypothesis allows deep ecology to draw the conclusion that human beings could hardly harm nature when they come to view it as literally part of themselves.[42] Such identification, a product of Self-realization, is to replace calculation as the hallmark of human relatedness to nature.

Naess recognizes that the human capacity for Self-realization is at least far beyond that of any other being, and may be unique. While all things might be able to unfold to their specific capacities,[43] only human beings seem to have the ability to *see* that urge in them, a knowledge that is crucial to the prospect for identification.[44] But this "uniqueness" should not be taken "as a premise for domination and mistreatment. Ecosophy uses it as a premise for a universal care that other species can neither understand nor afford."[45]

Commenting upon these ideas, Devall has noted, "From an ecological perspective all individuals or units are intrinsically made up of their relationships with other individuals or units in the ecosystem."[46] Since ecosystems are themselves interconnected, we see repeated here the idea that everything is connected to everything else. The earth, and perhaps the universe, exhibits the organic unity that we see within the single bodies that make it up.

Dolores LaChapelle prefers more poetic evocations, as indicated by the following "Meditation" she quotes:

> I am the sentient offspring of this rock . . . As the blood in my veins is but an inland sea, so the rock in my bones is but borrowed from the subterranean matrix in which I am re-immersed . . . Those stains of limonite and hematite now coloring this weathered cut will tomorrow be the hemoglobin that flushes my face with red. So now I, this rock parasite, return to praise my natural parents.[47]

Understanding ourselves as rock parasites may or may not be precisely what Devall has in mind when he calls on us to develop the "ecological self." This self may be defined as the *"state of being that sustains the widest possible identification."*[48] Usually, when asked who they are, "most people respond by saying: 'I am a Christian' or 'I am a male' or 'I am a carpenter' or 'a mother' or 'an American.' " But these "identifications" miss the big picture. "A person expressing ecological self would say 'I am a forest being.' "⁴⁹ But even being a forest being is hardly enough. "When I say 'the world is my body,' " Devall notes, "I present a metaphor and a fact."⁵⁰

The notion of the whole earth as an organic unity has important consequences for understanding the special meaning of individuation and diversity within deep ecology. If the earth is a unity in the same way a tree or a human body is an organic unity, then the higher the level of particularity, the less important the particular. Any one bodily cell is likely to be equal to another only in the sense of being equally trivial. The loss of one leaf means nothing to the tree. It would be only at higher levels of organization, for example, organs, that we could begin to speak about one part being as *necessary* for the proper running of the whole as another, species being the equivalent of organs for the purpose of our analogy.

Devall would have us develop a species identification; the triviality of the individual seems so deeply ingrained in him that it does not even seem to occur to him that many people, when asked in an everyday sense, "Who are you?" will give a *name* even before they give the social classification that Devall provides. That there should be a rich diversity of species is important, but the individuals who make up those species are to be seen primarily as essentially interchangeable and expendable.

Indeed, even the odd species may not be of that much importance. This organismic view explains how deep ecologists can be so critical of heroic yet artificial means to preserve endangered species such as that undertaken on behalf of the California condor. Zoo-bred and zoo-fed, the condors become appendages to the great machine that is modern society. They lose most of their meaning when they lose their place in the ecosystem that sustained them, and in the whole of nature.⁵¹

We have seen how the deep ecology notion of the equality in principle of all beings is connected with the aspiration to Self-realization. Underlying both is a notion of the organic unity of the earth, a unity that makes us all parts of one being. This observation helps explain why the deep ecologists are as attracted as they are to the notion of earth as "Gaia," that is, a great, single entity. But these principles require a significant change in our perspective on what it means to be an individual being and on the value of individual beings. What are the practical consequences of that change?

RIGHT LIVING IN THE WRONG WORLD

The practical consequences of deep ecology can be understood from short-, medium-, and long-term perspectives. One lesson that the more thoughtful deep ecologists have learned—perhaps from ecology, perhaps from the history of twentieth-century totalitarianism—seems to be the danger of expecting radical changes overnight. There is some healthy recognition that the greater the transformation of human life, the longer it is likely to take. Still, the environmental legacy they inherit allows them to *assume* that urgent action is necessary. Those things are best to do in the short and medium term that prepare the way for the desired long-term changes.

Short-term goals of deep ecology are of two kinds: coalition building along with other actions designed to change environmental policies, and individual life-style choices.

Coalition building is important for deep ecologists, as is appropriate to a minority view. Although critical of mainstream environmentalism in theory, they are quite ready to work with it in practice. Openness to various united fronts is a major theme in Naess's *Ecology, Community and Lifestyle*, more a political handbook on how to deal with friends and enemies than it is a philosophical work. Naess is greatly concerned lest deep ecology appear to have too rigid an ideology. Though the book begins with an eight-point platform for the deep ecology movement, that platform is as general in tone as anything adopted by the Republican party. It speaks of the importance of "richness and diversity" of life on earth, the need to limit human interference with this richness and diversity as much as possible, and the way in which such limitation will require fundamental changes in "basic economic, technological and ideological structures."[52] This last point is obviously the kicker, but refusing to suggest specific changes in the platform is just one small way in which Naess attempts to turn deep ecology into a popular program.

The book as a whole is an explication of this platform designed to appeal to a wide circle of possible allies. Supporters are instructed to be prepared both to confront (likely) enemies in ways most likely to make them friends, and also to be careful not to alienate those inclined to be friends by insisting on ideological conformity. Naess's philosophical "method" of "precisation"—beginning with very general formulations like those in the platform and only slowly and in stages exploring more precise meanings—is well designed to produce the maximum level of consent to deep ecology's propositions and to minimize conflict.[53] In Naess's forest there are many glades. For example, he takes pains to show that "A person's opinion about the ecological movement cannot be derived from the fact that he or she 'believes in the Bible',"[54] under the assumption that such people would be thought unsympathetic. That Naess is anxious for a red and green alliance is only to be expected; but he admits that deep ecologists can even learn something from economists, normally considered the hereditary enemy of environmentalists.[55]

Naess claims as a further strength of deep ecology in public affairs that it forces technical experts away from facts to "values and priorities" that they are usually unprepared to articulate and defend.[56] On the other hand, because deep ecologists have a clear understanding of "certain fundamental values" and a "total view" of how those values fit together and what their consequences are, they can "oppose nuclear power without having to read thick books and without knowing the myriad facts that are used in newspapers and periodicals."[57] Any movement that encourages its members to avoid facts and concentrate on certain fundamental values—which, in practice, is likely to mean slogans—increases enormously its potential membership. Even if Naess himself has not written *Ecology, Community and Lifestyle* in a way that is likely to have broad appeal, those who read it and take its message to heart will have a good sense of how to popularize their message.

What is the cash value of the platform and these coalitions? In specific public policies, deep ecology in the United States offers little that is new or particularly distinctive. We should try to leave nature alone as much as possible, to preserve as much of the wild as possible. To this end, a whole raft of federal subsidies should be eliminated: for public grazing land, for development of barrier islands, for farming. Agricultural practices need to be reformed and agribusiness ended.[58] Restoration of damaged ecosystems should proceed with extreme caution.[59] The United Nations needs to take a larger role in global ecosystem preservation.[60]

Compared with Commoner's technocratic centralization, such proposals seem modest and are likely designed that way to avoid falling into the trap of reform environmentalism's attempt to make nature safe for human beings. Still, such apparent modesty is more an indication of a doubt about the efficacy of conventional politics than it is an expression of ultimately modest intentions. Part of this doubt stems from the stress on localism to be discussed below; general policy recommendations are of little use when a major thrust of the argument is to take responsibility for one's own corner of the world. Another part comes from deep ecology's recognition that its kingdom is not, in fact, of the present world. Policy debates are assumed to take place on the basis of assumptions about our right to exploit nature that, the deep ecologists claim, are entirely alien to them.

Doubts about the value of politics as usual lead to the direct action or civil disobedience side of deep ecology, which Earth First! made its own. To some it may be surprising that the group, which came to public attention in 1981 by the lighthearted unfolding of a huge painted crack on the Glen Canyon Dam, should have moved on to life-threatening "tree spiking."[61] But violence against property was intrinsic to Earth First! from the start, having taken up Edward Abbey's "monkey wrenching" (i.e., disabling) heavy machinery by sugaring or sanding gas tanks or cutting down billboards. The nonviolence that fills deep ecology literature is, one might say, "nonviolence in principle"; it does not necessarily promote nonviolence any more than eco-egalitarianism does. There is ample room for exceptions. Devall and Sessions, while endorsing nonviolence, chastely allow "the decommissioning of a power generator or bulldozer" if they are "spontaneous acts."[62]

In fact, Devall keeps open the door to more violent forms of resistance. "I don't think anyone would have any qualms about committing sabotage against concentration camps, and yet everything done at Auschwitz was 'legal' under Nazi law. Ecotage also responds to principles higher than secular law in the defense of place."[63] Furthermore, Devall creates a remarkably repulsive, if increasingly common, moral equivalence between ecological problems and the Holocaust. Students of natural resource management are like "guards in Nazi death camps" because "their neutrality towards forests or wildlife or fish kills any natural feelings of empathy or sympathy."[64] Why, then, should we have qualms about sabotage against the places where such attitudes are taught and exhibited, if not also against those who have them?

The only "aspect of nonviolence" that Naess believes to be "required of all those who are ecologically engaged" is based on the premise that violence is likely to be counterproductive. Since "established decision making institutions" must for the moment be used to protect nature, they must not be alienated.[65] Of course, this decision represents a tactical judgment, and not a deep principle, and it is as a tactical judgment that Devall and Sessions seem most comfortable with it.[66] If it should ever happen that established institutions come to be populated by significant numbers of those who believe that signs of environmental deterioration are to be likened to *Kristallnacht*, this view of the counterproductivity of violence might change.[67]

Doubts about politics as usual mean that in the short term changes in personal "lifestyle" are the central focus. While Devall deliberately endorses the word "lifestyle" for its relativistic implications, there seem to be limits.[68] All choiceworthy lifestyles are guided by the motto "Simple in means, rich in ends."

The first thing to notice is that "Simple in means" does not involve a rejection of modern technology, despite the claim to be radically confronting the dangerous premises on which it is based. Deep ecologists advocate a different brand of modern technology—"soft" technologies, that supposedly work with nature rather than against it. It seems that for Gary Snyder, "modern tools and machines" such as airplanes, "sno-gos," and two-way radios are appropriately "soft," at least in Alaska.[69] But these are not isolated artifacts. They mean oil drilling and refining, plastics and metal manufacture and finishing, transportation infrastructures for the movement of goods. To have all such enterprises with less environmental impact is a formidable *technical* challenge, which suggests we will also continue to need engineers, and scientists, and all the complicated and expensive institutions that support and train them. Should further technological development ever seem unnecessary because technology does all we want of it, machines still break down.[70]

Perhaps it is best to say that deep ecology opposes technological excess and excess technology. It decries the crass materialism that defines human happiness according to an ever-increasing income or GNP. It reminds us that quality is not necessarily the same thing as quantity; that good does not have to be great. Although there is no lack of sense in taking on the excesses of consumerism, there remains the question of the foundation for judgments like these, and therefore of the nature of the edifice of which they form part. What is good sense abstracted from its context may be part of a problematic whole. Devall illustrates that whole when he presents the simple in means lifestyle.

> A lifestyle can be complex, offering varied challenges, many stimulating and intrinsically interesting conversations, activities, and situations without being complicated, hectic, or constrained by a feeling that we must manage each time-unit (each hour, each day) for maximum productivity or payoff. Voluntary simplicity is not self-denial but a more compassionate approach to living and consideration for the vital needs of other creatures. Simple living does not mean involuntary deprivation, enforced austerity, boring or tedious daily routines, or poverty of experiences. On the contrary, voluntary simplicity is often a necessary condition for maximum richness, intensity, and deepness of experience.[71]

It may say something about deep ecology's audience that such efforts are made to make "Simple in means, rich in ends" look pretty indulgent, although there is a mixed message on this point. Naess says, "It is not to be confounded with appeals to be Spartan, austere, and self-denying."[72] Yet he also links "Simple in means" with "Aristotelianism, Buddhism, Confucianism,"[73] all of which call in varying degrees for austerity and self-denial.

What does Devall define as a deep and rich experience? Following the consumerist implications of the right to live and blossom, he presents the basic proposition that "We affirm our style as a person by our pattern of consumption."[74] Devall does not seem to appreciate that at least a number of the religious traditions to which he has recourse as examples of "Simple in means, rich in ends" do not affirm the self in terms of property, and for that reason have little or no concern with property. The "ethic" of mere consumption—call it "shallow consumption"?—has no quarrel with Devall on the point that we are what we use. But Devall counsels us to change our consuming patterns to be richer, for example, by consuming less energy, or participating in fewer activities that "only a few can participate in."[75] Devall himself buys local beer, local salmon (fresh, never frozen), local milk and cheese. His house is furnished by "local craftsmen and artists."[76] "An oak fire in a fireplace is a desirable and intrinsically rewarding experience."[77]

Let us give deep ecology the benefit of the doubt. Contrary to what shallow consumers might think, let us assume it is not the luxury of local beer and fresh salmon, of touring Alaska or jetting to Australia, that makes experience richer. Neither does one have to live in northern California.[78] What is important is the cultivation of a sense of immediacy in our consumption. "Experiences can have intrinsic worth for us, or we can view them as instrumental for some relatively remote goal," Devall notes, and he is suspicious of remote or abstract goals.[79] Those experiences are rich in which we "follow the 'flow line,' the streams of energy with intense connection."[80] It just so happens that in northern California that means fresh salmon. In Pittsburgh it probably means pierogies and Iron City beer.

LaChapelle explains further what it means to go with the flow: "To live intensely, to live in the moment, is the point of it all. But this intensity disappears the moment that thought comes in."[81] We are to seek the moments where "the gap between the observer and the observed is not there. There is no separation—just the experience."[82] While not equally developed in all deep ecologists, this notion of unreflective, unmediated experience is a crucial link to the long-term goals of deep ecology. But first, we must fill in the middle, and transitional, goals.

"THE UNMAKING OF CIVILIZATION"

The medium-term changes deep ecology proposes flow from the new consciousness implicit in the lifestyle changes. They involve two main goals: the reorganization of politics and society along bioregional lines and a ritualization of human life to accompany a reenchantment of nature. Together these goals begin to define what one sympathetic commentator has rightly called "the unmaking of civilization."[83]

"Bioregions" are attempts to define appropriate human ways of life in accordance with allegedly natural constraints. Just as animals that inhabit different ecological niches have different characteristics, so human lifestyles need to vary to accommodate the demands of place. Where modern science and technology allow us to live in essentially the same way no matter where we are—eating the same food, dressing the same way, maintaining the same comfortable ambiance, whether surrounded by desert heat or arctic cold—the assumption behind bioregions is that "lifestyle" should respond to surroundings. Deep ecologists look in developing this idea to the cultural variations that exist among different primal peoples and how, for example, a desert culture will be organized very differently from a people who occupy a coastal plain. The diversity that bioregions are supposed to produce is thought to be a good in itself, analogous to the species diversity that Hardin has discussed.

Bioregional organization is part and parcel of deep ecology's critique of the nation state and its stress on localism and small communities. The large size and complexity of modern nations make it necessary for them to be highly centralized, bureaucratized, and materially interdependent. Against this, deep ecology proposes—in what Devall and Sessions describe as a continuation of a "minority tradition" in Western thought—self-reliance and self-determination for small groups and communities.[84] Naess outlines "certain properties which are considered positive" that have been developed by "green communities."[85] These include small geographic size, population limited enough that members of the community can know one another, direct democracy, economic self-reliance (with education primarily directed to this end [i.e., training in the arts and trades]), and small income and wealth differentials. In addition, "Counteracting antisocial behavior is done directly with friendliness. There is little direct influence from the outside which interferes with that order inside."[86] In other words, as Naess later makes clear, orderliness is maintained primarily through intense social pressures.[87]

Deep ecology also teaches that one of the primal human needs is a sense of rootedness. Gary Snyder has written eloquently and plausibly about the importance of a sense of place for a child's education and for subsequent healthy adult growth, lamenting the extent to which we are no longer "from" anywhere in particular.[88] In a telling critique of much environmental sentiment, he notes that it is not enough to want to "'love nature' or . . . 'be in harmony with Gaia.'" One must be grounded in serious knowledge of that bit of nature that is local and immediate—knowledge that we have even forgotten that we lack.[89]

While one of the supposed advantages of a bioregional perspective is that it puts human social organization more in accord with nature, there is actually much discussion among deep ecologists about just how one is to define bioregions.[90] For example, are they watersheds, or defined by plant species, or by historical/cultural divisions of the primal peoples who once occupied given territories? The possibilities are many, leading to a suspicion that, as entities drawn on a map, bioregions may be less natural distinctions than conventional choices, as arbitrary as national boundaries.[91]

But the geographic boundaries of bioregions may be of less moment ultimately than the cultural boundaries implicit in them. Here we enter into the second medium-term transformation that deep ecology would like to produce—a ritualization of life. Rituals and ceremonies will distinguish, reflect, teach, and justify the lifestyles appropriate to the various bioregions. The fact that the modern world is so lacking in ritual—or that existing rituals are the wrong kind—is one of its most important defects. The religious rituals and outlooks that predominate in the West are very much part of the problem. Although the development of modern science in the seventeenth and eighteenth centuries is widely regarded as a necessary condition for the development of the project for the mastery of nature, many deep ecologists, as we have seen, ascribe the changes to deeper causes as well. A common theme is the dangerous monotheism of Jewish/Christian/Islamic forms and rituals (i.e., their claim to a universal religious truth).⁹² For LaChapelle, the suppression of the organic and earthy "Mother Goddess" by the more abstract "sky god" in ancient Greece was bad enough, but as nothing compared with the harm done by the Christian suppression of *all* the ancient gods.⁹³ For the old gods were intimately connected to nature and to places—particularly caves and mountains—where, as LaChapelle sees it, human beings can experience the full power and mystery of nature. Early Christians engaged in a more or less systematic revaluation of values in regard to such places; rocks, springs, or mountains that were once sacred became "places to be feared and often hated," abodes of the Evil One.⁹⁴

Thus, the emphasis on place that is so important to bioregions takes on a religious and even mystical significance. While Snyder recognizes that one must "indulge in a bit of woo-woo" to call sacred some of these newly discovered sacred places,⁹⁵ other deep ecologists are happy to jump in where he cautiously treads.

LaChapelle is particularly adventuresome. To show what is wrong in the West, she introduces us to the Japanese "way of the gods," a phrase she uses in preference to Shinto, owing to the "unfortunate connotations to Americans because of state Shintoism, emphasized during the war."⁹⁶ Shinto, she believes, preserves a sense of the divinity of nature even under otherwise modern circumstances. She is impressed that in an underground hydroelectric complex "in a rough workingman's way station, the only decoration was a tiny bonsai tree with a scroll behind it—living nature enshrined."⁹⁷ It reveals how Shinto "has come down to us uncontaminated by self-conscious analyzing and thinking." (This remark would surely surprise the careful creator of that most unnatural bonsai.) Shinto's roots "in the living relationship of early man and nature" have never been cut, "while our Western culture had its living continuity cut at the time of Plato."⁹⁸

Blaming Plato reveals an important aspect of the deep ecology program for ritualization of life. For ritual proves to be an answer not only to monotheism and modern science but to the whole misdirected, anthropocentric tradition of Western philosophy. Plato made it possible for humans to conquer nature by giving us the categories (e.g., subject and object, or natural and conventional) that allow us even to *think* in terms of opposing ourselves to the world around us. It is once again Martin Heidegger, as LaChapelle understands him, who is "the only Western philosopher since Plato" to reassert the essential mystery of the world in the face of rationalism.[99] "Nothing religious is ever destroyed by logic; it is destroyed only by the god's withdrawal."[100] But the gods, Heidegger says, may always return.

What would it mean for the gods to return? We would then have a reenchanted world, a world where once again nature is animated and inhabited by spirits that humans must tend or cherish, respect or fear. Heidegger did not think the gods would come back simply if asked; the best we could do is be prepared for their return. But LaChapelle seems to believe that they are simply waiting to be invited—or perhaps willed into existence.

Deep ecologists are quite fond of the recovery or recreation of primal rituals, as well as of the invention of new primal rituals. LaChappelle commends the Pawnee Hako Ceremony, the Japanese Tea Ceremony, the Sweat Lodge Rite of Purification, and of course any personal rituals such as the heart may prompt, for which she recommends some musical selections. Even Christian feast days can be recovered, so long as they have pagan roots in seasonal festivals.[101] Lest one be too put off by the rather unbuttoned character of some ancient rites, LaChappelle notes in justification that it was the lack of orgiastic sexual rituals in the lives of rural nineteenth-century Americans that was a major cause of "hatred and feuds."[102]

Naess at least shows no great interest in the recovery of primal traditions, but in doing so his followers act consistently with his attempt to systematize a certain kind of progressive opinion. They want wisdom, and they will have it. Ours is by no means the first time to look to "natural man" as a means of social critique. But the deep ecologists manage the feat of doing so with little or no irony. Gary Snyder tells about educating young Inupiaqs in Alaska. On a historical scale, these kids are not that far from their primal roots, yet already there is an "Inupiaq spirit movement" that seeks to revive the old ways by, for example, putting up a "poster sized list of 'Inupiaq values' " in the classroom.[103] Snyder is too polite to wonder how the Inupiaq spirit could be revived in the English language and in accordance with German categories of thought. How much more serious is the problem for the deep ecologists—much further removed from their origins—as they travel the world over literally and literarily, searching out the values that will be useful to define their newly created sense of autochthony? It is only in an uncharacteristically weak moment that Snyder tries to justify such efforts by asserting that even primal peoples all know that their own "myths are somehow 'made up.' "[104]

Paul Shepard has faced this difficulty more directly. He agrees that we need a new paradigm of thinking that is *like* that of primal peoples, even if it cannot be the same. (Shepard calls them "cynegetic," or hunter/gatherer man.) But how are we to live within it, knowing we created it, with the same immediacy that primal peoples occupy their horizons? For if we return to the origins self-consciously, then we have not really returned to the origins; we have merely made a "lifestyle" choice that could be revoked at any time. To "shop for ideas that one may sift, sort, use, and cast off . . . is incompatible with the acceptance of those ideas as living principles."[105] Shepard argues that time can solve this problem:

> Though it may, indeed, be impossible to anyone already old enough to read to achieve the experience of a cynegetic and religious perception of the world in the sense described here, he can make it possible for his children in some small ways, and they can make it possible for their children in larger ways.[106]

If the deep ecologists were ever to become impatient, Plato knew that the elimination of literate adults would produce the same result,[107] and Mao and Stalin seem to have come in practice to a similar understanding. But in the spirit of Shepard's solution, we see why the deep ecology medium-term goals force us into a long-term look at what would be a desirable future for humanity.

In what follows we will be talking about some very remote possibilities. We will be looking at problems that might arise under circumstances that have never yet been known to exist. The highly speculative nature of what follows may seem to some to make it pointless. Why worry about such remote possibilities? In part, it is necessary to meet deep ecology on its own ground. Devall and Sessions endorse the consideration of a variety of long-range "ecotopias" as a way of thinking about how we should live with nature.[108] But more important, what is anticipated about the far future contains problems and tensions that are quite revealing about deep ecology's present intentions. For the constant recourse to the ways of life and ideas of primal peoples raises this problem: how compatible are such ways of life with the many things that deep ecology wishes to preserve from the modern world?

HUMAN ENDS AND THE END OF HUMANS

We know that the people of the future are to be organized along bioregional lines. In addition, there will ideally be far fewer of them. But how these few will live is still somewhat mysterious.

Paul Shepard argues that to know what is essential for the human future, we must look back to the hunter/gatherer way of life that occupied us for the vast bulk of our history, and further to the origins of that way of life in the even longer evolutionary development of humans out of prehuman forms. The social, economic, political, and cultural world around us today is the result of accident or force and conceals more than it reveals about what is essential to human beings. Shepard's story is a fascinating one, and he tells it well; rarely does one see as convincing a case made that prehistoric human life should be our ideal.[109] Indeed, the case is so well made that his look into the future of "cynegetic man" is almost incomprehensible.

For the cynegetic man of the future is to live much of his life in complex, highly urbanized settings that no hunter/gatherer ever lived in. The bulk of his diet will not be the food actually hunted and gathered but synthetics that no human being has yet to eat, produced by microbes and bacteria. Although hunting in the vast interior wild spaces left by dense urbanization along the coasts will be crucial to the education of young men, most will eventually forsake it for "academic, artistic, skilled or professional" studies; occupations that, as professions, are alien to past or present hunter/gatherer societies.[110]

In part Shepard recommends urbanization and artificial food production to make a return of huge wilderness areas possible in the face of a large population. But if that were his only reason, surely he could have called for radical population reduction with the deep ecologists, particularly because there is probably a commensurate amount of time needed for such reductions and for the long process of historical forgetting that Shepard sees as necessary before the cynegetic lifestyle can be authentic. Or perhaps with his evolutionary view he sees more clearly than the advocates of population limitation the importance of the drive to reproduce, and hence is less willing to limit it.

In any case, Devall and Sessions note a central problem with Shepard's account. It is not clear why—if Shepard has described human needs properly, and they believe for the most part that he has—people would want to return to the cities from their wilderness experiences. Devall and Sessions are content to believe that they would not.[111] But if Shepard is serious about the belief that they will, then he must think there is something in the character of the life that human beings have formed in the post-hunter/gatherer historical period that is worthy of preserving, something that human beings need. It is unfortunate that he has not considered more explicitly what this something is. His arguments about primal hunter/gatherer life would have us believe it is complete spiritually and comfortable materially, untroubled by scarcity or mere labor. Perhaps the mention of professional and academic careers tells us something important. Primal peoples do not tend to produce Paul Shepards, or the extraordinary and constantly expanding stock of information that his work depends on. Yet intellectual labors like his have very little place in what Shepard tells us about the essential psychic needs of human beings. The question "Who am I?" that he says we all must ask and answer for proper psychological development can, it seems, be perfectly adequately answered by the cave paintings of Lascaux.[112] There's no need for university libraries; indeed, they may well be harmful.

But if in respect at least to intellectual development there *is* anything to be said for the postagricultural or the modern development of humans, then we must take more seriously than Shepard does the conditions that have produced those results. To have doctors, chemists, lawyers, and academics cannot be taken for granted. There are certain preconditions in material requirements (such as accumulated wealth to the extent of allowing people to waste vast amounts of time merely educating themselves) and world view (such as the antimythic quest for truth that characterizes science at its best). Such preconditions may to a greater or lesser degree be antithetical to hunter/gatherer societies. Despite the fact that Shepard tends to dismiss our current constellation of culture, it seems to respond to at least some human needs that he implicitly believes to be genuine and legitimate.

As we have already suggested, Shepard would not be the first highly cultivated intellectual to idealize primitive life. But however common this posture, it raises the question of how consistent are the grounds on which modern life is being rejected and primal ways praised. One can almost say what one wants about prehistoric humans; how much is known with certainty? But a more willful historical blindness is at work in other instances. Take Naess's description of the small, close-knit community, held together by social pressure. He is curiously silent about the well-known defects of such communities when they existed in the past: their instability and sectarianism, their tendencies toward tyranny, oppression, war, and imperialism. Does a lurking belief in progress make him think such problems can be made to disappear? Will these tendencies not be all the more dangerous with the admixture of modern technology? For however "soft" technology may become, only the greatest of forgettings would prevent it from turning "hard" at a moment's notice.

Snyder honestly attempts to answer such objections. He understands that people might worry about the "parochialism, regional strife, 'unacceptable' expressions of cultural diversity, and so forth" that localism might produce.[113] He does not say that such objections overestimate the diversity and independence of the bioregional units. Unlike Hardin's simple hope that "tribes" would

coexist peacefully, Snyder accepts the vision of differing and independent units, and presents three arguments why this situation
would not be as unstable, oppressive, and potentially conflict-rid-
den a situation as we might expect from our historical experience.

First, part of the conflict we see in the world today stems from
universalistic beliefs that make us reluctant to leave others alone;
once again, monotheism is to blame. Get rid of that and you
reduce conflict. Second, although he concedes that conflict might
continue to exist, it could not be as destructive as that engaged in
by modern states. This must be an argument purely from size,
because as we have seen there will probably be no lack of technical
sophistication. Third, it is largely the development of "accumulated
surplus" that makes conflict possible. Some may use the surplus
aggressively; others may be tempted into conflict to get their hands
on it. As long as nobody has much surplus, nobody is likely to be
tempted to move in on a bioregion that is largely alien to them anyway: they wouldn't know how to make a living on it.[114] (It might be
a useful reality check in this context to think about the European
contact with the Americas.)

Shepard would add to these points that we overestimate the
extent to which human beings are inclined to fight with one another, since we observe them largely under circumstances of the psychic malaise caused by agricultural societies. Healthy
hunter/gatherers, he claims, don't even hunt other human beings—
let alone make war on them—unless population density is too high
or there is no big game to hunt.[115]

These defenses do not really get to the core of the problem,
which is the tension hinted at by the apparently innocent quotation
marks Snyder uses when he dismisses the problem of " 'unacceptable' expressions of cultural diversity." Normally, such marks would
suggest that Snyder himself does not mean to endorse the idea that
any expressions of cultural diversity would be unacceptable. But
the statement is ambiguous. He might mean that we should expect
all bioregions to conform to norms that he would find acceptable
(as Shepard's argument might suggest). Or he might be saying that
bioregional organization implies a willingness to say "anything
goes" as regards ways of life in other bioregions. The first possibili-

ty suggests a breathtaking optimism about human things that Snyder does not on the whole seem guilty of. But to see that the second possibility is problematic, we need look no further than at the
deep ecologists themselves.

That bioregions, most or all of the time, would be willing to live
and let live as regards the way of life of other bioregions is consistent with the rejection of "monotheistic" standards that purport to
judge all ways of life. Without such standards, it would be easier to
tolerate the bioregional equivalent of a national socialist regime.
We could for a start take our cues from Naess, who, even under
occupation, resisted the Nazis nonviolently. When he speaks of the
"very peculiar hypotheses" about Jews in *Mein Kampf*, that would
be an example of the proper way to characterize beliefs that
diverge from our own. "As most of us today do not accept any of
these hypotheses, we are unable to accept Hitler's norms on how
to treat Jews."[116] Peculiar hypotheses are *hardly* enough to start a
fight over; so long as most of us don't accept them, why bother
those who might? Bioregions might learn much about keeping the
peace from Naess's moderation.

But there are, on the other hand, the Bill Devalls of the world.
His belief that Nazi atrocities warrant violent resistance would, in
isolation, suggest the result of a powerful adherence to justice, or
at least of righteous indignation. But when he applies the same
standard to forestry students, we realize we are simply witnessing
anger. Whatever the cause, Devall presents us with a problem. So
what if most bioregions live and let live, as long as even one will go
to war to prevent tree abuse?

What if even one bioregion comes to believe that its way of life
is threatened by its neighbors? Or that its way of life needs expressions of manly courage that can be found only in conflict with other
humans? What if one bioregion is asked by some family within
another bioregion to help them right a wrong done them by their
tribe? Or if people find their way of life becoming more precari-
ous, owing to some catastrophic change in their bioregion? Or if a
particular bioregion has a highly developed sense of right and
wrong? What are the odds of such events not happening, over the
long or short term? What are the odds that they will not produce

conflict, if they do happen? The state is certainly not the be all and end all of human organization. But bioregions seem very unlikely to overcome the problems with it that they are designed to resolve.

Shepard seems implicitly to recognize the likelihood of such difficulties when he recommends an essentially *universal* urban culture. While that vision is obviously not acceptable to all deep ecologists, it is an attempt to deal with just those local instabilities that would tend to undermine bioregional organization. But if that is the case, then once again, Shepard has accommodated to something about human beings in his picture of the cynegetic future that he has not fully explained in his discussion of our past. Naess too seems to give tacit recognition to the existence of problems with mere localism when he makes the paradoxical argument that local autonomy can be served by having *fewer* levels of government through which decisions must pass (i.e., by greater centralization of power).[117]

If there is no global organization with the power to enforce peace among the bioregions (i.e., an organization that would not itself be bioregional), what will prevent ethnic, tribal, religious, or even national conflict from being as much of a problem in this new world as it is in ours? Will the people of the future be without jealousy, self-love, honor, excessive pride, love of power, lust, fallibility, misperceptions? Are all these things that can produce conflict merely curable pathologies, or are they part and parcel of what makes us human?

A sense that perhaps these traits are indeed coeval with our humanity may explain the need to make the non-human Sasquatch an ideal, as the epigraph for this chapter suggests.[118] Deep ecology looks not just to a new life for human beings but to a new species altogether. Aristotle noted long ago that the human capacity for speech and reason, *logos*, made it possible for humans to be either the best or worst of animals.[119] With post-Aristotelian history in mind, the deep ecologists have plainly decided that on balance it acts for the worst. At the furthest edge of their thought, they look to a human being who has overcome the limitations of *logos*.

The importance of deep ecology's sustained attack on *logos*, on both modern and classical rationalism, cannot be understated. It has become a truism of social criticism that a certain *kind* of reasoning brings with it the evils of technology, variously described as "calculative," "economistic," "scientistic," "technocratic," "domineering," or "means oriented." While the deep ecologists subscribe to such criticisms, their critique goes even deeper. Reason becomes the number-one enemy. LaChapelle endorses the proposition that "This rational thought is out to kill us and is just as dangerous as a cobra."[120] Devall is likewise impatient with reflection: "I think deep ecology is best expressed, not explained."[121] Curiously, Buddhist and poet Gary Snyder seems to have the most respect for Western philosophy. He at least is reluctant to condemn it wholesale. But what saves it for him is the charming but rationally devastating reinterpretation of philosophy as the wisdom of Occidental elders: *"Books are our grandparents!"*[122]

Such a result may seem odd from a movement that called itself deep because it claimed to question, in the fashion of philosophy at its best, what is too often *un*questioned in the world around us. But it is ultimately consistent with the way in which Naess and his followers have attempted to popularize their moralistic program of reform. Naess presents his ecosophy with the "main goal" of emphasizing "the responsibility of any integrated person to work out his or her reaction to contemporary environmental problems *on the basis of a total view*."[123] In other words, one's "reaction" to a given issue is predicated on knowing the ultimate answer in advance, as is consistent with the adoption of a platform and the lack of interest in mere facts. Furthermore, he says, "a basic positive attitude is articulated in philosophical form. It is not done to win compliance, but to offer some of the many who are at home in such a philosophy new opportunities to express it in words."[124] Translation: rational argument is not going to convince anybody, but if you are already inclined to agree with us, here is how you should talk about things. The platform is designed to suggest views that are "basic," not "in an absolute sense, but basic among the views that supporters have in common."[125] If there were a *deep* ecology that persisted in asking why and how, it would show the shallowness of those who have appropriated that name. Even if Naess is right in his implicit judgment that there is not much chance for a popular movement based on the proposition that people should have to sit down and *think* about our relationship to nature, that would simply all the more expose the pretentious philosophical talk with which the deep ecology campaign is surrounded. Far from its highest role of questioning all opinions, philosophy for Naess is to be used to articulate a "total" view that is compatible with preexisting attitudes or "reactions." This system is a tool of the political reform program; it questions in order to find justifications. We have seen all too clearly how "philosophy" can be employed in this way, in the totalitarian regimes of our century. Naess may think he avoids such consequences by modesty concerning the possibility of an absolutely complete systemization of opinions. He does not claim to have all the answers. Still, when the object is no longer to understand the world but to change it, one should, as honest Marxists do, cease speaking of philosophy at all and simply use the term ideology. Of course, the end result would be the same either way. Henryk Skolimowski, an essentially sympathetic eco-philosopher, has accused Sessions and other deep ecologists of adopting a "party line" such as he experienced in Communist Poland. Antianthropocentrism becomes "an ideological dogma—deviate from it, and we will shoot you."[126]

What purpose does this ideology serve? The critique of reason combined with the cultivation of unreflective experience means that in effect, we are being told to emulate the way in which unreasoning animals live in the world. "Sasquatch is alert to the moment, attuned to sounds, feelings, changes in the forest, while we show our insensitivity to the moment when we ride our motorized vehicles or jog plugged into our Walkmans."[127] Can it be doubted that a squirrel burying a nut is alive to all the nuances of his surroundings, totally immersed in the experience, and living so much for the moment that he probably will not remember where the nut is buried?

Bioregions and ritualization may appear to stand in tension with these "animalizing" tendencies, as they seem to involve distinctly human capacities for organization and activity. But the more we imagine the success of this part of the program, the more a likeness to unreflective animal existence appears. The peaceful coexistence of bioregions begins to make some sense if we imagine a variety of posthuman species that live such different lives from one another as to make interaction among them increasingly less likely or meaningful. Grizzlies don't try to muscle in on polar bear territory. Likewise, a powerful ritual becomes "second nature"; one can hardly conceive of not doing it. From there it is a smaller step to the dances of bees, the songs of whales, or the mating rituals of penguins.

Naess too suggests an entirely new way of living in the world for humans and animals alike; his vision and Devall's are two sides of the same utopian coin. In a passage explaining how fully developed Self-realization would look at the natural world, he notes that those who have it

> see a lonely, desperately hungry wolf attacking an elk, wounding it mortally but being incapable of killing it. The elk dies after protracted, severe pains, while the wolf dies slowly of hunger. Impossible not to identify with and somehow feel the pains of both! But the nature of the conditions of life at least in our time are such that nothing can be done about the "cruel" fate of both. The general situation elicits sorrow and the search for means to interfere with natural processes on behalf of any being in a state of panic and desperation, protracted pains, severe suppression or abject slavery. But this attitude implies that we deplore much that actually goes on in nature, that we deplore much that seems essential to life on Earth. In short, the assertion of [the hypothesis that higher Self-realization leads to higher identification] reflects an attitude opposed to any unconditional *Verherrlichung* [glorification] of life, and therefore of nature in general.[128]

The sentiment Naess describes will surely be familiar to many; what is remarkable is not the sentiment but what he makes of it. When he says that "at least in our time" nothing can be done about the situation of the wolf and elk, there is an implication that perhaps there will come a time when something *can* be done. Naess may or may not believe the fate of these animals cruel, but he is ready to discuss what might be done to improve on nature. These changes go well beyond anything ever imagined by Francis Bacon, the archenemy of deep ecology for his advocacy of the conquest of

nature. He thought merely that such control of nature could benefit human beings. In this passage Naess imagines a pacification of
existence that would extend comfortable self-preservation to all
beings.

Why take seriously such extreme charity, or why give a moment's
thought to Devall's aspiration for a new kind of being to replace
humanity as we know it? Perhaps he represents merely a new form
of the Frankensteinian aspirations of modern science. Perhaps we
take these dreams and Hans Moravec's—quoted at the beginning
of this chapter—too seriously. The seasoned skeptic, sipping an
artificially sweetened and flavored beverage, sitting in an air-condi-
tioned room, prepared to type his criticisms into the word proces-
sor—has heard with his hearing aid–enhanced ears many such
promises before and knows in his pacemaker-regulated heart, and
indeed has seen with his own contact-lensed eyes, that such things
do not happen.

It must be admitted that the post-necessity, postbiological and
the posthuman futures are remote possibilities, even if the skeptic
overstates the case. But the aspiration to create a new kind of
posthuman being suggests that deep ecology goes far beyond modern science and technology by promising us comfortable self-
preservation through the overcoming of the constraints of *human*
nature. Human beings have various capacities and desires that
make them hard to satisfy. The project of modern technology was
to satisfy or moderate those desires that most compromised our
ability to live peaceably together. The deep ecologists accept that
goal. But they believe that our ability to formulate it, and to develop the means to achieve it, will forever stand in the way of its
achievement. Hence they look to the creation of happiness only
with the arising of a being who cannot be unhappy. The postbiological world of the robots, and the posthuman world of Sasquatch,
are simply two sides of the same coin.

The aspiration to make of human beings a being incapable of
being dissatisfied is a ne plus ultra of totalitarian thought. It is not
so simple as mere childish hopes.[129] Recent history has no lack of
these revolutionaries whose humanitarianism is indistinguishable
from misanthropy because they love a kind of being that will sup-

plant mere humanity, be it a species being or a superman. Nothing daunted by the awful results of these efforts, progressive thought presses on to ever new imaginings of futures from which humans as we now know them are excluded.

Let us sum up these considerations. The deep ecologists would have us think that the modern world has distorted our vision of human nature. To believe the "unmaking of civilization" an undesirable state of affairs is discounted as merely a result of that distortion. But given deep ecology's tacit reliance on aspects of the civilization they want to unmake—be it snowmobiles, professions, global institutions, or the moral capital that makes Nazism particularly vile—it seems most accurate to say that our world is not so much against human nature as it is the result of the selective development of some human capacities, and the satisfaction of certain human desires, at the expense of other capacities and desires. Deep ecology may justly enter the picture as a reminder of what we have lost or sacrificed in the technological and materialistic culture that so many now aspire to. But has any known culture done justice to all human capacities? Do we really have good reason to believe the totalitarian promise that some paradigm shift in our thinking, some rearrangement of social, political, or economic forms, would eliminate wholesale what seem in fact to be the conflicting tendencies of our nature? Is there not, in the belief in the efficacy of any deliberately designed transformation, a remnant—highly ironic in deep ecology—of the anthropocentric belief that human beings are masters of their fates and molders of their destinies? Can any existing social, political, or economic institutions not turn into grave problems when those problems are defined from the perspective of the unmaking of civilization, or indeed of the unmaking of humanity?

These many unresolved tensions within this final aspect of the deep ecology argument simply confirm and magnify the utopianism that grounds this school of thought. It may appear that their evidently utopian goals would prevent the movement from ever catching on more broadly. Why would sensible people ever buy into such an outré way of looking at the world? It will be tempting to see this school of thought as just another academic and intellectual fad.

But I think that judgment is in error. As already noted, to the extent deep ecology becomes entrenched in the academy, it will mold the views of future teachers, decision makers, opinion leaders, and citizens. As doubts about the legitimacy of Western culture and thought spread in higher education—doubts that deep ecology shares and encourages—more people will be intellectually prepared to accept their message.

But more important, it is perhaps a conceit of intellectuals that the bizarreness of an opinion is going to discourage its wide acceptance. The essence of reform movements is that they start on the fringes, and while at times moving to the center means moderating the message, sometimes the center itself moves. There is evidence that such a transformation may be in the works in relation to the messages of deep ecology. Only a small number of people may subscribe to deep ecology in its entirety, but a whole constellation of ideas closely related to it are in the process of becoming the "common sense" view of environmental issues. Increasingly we see attitudes shifting toward a noninterventionist stance as regards the environment and a greater sense of human equality with other beings that is not unlike bio- or ecocentrism. *Jurassic Park* may not have been on the *New York Times* best-seller list for three months *because* of its deep ecologylike teachings, but the set speeches presenting those ideas were apparently not enough to turn off its many readers. Deep ecology is not the same as animal rights, but deep ecologists would sympathize with a suit to prevent the transfer of a Cleveland Zoo gorilla to the Bronx Zoo for mating, on the theory that he had only recently found happiness with a nonfertile mate after many years of being a loner. Not only was this Romeo and Juliet story played straight in the local paper, but the zoo delayed its plans for a time.[130]

Opinion polls suggest the same tendencies. In 1985, 46% of adults polled thought not merely that medical experiments on animals were cruel or unnecessary but that they violated the animals' rights.[131] In July 1991, while a bare majority of registered voters thought that protecting endangered species was less important than protecting jobs, a substantial minority—34%—thought it more important.[132] A 1989 national adult poll suggests that, of those who are willing to pay higher taxes to save endangered species (38%), 64%—in good egalitarian fashion—would not distinguish among species to be protected.[133] People who hold such opinions are likely not aware of the reasons deep ecology would give to justify them. But if they ever hear those reasons, the fact that they have already drawn the conclusions will surely predispose them to take seriously the deep ecology arguments.

But these arguments are fatally flawed. Deep ecology needs to think more about the following observation from Gary Snyder—as does Snyder himself: "To be truly free one must take on the basic conditions as they are—painful, impermanent, open, imperfect—and then be grateful for impermanence and the freedom it grants us."[134] Far more so than the modern thought it condemns, deep ecology is in revolt against conditions as they are in the name of pleasure, permanence, and perfection.

The environmental popularizers we have examined have each played a role in the development of the widespread public "concern for the environment" that is such a noteworthy aspect of politics in the United States and many other parts of the world. But again and again, we have seen how these popularizers fail to treat adequately the ethical and political questions that must be at the heart of any such concern. What we have been taught to be concerned about has been defined by utopian visions of the future.

Starting from such shaky foundations, we should not be surprised that when we come to practical discussions of this or that environmental issue, we find our usual categories to be inadequate and frustrating. The principles that we hear enunciated seem to have little to do with the policies actually adopted. "Protecting endangered species" means looking after a few favored animals; "hazardous waste cleanup" means endless lawsuits. Simplistic dichotomies and vague syntheses are the order of the day: we are threatened with "jobs or the environment" and placated with "jobs and the environment"; "health before profits" is one day a rallying cry, and the next it is "health and profits"; technology and nature are in violent opposition, technology and nature can learn to coexist. Because we have little or no abiding sense of what we want of our relationship with nature and the world around us, we are the victims of every new report, study, or experiment on what we are doing to it or it is doing to us.

This situation is not a healthy one. There may be some comfort in the fact that self-professed environmentalists are not the only ones trying to get the ear of the public for the discussion of environmental issues. There have been authors—not nearly so many, or so influential—who have tried to challenge the environmental popularizers' definitions of the source and character of, and solutions to, environmental problems. It takes at least two to make a public debate; have these critics done their job? Can we turn to them for a better way of thinking about the environment?

CHAPTER FIVE

Something More Than Natural

... for though we love both the truth and our friends, piety requires us to honor the truth first.

Aristotle, Nichomachean Ethics[1]

It was an admirable place ... in which the many tongues of Nature whispered mysteries, and seemed to ask only a little stronger puff of wind to speak out the solution of its riddle ... [I]t was just the nook, too, for the enjoyment of a cigar.

Nathaniel Hawthorne, The Blithedale Romance[2]

THUNDERING SILENCES

Predictions of global disaster "if present trends continue" were once again in the minds of Donella Meadows, Dennis Meadows, and Jørgen Randers, three of the four authors of *Limits to Growth*, when they published *Beyond the Limits* in April 1992.[3] Or perhaps they had never made any predictions. With stunning revisionism, they claim that their first effort was not a "prediction of doom" and not even "a prediction at all." Instead, it was "about a choice," a choice that contained "a message of promise."[4]

Apparently, our "choices" have not changed much in 20 years. The same stringent policies that needed to be adopted by 1975 need to be in place by 1995 if we are to have what is now called a "sustainable future": population limitation, vast increases in efficiency and recycling, control on capital growth.[5] Delay them *another* 20 years, and the computer again paints a bleak future.

Such results are hardly surprising, as this new analysis is based on essentially the same computer model as was used in *Limits*. *That* is perhaps a bit surprising; after all, the ultimate defense of that model at the time was that it was the best available, not best simply. Yet let us grant for the moment that 20 years later this model remains state-of-the-art. Let us even grant that the computer runs might tell us *something* true about the world. With these concessions made, the most troubling thing about *Beyond the Limits* comes into relief: it refuses to make systematic acknowledgment of and response to the multitudinous criticisms made of the earlier analysis.

The book contains scattered references to objections leveled against *Limits* and some desultory attempts to answer them. A few specific numbers in the model are changed. But little in *Beyond the Limits* even hints at the body of literature that argues that its methods and results are fatally flawed.

One might think, for example, that in the sequel the authors would discuss for a wider audience some of the interesting issues aired when the original MIT team answered their critics in *Models of Doom*.[6] But not only is that debate not reviewed; its very existence is suppressed. The annotated bibliography in *Beyond the Lim-*

its does not include any reference to *Models*, although it might have been appropriately included under three of the five headings by which books are arranged. The only mention of *Models of Doom*, in a footnote, simply lists it as an example of a study that used the model to test various "what ifs."[7] Some of the criticisms put forward by *Mankind at the Turning Point* are answered in passing, but the work is neither mentioned nor listed in the bibliography, despite the fact that there is a special section for "works by and for the Club of Rome."[8]

If *Beyond the Limits* were mere polemic, such omissions would not be hard to understand. But it presents itself as popularizing serious social science and policy analysis. Its authors purport to be interested in "truth telling."[9] Yet it is one of the well-known and well-respected traditions of science that disagreements be aired openly and directly; part of the strength of one's own case is the ability to answer or refute criticisms brought against it. Surely the public could be made aware of how this process works.

Even by the standards of the more mundane world of politics, there is something lacking in *Beyond the Limits*. While there are apparently few depths to which debate over public issues in the United States will not sink, it should be noted that the silences in this sequel do not prevail uniformly in all questions that provoke public controversy. Opponents and proponents of gun control *do* try to refute each other's readings of the meaning of the constitutional "right to bear arms." Those who are "pro-life" and those who are "pro-choice" *do* take explicit issue with each other over such things as a constitutional right to privacy, or when life or personhood begins. People who approve of affirmative action policies *do* debate the meaning of equality and the role of government in promoting equality with those who disapprove of affirmative action.

Analogous debates about the meaning and goals of environmentalism will be necessary if we are ever to confront the implications of the crusading utopian moralism that is the dominant strain of contemporary environmental thinking. Yet environmental popularizers tend to assume that critical disagreement springs either from ignorance or from a desire to protect well-entrenched, narrow interests. If the former, the answer is education—another book that details the horrors of our impositions on the environment. If the latter is the case, then all that needs to be done is to point out the supposed bias. In neither case is it necessary to meet or refute the arguments on their own terms.

Some responsibility also needs to be laid at the feet of the critics, since it takes two to argue. The green crusade has been so successful that few want to be, or even appear to be, definitively outside the fold. Hence, many would-be critics are perfectly happy to pay obeisance to the proper environmental gods ("we all want clean air") as the price of being heard at all. There are benefits and costs to this strategy. The most active and extreme proponents should not be allowed an ideological "veto" over who gets to be called "an environmentalist." George Bush as president had as much right to define what he takes to be the hallmarks of concern about the environment as any paid Washington lobbyist. Unless that definition is made carefully and convincingly, however, in practice one will still buy into, or be judged by, the "other side's" assumptions.

Another problem the critics face is sheer numbers. Environmental popularizers sometimes write as if they remain the embattled intellectual minority they were in the 1960s. In fact, over the last 30 years there have been relatively few systematic attempts to critique environmentalism. Doubtless for some time this reflected an arrogance on the part of "mainstream" thinkers who could dismiss the newcomers as cranks. But even as environmentalism has grown in strength and importance, there has been only a slight increase in studies designed to examine its principles and purposes in a thoughtful yet critical way.

We turn now to examine a sample of such critical books. Here too for the most part we will be looking at popularizers—authors who have tried to convince the public that environmental claims for one reason or another don't add up. Their range of success varies more widely than we have seen in the previous cases. Some of the books we will discuss made a significant splash, with favorable reviews even in such general readership publications as the *Times Book Review* or *The New Republic*. A few got most of their attention from conservative publications. Others sank more or less without a trace. Whatever influence these authors might have had—and my own judgment is that to date it has not been proportional to their merits—the question would arise as to whether they have helped frame their doubts about prevailing environmental ideas and ideals in such a way as to lay the foundation for meaningful, ongoing debate. While the lonely few who have attempted such confrontations deserve a great deal of respect for standing against the tide and holding open questions that would otherwise be closed, there is reason to think they have in fact not always been skilled at getting to the heart of the problem we have seen posed by the environmental popularizers. Mostly they have tended to focus on the scientific flaws of environmentalist arguments. This is a crucial topic, but it does not touch the utopian ideals that are the real soul of the movement. Even when those ideals are noted, they are rarely well understood; the debate quickly degenerates into claims and countercharges about who is for or against progress.

WEIRD SCIENCE

The extreme conclusions of environmental disaster that have over the years been the stock in trade of environmental popularizers have invited attempts at more sober assessments of what science can tell us about what we are doing with and to nature. John Maddox's *The Doomsday Syndrome* (1972),[10] George Claus and Karen Bolander's *Ecological Sanity* (1977),[11] Dixie Lee Ray's *Trashing the Planet* (1990),[12] Ronald Bailey's *Ecoscam* (1993),[13] and Michael Fumento's *Science Under Siege* (1993)[14] are prominent examples. Julian Simon has concentrated on resource, population, and economic issues in *The Ultimate Resource* (1981)[15] and *The Resourceful Earth* (1984), which he edited with Herman Kahn.[16] Edith Efron's *The Apocalyptics* (1984)[17] and Elizabeth Whelan's *Toxic Terror* (1985)[18] place their discussions of cancer and health threats within the larger context of the environmental movement.

It is noteworthy that most of these authors are outside of the academic world that has been such a fertile plot for environmentalism's growth. John Maddox, though he taught theoretical physics at Manchester University, was editor of the prestigious British science journal *Nature* when he wrote *The Doomsday Syndrome* and has had a long career as a science journalist and broadcaster. Karen Bolander, with a doctorate in clinical psychology, had a practice of individual and family therapy; George Claus was a medical and botanical researcher. Edith Efron, Ronald Bailey, and Michael Fumento are journalists, and Elizabeth Whelan, who holds a doctorate in epidemiology from the Harvard School of Public Health and was a research associate there, is executive director of the American Council on Science and Health. Herman Kahn ran the Hudson Institute think tank. Dixie Lee Ray has been governor of Washington state, chairman of the Atomic Energy Commission, and assistant secretary of state in the U.S. Bureau of Oceans, in addition to being on the zoology faculty of the University of Washington. Julian Simon is a professor at the University of Maryland.

This "outsider" status is both a strength and a weakness. Clearly it helps these authors question the regnant environmental orthodoxies. But it also means they are often writing, as we saw happening with the environmental popularizers themselves, about matters well outside their nominal areas of expertise. This troubles the critics more than it does their opposite numbers, moving them to discuss why those who *do* have the relevant knowledge seem disinclined to call attention to the abuses of scientific information these authors believe they have found. Claus and Bolander, for example, cite the high degree of scientific specialization, the breakdown in standards for refereed journals when referees act as partisans of a particular view, and the corruption that comes about when science attempts to serve powerful interests.[19] (Notice the overlap with the claims that Carson put forward on the other side.) Elizabeth Whelan adds that serious scientists are likely to be uncomfortable with the "instant analysis" and simplification that play such an important part in media coverage of science, and hence in setting the public perception of what "science" says. She also points out how criticism of the wrong sort can threaten funding, while noting perceptively that for many scientists the way their work is used by others is likely to be of little interest, so long as their research is not hindered.[20] Bailey too speaks of the effect of scarce research funds and how that can lead to the "politicization of science."[21]

We should not forget that the environmental popularizers would argue that the reason they are not criticized more widely by the scientific community is that their findings and ideas are accepted by that community. Doubts about this claim are possible because of the work of these critics. Whelan, for example, demonstrates how the now iconographic "disaster at Love Canal" evaporated as a public health crisis as soon as there was serious scientific scrutiny of the case.[22] Maddox gives the missing context for Ehrlich's hysterical predictions about food and population crises.[23] Claus and Bolander provide exhaustive documentation for the case that science became politicized in the debate over pesticides, showing how DDT, another environmental icon, was demonized.[24] Efron demonstrates a like politicization of cancer research.[25] Fumento lets the air out of the overinflated Alar scare.[26]

The list of environmental crises that weren't could be a long one indeed. Sadly, the impact of these works has not generally reflected their importance; these writers have remained voices in the wilderness. As noted in the introduction, only very recently have signs appeared that a general discussion of the poor quality of the science that has informed environmental thought and action will begin.

It would be impossible to examine here all the particular disputes over scientific evidence that these authors have raised with environmentalists, although some of the information they present has already been mentioned in these pages. Sometimes they attempt simply to reopen questions that environmentalism has tried to close; in other instances they suggest how established scientific truth runs counter to the claims put forth by politicized science. But whether the scientific information used by environmentalists is simply wrong or merely dogmatically held, these critics are forced to wonder what, if not good science, serves as the foundation for environmental arguments. What motivates people who are so often scientists themselves to see science through such distorting lenses, or to ride roughshod over uncertainties in their quest for making a convincing case?

In answering this question, these critics show a high level of agreement. Unfortunately, the consensus forms around one of the great misunderstandings of environmentalism, which has been an important roadblock to debate about environmental goals. For all agree that opposition to technology, and hence to "progress," is one of environmentalism's core ideas. This reading gives them some insight into the problem posed by environmentalism—but it is not enough.

Maddox writes that the preoccupation of environmentalism with distant calamities "usually suggests policies of inaction . . . In this sense, the environmental movement tends towards passivity, true conservatism," as opposed to the "vigorous and expensive" policies necessary to solve more immediate problems that threaten human well-being.[27] But perhaps, he speculates, environmentalists oppose action because the technological means by which conditions might be improved are seen as "out of control" and themselves posing the greatest threats to human life.[28]

Claus and Bolander cite "opposition to technology" as one of five major principles of environmentalism. They see environmentalists as advocates of "de-development," nostalgic proponants of days gone by who are "themselves filled with inertia and lack imagination."[29] They link this attitude with another of their major themes—the "anti-intellectualism" of environmentalists. While granting the limits to what reason can accomplish, Claus and Bolander argue that some environmentalists reject reason altogether.[30] Finally, opposition to technology could be linked with another theme they discuss—the way environmentalism depends on and encourages a general despair about the human prospect.[31]

Efron believes that "environmentalist" is a misleading title for many of those in the "environmental movement"; the more extreme elements are in fact "apocalyptics."[32] That is to say, in the manner of those who have for generations predicted that the end is nigh, environmental apocalyptics believe that only a complete reformation of human affairs can keep us from destroying ourselves. Efron cites many targets for the wrath of the apocalyptics, among them the "constellation of science, technology, industrial production, the marketplace, and capitalism."[33] Fumento too puts "fear and loathing of technology" prominently among a number of motivations he discusses.[34]

Whelan agrees that environmentalism is motivated in part by "a war against progress" through which an elite seek to protect what they have achieved.[35] (We will speak more of the class implications of this kind of analysis below.) Bailey argues that environmentalism is home to "modern antitechnology zealots."[36] Finally, Dixie Lee Ray somewhat confusingly sees environmentalists both as protectors of the status quo and as "anti-development, anti-progress, anti-technology, anti-business, anti-established institutions, and, above all, anti-capitalism"[37] (i.e. "anti" all the things that define the status quo in the United States).

Elements of these characterizations are right on target. But as we have seen, to call environmentalists antitechnology or antiprogress or antidevelopment is to beg crucial questions of what the movement wants—and, not so incidentally, to block the critics from taking a closer look at what they themselves stand for. It is true that one finds in environmental thinkers doubts that many technological developments we take for granted are unalloyed goods. But the critics mistake criticism of this or that technology, particularly those central to our present way of life such as cars or fossil fuel energy consumption, for a wholesale rejection of technology. To think rejection of these particulars amounts to a rejection of technology or progress per se is to miss the significance of the utopian plans that these thinkers have formulated for restructuring society precisely in order to maximize the good that can be achieved by technology. Barry Commoner wants to harmonize the technosphere and the biosphere. Paul Ehrlich wants fewer people in part so that there can be greater freedom for technological development, since fewer people means less impact per technology. E. F. Schumacher wants to achieve all the promises of modern materialism better than we have so far been able to. It seems to be left to the deep ecologists rather than critics to point out the absolute dependence of "shallow" environmentalism on modern technology. But as we saw, even that is the pot calling the kettle black.

To mistake the position of one's opponent so thoroughly never aids the seriousness of a debate. The environmentalist popularizers have taken advantage of this error by pretending that only their critics are "technocrats," believers in technological fixes, or "cornu-

copians." Vulnerable precisely on the charge of their own technological utopianism, they take this chance to turn that issue back
upon those who criticize them, so that environmentalists can
appear to be the "realists." When critics acknowledge specific
problems with the way things work today, they are likely to argue—
no less than do the environmental popularizers—that more, different, or new science and technology will solve them. But the critics
give even less attention than the popularizers to the political or ethical assumptions that make this improvement possible, because
they apparently assume that existing political and economic
arrangements can supply whatever is lacking.

Both sides are less than forthcoming about the serious questions
behind the role technology does or should play in our lives. Reasonable people are entitled to question just what today's technology has accomplished. When the critics defend the present
constellation of technology and development—of progress—
against environmental criticisms, they of course do not claim perfection. But in response to the hysteria they are attempting to
counter, present difficulties tend to be treated as little more than
glitches. It is as if the mobility and choice provided by a car are its
essence; traffic jams, exhaust fumes, and highway deaths are merely accidents. The critics remind us that progress as hitherto understood in the West has led to longer, more prosperous lives for more
people than the world has ever seen. But when they speak of long
life, problems of aging are left aside. When they point out the
undeniable benefits of general prosperity, it is without serious
recognition of the aimlessness that increasingly seems to characterize materially prosperous societies. When they highlight how we
have accommodated and benefited from population growth in the
past, it is as if there were not already obstacles to distributing sufficient goods and services.

Both sides accept uncritically the materialistic and progressive
assumption that the royal road to human happiness and peace
leads through ever increasing material comfort, safety, and prosperity for an ever increasing percentage of people. As a result, in
this fruitless debate about progress, both sides are willing to overlook what should be obvious: when we use technology to solve one

problem, we will open the door to another problem. Petroleum and electricity saved the whales by making whale oil lamps obsolete. Petroleum and electricity also allow more sophisticated means of hunting whales, so that they are still threatened.

But both the environmentalists and their critics might respond to this point by saying that, if only we do things right, problems will get *smaller* as each old one is solved, and life will get better and better in the process. Is it possible to express doubts on that score without being dismissed as a crank? It is curious how freely we criticize the world we have made, up to the point that our ability to constantly improve it is questioned. Cars were wonderful solutions to the problem of urban horse wastes, but horse accidents did not cause the same level of damage to life and property as do cars. The parents whose child took the family cart for the evening had less to worry about in that respect than those who loan the family car. And while they had to worry more about the possibly fatal consequences of infection that might come from even a minor horse-drawn accident, they would never be faced with the truly terrible decision to end life support for a child all but killed in a major accident. And so on. Perhaps there is an "ethical homeostasis," relating to the moral challenges life presents to human beings.

It is no argument to say that we would not choose—as most would not—to return to the conditions of some earlier age; we are all the victims as well as beneficiaries of the way of life we know best.[38] We can grant with the critics that people *do* live longer, that food production is increased and many conditions of life improved. But the very same science or technology that produces these results has its darker side. Furthermore, unless we are sure that "longer" and "wealthier" are simply to be equated with "happier" and "better," we should perhaps give two cheers for these accomplishments, and not three. By letting their defense of the underlying values and assumptions that represent the best hopes of the status quo remain implicit, it may be that the critics have failed even more than the environmentalists to think seriously about what human beings can and should want out of life, and about the problems that seem necessarily to arise from conflicts among desires, or between our desires and what is possible.

The shared failure to address such fundamental questions explains why, despite its utopian character, environmentalism can still appear to be a "mom and apple pie" issue. Even the wilder pretensions serve familiar purposes. Deep ecology's biospherical equality "in principle" is only an extension to the nonhuman realm of the comfort we want for ourselves; why not save caribou from wolf, and wolf from starvation, if it were possible?

In short, painting environmentalism as antiprogress and antidevelopment leads to a debate in which no one need think very seriously about the assumptions behind our current way of looking at our purposes in the world, or about alternatives to those assumptions. It has allowed the critics to share a measure of the utopianism of those they criticize.

Do the arguments adduced thus far mean that the deep ecologists are right that all non-"deep" environmentalism is little different in principle from the materialistic progressivism it purports to oppose? And if it were the case that environmentalists and their critics were more in agreement than *either* side now thinks, would it be good news or bad news? If there were such agreement, couldn't we concentrate on what are apparently much more tractable questions of the best means to reach those goals? If environmentalists and their opponents are both believers in material progress, why not rejoice that more fundamental disagreements do *not* exist? Would not it then be more likely that all sides can get together and agree about what needs to be done? Who doesn't want people to live longer, healthier, wealthier, happier, and more productive lives?

In fact, the consensus is not that comprehensive, nor are disputes over means necessarily easy to settle. Despite the similarity in broad goals, there is a crucial point at which the critics and the environmental popularizers diverge. The critics are not tempted by the quest for material progress into the totalitarian mentality of so many environmental popularizers. Why not?

Honesty requires the admission that because the critics speak so little about politics and ethics, it is not clear that they *know* why not. But hints are seen in the frequency with which they defend capitalism from the environmentalist attack. It is necessary, but not sufficient, to praise the market for its ability to produce the wealth that allows us to protect the environment. It is more to the point to recognize how free markets point to freedom generally as a good that transcends the lip service environmental popularizers sometimes pay to it.[39] Once individual liberty enters the picture, it is nearly impossible to identify and justify a single, substantive purpose or goal that would promote the totalitarian ordering of society. If left free to do so, people will lead their lives in very different ways. (They may coalesce in some great crisis, which is another reason why that mentality is promoted by the environmental popularizers.) These differences are a constant reminder of the potential for conflict among various goods, both among people and within our own desires, *even* if all the goods in question tend to be defined in materialistic terms. Of course, they do not have to be so defined.

Such conflict has consequences for the shape of politics and society, just as does the environmental attempt to arrange matters so as to eliminate it. "Organic growth" means that any inability of the parts of a whole to work together for a common purpose signals disease. But those who do not seek to transcend such differences will be more likely to favor the politics of liberal regimes, where a private sphere of diversity is marked off and where the public realm both limits and is limited by the resulting conflict.[40]

Here, then, we can see that the deep ecologists miss an important principled difference between environmentalists and their critics. It is a sign of their immersion in utopian thinking that they should be blind to it.

Perhaps one reason why the critics can only hint at the significance of liberty is the relatively narrow conception of a good life that they put forward. They seem impatient with aspirations that go beyond material desires and that may place them in a less prominent light. They see environmentalism as treading in the spiritual realm, with an excessive or misplaced reverence for nature, and they don't like it. For example, Fumento speaks of the "cult of the natural" and "environmentalism as religion."[41] Dixie Lee Ray notes that "activist environmentalists . . . also tend to believe that nature is sacred and technology is a sacrilege. Some environmentalists appear to favor taking mankind back to pantheism or animism."[42]

Is such criticism based on pure skepticism of any religiosity, or on a sense that there is something wrong with environmental spirituality as such, or from a desire to protect conventional religious beliefs? The point is usually not developed enough for us to be sure, but it suggests another area in which critics and environmentalists are talking past each other.

Deep ecology is the best test case, as the most overtly "spiritual" school of environmental thought, with its desire to "re-enchant" nature.[43] But do the deep ecologists think nature really *is* enchanted, that trees, rocks, and animals have spirits or souls, or that God or gods watch over them? One hint that they do not is seen in their trying so hard to see the world in terms of organic harmony. Animists and pantheists more often see contending, sometimes chaotic forces at work. They do not expect that humans will readily find a peaceful place in this universe, and simply hope to minimize the extent to which they will get caught in a minefield of contending powers that are far greater than their own.

Thus, the deep ecologists are not so much attempting the recovery of primal truths on their own terms as they are consciously or even dogmatically adopting a set of beliefs that are amenable to a certain "lifestyle." We are to adopt these beliefs out of a supposed need to posit or to will certain things as good or as divine to produce the behavioral changes that will save ourselves and/or nature. It is obvious that such attempts to overcome "anthropocentrism" must fail to the extent that it remains human beings who do the valuing. What remains concealed in this common criticism is the view held by critics and criticized alike that our will is the ultimate source of good and right. One hears little of gods of nature or a God of nature that reveal to us how to live. Nothing is said of nature as a normative standard along the lines that Socrates or Aristotle investigated nature. As a result, the shallowest of technocrats or the deepest ecologists are treating nature as stuff to be valued by the human will, whether they see it as storehouse or sanctuary. All too often, then, we are left with a choice between "woo-woo" about nature and "gee whiz" about technology. Even the awe we are encouraged to feel in facing nature is distorted by being placed in this context, since such fundamental willfulness is hardly compatible with the humility that awe would otherwise produce.

Whatever their limitations, the critics who focus on the scientific inadequacies of environmental arguments perform a crucial service. They restrain us from being stampeded into radical reform on the basis of incomplete or mistaken information. When it comes to answering the crucial question, "Just how bad is the environmental situation?" they give us reason to doubt that the situation is as dark as it is often painted. They provide a broader perspective that shows how today's crisis is likely to be forgotten tomorrow. But while they realize that the ground upon which environmentalism rests is not narrowly scientific, they do not fully understand the nature or significance of its political and ethical underpinnings. Such factors cannot be dismissed as the intrusion of mere politics or individual values into what is properly a debate to be settled by science itself.

Science helps us know what is possible among those things we want to do or avoid. Science can also help develop the means we will employ to reach the chosen ends. But as modern science understands itself, it cannot determine a choice among ends. And that is the nature of the choice environmentalism presents to us. Environmentalism, as with any other political or ethical "ism," is offering us visions of a good life and must be judged on that ground. Modern science's self-imposed inability to make such choices may be a great weakness, but it is a condition that must be acknowledged and respected. All the same, we cannot conclude from it that there is no rational way to make distinctions between the outlooks on the human good that compete for our attention.

But the environmental popularizers and the critics of their science rarely take this last step with sufficient clarity and completeness. For example, Julian Simon knows that there is "necessarily a moral dimension to these decisions over and beyond whatever insights science may yield."[44] In the case of the population questions that interest Simon, these values include how much to take account of near- versus long-term costs and benefits, the extent of altruism and selfishness, how much space and privacy is desired, the legitimacy and extent of a right of inheritance, the inherent value of human life, the importance of animals and plants versus people, and the importance of individual freedom.[45] But these crucial points got lost in his famous bet with Ehrlich, creating the impression that the ability of each to predict the future was the central issue. Simon may well be correct that such a bet would popularize his argument better than a debate about the moral dimension, and to some extent he is forced by Ehrlich's own case to meet him on this ground. But so doing covers over his real disagreement with Ehrlich, which is defined by their different visions of how they want the world to be. The critics no less than the environmentalists owe us a more careful treatment of this crucial topic.

ARISTOCRATS' NATURE

Another group of critics focuses more directly on this vision by focusing on the politics of environmentalism. Accepting the proposition that environmentalism is at root antiprogressive, they provide a class analysis of the movement, painting environmentalists as "haves" who want to protect what they have—not merely from the "have nots" but from others who are in the process of getting.

Bernard J. Frieden's *The Environmental Protection Hustle* (1979)[46] is one of the best examples of this genre. In 1975 Frieden, who had been director of the Harvard and MIT Joint Center for Urban Studies and had served on White House urban task forces under Presidents Johnson and Nixon, went to California to study how national policies were dealing with the acute pressure on housing needs caused by the recession of 1974–75. He found that local zoning and building permit decisions made under the influence of environmental interests were having a much greater impact on the housing situation in California than he had expected. Instead of trying to reach accommodation between the legitimate need for housing and legitimate concerns about preserving the environment, local governments were drastically and irrationally reducing available housing choices and increasing the cost of housing, in the name of environmental protection.

Frieden presents detailed and devastating case studies to support his contention. For example, Marin County blocked development by getting the federal government to create parks within its borders, and then blocked access to those parks.[47] Palo Alto tried to preserve open space by purchasing undeveloped property on the outskirts of town, but then resorted to zoning regulations that effectively prohibited development when the price of buying the land in question proved to be too high.[48] A proposed subdivision in the foothills of Oakland was transformed from one that would have provided reasonable cost housing for 2,200 families to one providing 300 units of expensive or luxury housing to preserve more open space.[49] A county environmental impact statement for a development around Mt. Diablo cited the need to protect animals not known to be on the site, known not to be on the site, or if on the site known not to be endangered.[50]

Two aspects of the problem he documents seem to concern Frieden most. In the extensive processes of review and negotiation to which any large building project is subject, all interests—those of the developer, potential workers, current residents, environmentalists, the local government—are represented. All, that is, *except* the interests of those who would like to be able to buy new homes at reasonable prices. This fact, plus the generally unsavory reputation of property developers, can create a significant bias against development. Yet people need to live somewhere; where are they to go? As Frieden sees it, a second major problem is that environmentalists opposing development play fast and loose with the arguments they use to answer this question.

Thus, he notes, environmentalists oppose development of rural or undeveloped land in the name of preserving scenic areas, endangered species, or farmland. But they also oppose development of remaining vacant areas within cities in the name of preserving open space. They oppose development of valley areas, since those soils are better suited to farming, but also oppose developments on hillsides because they might cause floods or landslides. They oppose suburban development because it is wasteful of land and increases commuting and car use, but also oppose high-density development near suburban job centers, even with good connections to public transportation.[51] Is there any kind of principle behind this seemingly unprincipled opposition, except an animus against any growth or change? Frieden does not have an easy time with this question. The heart of his analysis is that the environmental groups active in the controversies he studied had "upper middle-class membership with strong representation of professionals, executives, scientists, and engineers."[52] These are not by and large people who have to look for modestly priced housing; they *are* people who might find the development of lower-cost housing in or near their neighborhoods threatening to the amenities they have come to enjoy, or to the value of their own property. The rubric of "environmental protection" thus becomes a substitute for the kind of status-conscious zoning and exclusionary legislation that was well established during the 1950s. The very broadness of the concept of "the environment," Frieden perceptively notes, makes it all the easier to justify a variety of manifestations of selfishness.[53]

Surely class bias was evident, Frieden notes, when a 1972 survey of Sierra Club members found 58% strongly or "somewhat" opposed to the club's paying attention to the "conservation problems of such special groups as the urban poor and ethnic minorities."[54] Environmentalism as a movement is of more interest to American elites than to the population at large. Extensive efforts have since been made to link environmental issues with "race, class and gender" themes perceived by those same elites to be the keys to attracting nonelite support. But such outreach has not been sufficiently successful to prevent the charge of "eco-racism" from having sting still today.

Frieden explodes the presumption that environmentalists always represent the public good against the "special interests" that oppose them. But it must be added that it is politics as usual in the United States for special interest groups to try to attract the wider support they need to be effective by claiming that their concerns are linked to the broader public good. And in a complex, highly interdependent society, many such claims have legitimacy. As a special interest, environmentalists are no less entitled than other special interests to press their cases on the public. Indeed, if all they could be charged with were the desire to protect their property— even to the point of selfishness—it is not clear that one has accused them of doing anything but living up to one of the fundamental expectations upon which American politics is built.

Would Frieden, then, have any grounds to criticize environmentalists if they honestly admitted to being just another special interest? Perhaps not; the opportunism of their arguments at least would come as less of a surprise. Environmentalists, or those who make environmental arguments, simply know how to work the system. We may regret the system works that way, but we cannot blame environmentalists for *that*. On the other hand, there may be an implicit populism in his case—a sense that by acting as he describes, environmentalists are getting away with something they should not, a sense that the "little guy" is being taken advantage of.

More recent "public choice" criticisms of environmental policy attempt to supply more overtly the basis for a political judgment that Frieden fails to bring to the fore. Such authors suggest that policies like CFC phaseouts or the 1992 Clean Air Act amendments have little to do either with science or with environmental ideology, and a good deal to do with the interests of government bureaucracies and the powerful economic constituencies they come to represent.[55] So far, at least, Frieden essentially anticipates them, but the public choice authors are alive to the centralizing and planning mentality that is at work within environmentalism and that seems to escape Frieden's notice.[56] Frieden disputes the particulars of the "no-growth" plans but not their legitimacy as tools to control development.

Yet it is always the prospect of "The Plan" that provides the opportunity for the reconciliation of the apparent contradictions environmentalists fall into when they critique particular development projects. Are they inconsistent in their positions on urban versus suburban development? That is because only a regional plan can settle such issues. Do they waver between citing local and regional effects? That is because there is no state plan to direct the relationships between these potentially competing levels. Can one imagine conflict between state plans? That only shows the need for a national plan. International conflict? That's why we need global planning. The strength of Frieden's argument is in the particulars of his case studies of the impact of environmentalism on such a basic need as housing. But his understanding of the broader significance of the movement remains limited.

William Tucker's *Progress and Privilege* (1982)[57] examines environmentalism with a wider view and a somewhat greater degree of sensitivity to the theoretical questions of morality and politics raised by its vision of the human good.

Tucker spends a good deal of time on the scientific inadequacies of environmental arguments, but his distinctive contribution rests elsewhere. He begins with just the attempt to define what he means by "progress" that was lacking among the critics who concentrated on environmentalism's scientific failings. "Progress is the process whereby each generation tries to make life better for itself and for the next."[58] Later he adds that today it is generally understood in terms of material progress, "the improvement of our material conditions."[59] He recognizes that environmentalists can claim to be supporters of progress so defined but argues that their understanding of it is built more on preserving what we have rather than on "moving into the future."[60]

Far from being interested in progress, Tucker charges, environmentalists want to preserve aristocratic privilege. This charge has two parts. First, taking over an argument that was popular with more hardheaded elements of the Left in the late 1960s and early 1970s, Tucker argues that environmentalism represents an alliance between big money and the upper middle class against the poor and working class.[61] The rich have always been able to lock up the land and resources for their private use. Now, in alliance with the upper middle class, government is used, for example, to sequester land for the enjoyment of the small minority who can afford a "wilderness experience," while the working class—who would get the mining, logging, drilling, or associated jobs—lose out. The same thing happens whenever we fail to develop land, resources, or technologies in the name of environmental preservation.

This line of thought outraged environmentalists, who felt, with the book's arrival during the early Reagan years, that they were being kicked when they were already down.[62] How could environmentalism be an elite phenomenon when polls show everybody wants clear air and clean water? But Tucker was on to something; he saw the "greening" of big business well before it became obvious to all. He points out that there is really much less reason for conflict between *big* business and environmentalism than between *small* business and environmentalism. Big business can afford the costs of more stringent environmental regulation and will not mourn its anticompetitive tendencies.[63]

Here again we see hints of populism. That theme becomes explicit when Tucker introduces a second sense in which environmentalism is aristocratic: that its fundamental world view is one characteristic of actual or presumptive aristocracies. Aristocracies, as Tucker describes them, are conservative (i.e., interested in protecting the status quo), anti-industrial, antiscientific, antimaterial, agrarian, and oriented toward stewardship. All in all, he provides a not implausible reconstruction of the aristocratic world view, and there does seem to be a good deal of overlap with the stock critical charges against environmentalism. This line of thought allows Tucker to make some thought-provoking arguments, such as tracing one strain of the "limits to growth" argument to a back door triumph of the Southern agrarians.[64] In another instance, he suggests that Commoner's view of nature is very like the nineteenth-century doctrine of "vitalism," which asserted that the principle that animated mere matter such that it became life would forever remain mysterious.[65] In another, he links the love of wilderness and the murky religiosity that comes to surround it with Rousseau and nineteenth-century romanticism.[66]

As illuminating as such suggestions might sometimes be, they are both scattershot and not always consistent with his central thesis about environmentalism's antiprogressive and aristocratic biases. For it is difficult to imagine the shape of an aristocratic *ethos* that has roots simultaneously in vitalism, romanticism, Marxism, Eastern religions, Southern agrarianism, and various other strains of thought Tucker links to environmentalism. Furthermore, how could a movement so concerned about issues of physical health and well-being be considered antimaterialistic? However much environmentalists abuse science, the central place for science in their rhetoric makes it hard to see how they can be antiscientific in the simple sense Tucker suggests. Can calling for radical reorganizations of global political, social, and economic arrangements be conservative? And even if one wants to speak of a "radical conservatism," is the environmentalist love of big government and planning consistent with the aristocratic and conservative quest for personal freedom and local autonomy?

What is most problematic in Tucker seems finally to go back to progress. It is simply mistaken to see only preservation and conservation in environmentalism. For that which they do seek to preserve, be it fossil fuels or virgin rain forests, can be preserved only by what they regard as fundamental improvements, and radical changes, in how human beings live and the way they relate to the environment. Yet by the end of Tucker's book, one almost wishes that environmentalists really did represent the serious challenge to progress he makes them out to be, for then there would be someone to stand up to thoughtless assessments like the following:

> In truth, we could do wonders. The extraordinary possibilities of genetic engineering, the potential that biology and the world of microorganisms can be harnessed into human service, the hope for a clean and safe nuclear power, the almost limitless possibilities for using direct energy of sunlight, the hope of improving our efficiency and stopping the waste of resources—all this offers us a vista for improving the common lot of humanity that few generations have ever been privileged to see . . .
>
> The Age of Environmentalism has been a respite, a period when we took time from the business of the world to learn to enjoy nature, appreciate the limits of our accomplishments, and reset our bearings. We are the wiser for it and have environmentalism to thank. But such interludes cannot last forever. History is calling us. There is still much to be done for the progress of humanity. It is time to begin again.[67]

Commoner and Tucker might disagree only on the particular technologies that are to produce such "wonders." When the ediface we are to build is made up of wonders, how firm a foundation are "hope" and the call of "history"—particularly when history is not exactly a story of the unambiguous good that comes from new technology? We are left to choose between Tucker's hopes and the hopes of an environmentalism that, despite all his most telling criticisms of it, has left us "the wiser." That is to say, we have a choice between two forms of technological Coue-ism. Is Tucker's really to be preferred only because he promises that we can have it all simply by returning to business as usual?

RISK AND RELATIVISM

Is there a way of appreciating the distinctive character of environmental ideas without falling into this barren debate about progress? In *Risk and Culture* (1982) Mary Douglas and Aaron Wildavsky argue that a cultural analysis of risk perception provides the key.[68] Douglas, a British social anthropologist, taught for many years at London University before holding a variety of distinguished positions in the United States. Wildavsky was an eminent political scientist of extraordinarily wide-ranging interests, from the Bible to budgeting, who spent most of his teaching career at the University of California, Berkeley. They begin with a simple question: given that life is full of risks, why do environmental risks become subject to vast controversies or efforts at amelioration through public policy?

The easy answers, that we pay more attention to the environment because it presents us with high risks, or risks imposed on us involuntarily, or risks with irreversible consequences, turn out to be inadequate.[69] Our perceptions of risk, and our responses to perceived risks, usually have little to do with statistical probabilities of how likely a given event is to take place. The risk of being killed in an auto accident is hugely greater than that of being killed in a nuclear power accident, but people do not picket auto plants for that reason. Is it because I *choose* to drive a car, but nobody asked me whether I wanted nuclear power? But I did not choose to live in a place and time where I needed to drive to make my living, nor did anyone consult me about the road conditions that may be a prime cause of an auto accident. Or is it because the results of auto accidents are serious for individuals but not for large segments of society, as the result of a nuclear accident would be? We can say that only because we have grown accustomed to the daily carnage that takes place on the roadways.

Risk, Douglas and Wildavsky argue, is not something that can be understood simply by estimations of probabilities or consequences. What we fear and what we want to avoid are social or cultural constructs.[70] That is to say, our ideas about risk are the products of our particular way of life.

Wildavsky and Douglas remind us that many societies have paid a great deal of attention to the way "pollution" threatens our physical well-being and relationship with the world around us. Other cultures find pollution in things like eating the wrong kind of animal or having sex at the wrong time rather than in smokestacks.[71] The particular form pollution concern takes in the United States is largely determined by three modes of social organization within our society—the individualist, the hierarchical, and the sectarian.[72]

In the United States, the hierarchical and individualist modes of social organization define the center. Bureaucracies are the prime example of hierarchy, while individualist organization refers to relationships defined by the market. Each has its own way of defining risks. Where hierarchies, for example, define risk in terms of threats to the integrity of the organization, individualists see risks in threats to the success and well-being of individuals.

These two centrist modes of organization stand in contrast to the sectarian—religious or secular—which defines *itself* as being an outsider or "border" organization. Its stock in trade is not merely criticism of the center but criticism of all existing institutions, which are regarded as essentially coercive. Only entirely voluntary associations satisfy sectarians, but how are those associations to be held together? Apocalyptic visions of the future, along with a mentality of "us" against "them," serve the purpose. While some environmental groups act like hierarchies, Douglas and Wildavsky admit, many other such groups have the organizational form and beliefs characteristic of sectarianism. To satisfy the demands of cohesion they must constantly be on the lookout for new enemies and new threats to human well-being that are being ignored by the center. If biotechnology fades as a threat, then beef will be our downfall. If nuclear winter melts away, then there is the endless summer of global warming. If wildlife is not disappearing because of pesticides, then it is threatened by ozone depletion. Today's crisis is not chosen cynically or casually by the sectarian but out of the necessity of maintaining cohesion by validating both the sect's distrust of the center and its apocalyptic expectations.[73]

Douglas and Wildavsky present a concise summary of the difference social organization makes for risk perception as between the center and border positions:

The center sees the future as continuous with the present. It has numberless ways of discounting information to the contrary. It expects disturbances and setbacks in the normal course, but it also expects to weather them. In the long run it is optimistic. The border foretells imminent disaster. It does not believe in the long run, and in the short run it is pessimistic. Paradoxically perhaps, it is optimistic about the perfectibility of human nature. Since the border is committed against institutions, it must fall back on faith in human goodness as the basis for good society. When its prophets inveigh against human wickedness, they are calling upon the people to return to their essentially human power of moral regeneration. The center does not worry about possible irreversible damage to nature emanating from its own technology but rather about the possible irreversible destruction of its social systems.[74]

If environmentalism represents a sectarian outlook on the world, then how has it come to be accepted so widely in the United States? It is paradoxical that a sectarian position should come to be mainstream. Douglas and Wildavsky present a host of factors that have brought about this result. Over the long haul, America has always had strong sectarian tendencies; our beginnings are to be found in various kinds of religious sectarianism. More recently, such tendencies have come to the fore again because of the general postwar increase in wealth and education, which allows sufficient numbers of people to hold unconventional opinions so that holding such opinions almost becomes conventional. Added to that they cite specific events like the civil rights movement, the Vietnam War, and Watergate, which fostered distrust of "the establishment." Finally, the rise of mass mailing technology has made the construction of voluntary organizations easier, while the development of "public interest law," a good deal of it funded by government, has given adversarial organizations ready access to power through the same legal system that in principle they despise.[75]

Douglas and Wildavsky make an outstanding contribution to understanding environmentalism. They substantiate the central role of widely different value judgments in environmental disputes. And they do so not on the basis of a dogmatic assumption of the importance of ideas, but rather by showing how starting with common, practical organizational problems one is led to see how different value structures support different styles of organization.

Identifying these differing premises is no small thing. But even if Douglas and Wildavsky have done so in a complete and satisfactory way, their analysis suggests a simple question that they have a great deal of trouble answering. Is any one of these perspectives right? Strictly speaking, the assumptions of their analysis do not permit such a question. The authors claim, reasonably enough, that they can show both the consequences of preferring one form of organization over another and the internal inconsistencies that arise from each.[76] But to choose one or the other as a more satisfactory form of organization would simply betray their own cultural bias.[77] Indeed, they acknowledge that any attempt even to discuss how institutions can accommodate diverse perspectives most successfully betrays a culture-bound outlook.

Yet at the same time, they claim that they do not want their cultural analysis to be a "conversation stopper," allowing no further judgment once the social conditions of the position in question have been articulated; they realize that this would relativize their own analysis in a way they are not happy with.[78] So they advocate "a many sided conversation in which being ultimately right or wrong is not at issue."[79] That this would satisfy none of the perspectives they discuss may be an advantage. But for all the hardheaded analysis of *Risk and Culture*, it is also not a very practical response.

We know we will spend money or pass laws in the face of some risks but not others. Even granting that we select those risks influenced by cultural biases, even granting that we will judge the success of our policies influenced by cultural biases, what do we say to the man who whistles to keep elephants away in the heart of Manhattan? Surely he is expending a great deal of unnecessary energy. Is global warming simply the perfect foil for the apocalyptic needs of sectarian organizations? Or is it the sort of remote threat that hierarchical and individualist organizations tend to be blind to? We will find that we spent our money to purchase unnecessary protection or failed to deal with a genuine threat.

Practical necessities force the question "Who is right?" on us, that is to say, practical necessities require us to confront the differing visions of border and center in a way that investigates the truth of each vision of the world. However compelling their description of these visions, Wildavsky and Douglas will not have really completed their job until they make a reasoned judgment among them.

Neither environmental popularizers nor their prominent critics present us with a fully satisfactory way of thinking about our relationship to nature. But something can be learned from the characteristic flaws in their arguments about how a new beginning might be made for thinking about this difficult topic. On the one hand, to avoid dogmatic arguments over what science can tell us about the environment, we need popularizers who have a greater appreciation for the merits of science as an exercise in critical thinking and modest steps towards a limited truth about the world, along with a better sense that scientific information is not the only rational basis for policy-making. On the other hand, environmentalists have been guilty of a moralistic simplicity about human desires and aspirations that has led them to dreams of political and social totalitarianism, while their critics have been too inclined to believe that something called progress will solve our problems. In either case, we need a greater appreciation for the complex and contradictory tendencies of the human soul.

———

How, then, can we begin to think in a better way than we have been thinking about "the environment"? My purpose in raising this question is not to suggest some new environmental "theory" that if "applied" properly would solve all the difficult problems we have come to believe we face. I have no wish to replace one ism by another. But the difficulties with the prevailing ways of thinking about the environment that this book has documented suggest alternatives that deserve exploration.

Clearly, environmental popularizers need to develop new expectations about their job. It would be too much to expect that these writers would suddenly become disinterested chroniclers, given the passionate concern that often motivates them. Nor should we want to purge their works of the literary and rhetorical strengths that convey so well their sense of excitement and urgency. But it is not too much to ask, particularly when authors are themselves scientists, that such concern go along with more respect for the canons of evidence and objectivity that go by the name "the scientific method." The recent work of James Lovelock is instructive in this respect.

Lovelock is an independent British scientist and inventor who developed the electron capture device, a tool that has been crucial to the measurement of tiny amounts of substances such as CFCs or pesticides.[80] Thus, he is in part responsible for the fact that environmentalists have been able to focus on the existence of once unmeasurable contaminants as indicators of environmental degradation. But he is also father of the Gaia hypothesis, an idea he began to develop when he was a NASA consultant working on instruments for the detection of life on Mars. He speculated that the presence of life on a planet would have profound consequences for the makeup of its atmosphere. Out of that, the Gaia hypothesis was born.[81]

The Gaia hypothesis is the ultimate expression of the idea that everything is connected to everything else. It suggests that the earth as a whole represents a system that regulates itself in such a way as to provide conditions that are amenable to life. Hydrologic, atmospheric, and even lithospheric systems all work on and with living beings, and living beings work on and with them, to maintain conditions broadly favorable to those beings. This hypothesis is as yet very far from being the orthodox position among scientists, and my purpose here is not to endorse it on its merits. What is important is how Lovelock has gone about popularizing his work.

There is no doubt that the Gaia hypothesis has attracted in part a rather loony following. But a closer look at Lovelock's writings suggests that he, more than the majority of environmental popularizers, has managed to produce serious treatments of scientific issues that are immensely readable and interesting in part because they show respect for the scientific method even as they present the kind of grand theory of which the scientific community—not unreasonably—tends to be highly suspicious. His *Healing Gaia* (1991), very nearly a coffee-table book, largely maintains these high standards.[82] What accounts for this feat?

First of all, where the professional publications of the popularizers we have examined are often well removed from the subjects of their popularizing efforts, Lovelock has published a large number of articles about the Gaia hypothesis, or various aspects of it, in professional journals and other publications. Indeed, it was *first* articulated in such a forum, and only later did Lovelock start writing about it for a broader public.[83]

As a result, he has had to think through the consequences of his hypothesis to meet the rigors of professional review and comment, in addition to knowing how to make it comprehensible to the layman. Lovelock does not claim to be an expert in all the fields upon which the Gaia hypothesis impinges, but he has willingly opened himself to the criticism of his peers in those areas. He understands the difference between thoughtful advocacy and polemics.

Nowhere is this characteristic more evident than in his willingness to discuss criticism of his theory in his books, and to answer it or revise his theory as necessary. His early formulations of the Gaia hypothesis, for example, seemed to imply that he endorsed teleology—broadly speaking, the belief that nature exhibits purposive motion to certain ends. This way of thinking is anathema to modern natural science, and observers have noted that when Lovelock explicitly abandoned it, the scientific community became much more willing to listen to him.[84] Whether or not such revision was a good idea, Lovelock rethought this issue, recast the Gaia hypothesis accordingly, and shared the process with his readers. As a result, the lay reader gets a wonderful sense of how science operates as a community of researchers making a common effort to improve their understanding of the world.[85]

Lovelock's desire to present his hypothesis in the most convincing way possible is also tempered by a fine critical sense. Though he need take second place to no environmentalist in his concern for the well-being of nature, he has not followed the crowd in his understanding of what constitutes serious threats to it. Starting from his picture of the total terrestrial system, he presents some cogent arguments as to why we can easily overestimate the ill effects of such things as acid rain, ozone depletion, or nuclear energy.[86] Even his debunking is done with a caution appropriate to the uncertainties of the issues at hand.

Whatever the future of the Gaia hypothesis, popularizers could learn from Lovelock's example. Without being a narrow specialist, he keeps himself sharp by maintaining a close connection between his professional and popularizing work. He lets his readers in on the debate and uncertainty attendant on the position he advocates. Still, there is something missing from his writing as well. Lovelock has a sense that his point of view raises some serious moral as well as practical issues about what human beings do to nature, but his ethical speculations are not the highpoint of his writing. He has the grace to be visibly uncomfortable with them himself. Gaia gives us an Olympian perspective from which point of view what human beings do or fail to do appears trivial—at best, only of concern to us and a few other newcomer species. Yet Lovelock combines this outlook with a conventional, and very English, sentimentality about the nice things in life.[87]

The one extreme may call out the other. "This too shall pass" may be the height of wisdom, but it can easily frighten us into holding on mindlessly to whatever we have. The tension in Lovelock's position at this crucial point is typical of one of the biggest problems we have had in thinking seriously about ethics and politics in relation to the environment. That problem is that we are trying to think about the environment.

What is "the environment"? Words seem to be useful to the extent they discriminate—this and not that. What is *excluded* from "the environment"? What isn't part of it, or relevant to it? A college environmental science text says that "environment" means "The combination of all things and factors external to the individual or population of organisms in question."[88] This definition suggests lots of interlocking environments; the blue spruce is part of our environment and we are part of the blue spruce's environment. But therefore the word really refers to all that is the case, as one adds up all the external environments and their connections. Given the crucial role played in terrestrial ecosystems by the sun and moon, it seems arbitrary to confine "the environment" to the limits of our globe. We can't even limit "environment" to everything that exists at a given moment, since future and past seem so important in our judgments of what kind of "environment" we want to restore or avoid. Do we do anything more than sin against customary usage if we call an "environmental problem" an "everything problem," or rename "environmentalism" "everythingism"?[89]

I think not. Indeed, so doing clarifies why those who attempt to deal with "the environment" find themselves so consistently drawn to totalitarian schemes. For the environment *is* the totality; to solve environmental problems requires that we try to solve all problems at once. It assumes, because everything is connected to everything else, that the diversity of the world is ultimately reducible to a unitary "environment" that can be dealt with as such.

This madness defines the poles between which so much environmental thinking oscillates. At best, thinking about everything at once is going to be difficult and frustrating. It is hardly surprising if, having set ourselves this absurd problem, but having refused to acknowledge its absurdity, we should grow contemptuous of our stupidity and be tempted to think, in the manner of many deep ecologists, that the whole show would be better off without us.[90] Or we can be as easily led to the other extreme and attempt to "manage" the environment with an intensity that has never before been seen in human affairs, as per Barry Commoner. We seek enough power and control to deal with . . . everything. "We are as gods and might as well get good at it," as the Whole Earth Catalog pronounced. Thinking in terms of "the environment" invites us to multiply endlessly the arenas for the exercise of our powers, and thereby encourages dissatisfaction with whatever we *have* accomplished.

If we simply purged "environment" and its cognates from our vocabulary, we would have to talk about specific problems all the time: sulfur dioxide pollution in urban areas, or the decline of desert tortoise populations in Nevada. Such instances would no longer be icons of something bigger. They would be in themselves the focus of attention. We would then have to know something about what we are talking about; Gary Snyder is correct that "environmental concern" however heartfelt gets us nowhere. The reasonable desire to appreciate nature's complex interconnections and avoid academic specialization would not have to be sacrificed; there is a middle ground between trying to think about everything at once and thinking about only the head of the leech. But forced more to deal with specifics, we would find it harder to multiply them endlessly, and it would be more to our advantage to make decisions about what we can and cannot reasonably do to address situations that we have judged are more or less important.

Environmental policy-making must involve the creation of priorities. It is the open-ended rubric of "the environment" that makes such decisions appear, as they often do, arbitrary. Why make heroic efforts to save the California condor when "the environment" is filled with other endangered species? Why not spend that money, and much, much more, on cataloging *all* species, so we can have a better idea just how many are threatened? But this is the logic of avoidance. I cannot organize *all* my files until I buy file boxes, but that means first I have to go to the store, but I can't go to the store without first going to the bank to get money, but I can't go to the bank yet because there is no money in the checking account. The fact that I could clear out one drawer at a time is easy to forget. If we define the scope of our concerns more narrowly, we can more likely create defensible priorities. Furthermore, without the presumptive unity of "the environment," we will be more open to appreciating the trade-offs that our conflicting desires and nature's constraints create for us.[91]

The replacement of "environmental concern" by specific problems of the interaction of humans and nature seems to have been in Rene Dubos's mind in his later work. Best known for the much misunderstood phrase "think globally but act locally," Dubos was a major figure in the development of contemporary environmentalism and deserves more attention than he will get here. Unlike many of his fellow popularizers, Dubos was not afraid to change his mind, and as a result he has occupied a number of "niches" within the environmental movement, making it hard to produce a fair overview of his thought.

Born in France, he held positions at Rutgers, the Harvard Medical School, and, for 44 years, at Rockefeller University in New York. As a research doctor he was responsible for some of the early developments in antibiotic therapies. In the 1940s a general examination of the relationship between human disease and the environment began to take him in new directions. He became a vocal critic of the hope that we could or should seek to eradicate disease,[92] and later argued that modern technology was creating a world in which human beings were not biologically programmed to live.[93] In 1972 he wrote, with Barbara Ward, *Only One Earth: The Care and Maintenance of a Small Planet*.[94] Commissioned by the United Nations, the book set much of the ongoing agenda for official UN environmental action, with its condemnation of industrialization and the market, its suspicion of the West, and its calls for redistributionist policies.

Yet having become a mainstay of many such international efforts, he was for a time disenchanted with them. He came to see them as "a waste of time," because they produced only vague and high-sounding statements to cover partisan and ideological disputes among various UN factions.[95] Even that position needed subsequent revision. International conferences could be object lessons not just in common problems but in the diversity of human situations and institutions. Hence they could demonstrate the danger of "globalization," a trend toward imposing uniformity when trying to solve the world's problems. International conferences gave opportunities for people to gather and share information about their particular situations that might prove to be useful to others. But there was no point in searching for grand schemes that could be applied everywhere.[96]

Hence Dubos's interest in local matters. In his later writings, Dubos exhibits a poetic sensibility toward the myriad combination of human and natural relationships that make up the local. He is entranced at how "natural" landscapes inform and are informed by the many ways of life that human beings pursue, as in the distinctive looks of the French or English countrysides.[97] Indeed, most of what we experience as nature is really a result of nature and humanity working together. Yellowstone is a national park because of the rail barons, the last old growth forest in Europe is a remnant of aristocratic privilege, the stark beauty of Greek landscapes is a result of deforestation and erosion, the American Great Plains may exist because of the hunting fires of Native Americans, and many of our wildflowers are here only because of "European imperialism." Our relationships with nature, Dubos helps us to see, are no less various and ethically complex than those we have with our fellow human beings; indeed, it may not do to separate the two too decisively.

Dubos admits to having caused some consternation in this respect as a lecturer on college campuses in the late 1970s. "Faculty as well as students were surprised and somewhat annoyed when I suggested that, instead of being exclusively concerned with the nation or the world as a whole, they should first consider more local situations."[98] What sort of local situations did Dubos have in mind? He mentions not only local fields and streams but also "the messiness of public rooms on their campus and the disorder of their social relationships."[99] Little wonder an "environmentally concerned" audience would be annoyed; who wants to hear it's time to clean up his room?

"Think globally, act locally" is Dubos's attempt to encapsulate his thinking on globalization, diversity, and localism. Although it has been taken to mean we should do our part at home to solve the world's environmental problems—101 things to do to save the earth—that seems to misunderstand Dubos's intention. If "global thinking" is to avoid globalization, it must appreciate the widely differing ways in which human beings interact with the world around them to address common needs like food supply, clean water, pleasant surroundings, decent behavior. It would therefore be foolish to define our fundamental relationship with nature in terms of "global challenges."[100] Ultimately, the only justification for so doing comes down to the threat of global destruction. Leaving aside the scientific uncertainties, it is easy to see how creating the perception that the whole earth is under the gun, that everything is at stake, is likely to be a ready excuse for the worst kinds of extremism. Short of that terrible consummation, we prepare the way for defeat, despair, and cynicism as we are forced by the way we define it to confront an impossible problem. We increase the sense of individual powerlessness, when only a moment's thought is needed to realize that my action—for better or worse—is unlikely to be meaningful on a global level.

That global thinking is for Dubos precisely not a call to global action casts the proper light on what we might reasonably expect from the local action he commends. We are capable of finding enough problems in that part of nature that is our own figurative (or even literal) backyard to keep us busy for many years to come, if we no longer have the excuse of looking far away to complain about how difficult somebody else is making it for us. If many people take this route, so much the better; if fewer, then at least some corners will be more pleasant and livable.

For those who are convinced, or hopeful, that our civilization is on the eve of destruction, such a course will sound like putting one's head in the sand. But perhaps the possibility that some catastrophe of nature will bring all we do to nothing is simply an unlikely, yet not impossible, fact of life. To make it the starting point of all our thinking provides too easy an excuse for doing nothing, or doing far too much. Metaphorically speaking, I could refuse to mow my lawn for fear of being hit by a meteorite, staying inside to eat my salmon before an oak fire. Or I could hold out until the government sets up a satisfactory space shield. Or I can do my job and mow my lawn.

All the talk about problems of unprecedented scope, all the fearful celebrations of our power, all the hand wringing about the death of nature are distractions from the day-to-day situations and problems of people all over the world. If we do not allow ourselves to be misled by the totality of the environment, and if we do not give in to utopian hopes for a perfect world, we see that what faces us are the same fundamental questions and aspirations of human life that have always faced us. Messy rooms and messy social lives are hardly new. The human characteristics that are the sources of our fears and our hopes about what we are doing with nature—our greed or altruism, our domination or care, in short, our vices and our virtues—were not born with, or first recognized by, the environmental movement. We do not need to explore new ethics for mere survival, nor revive or imagine old wisdom for saving the earth. We need to take care to live decently with an eye to the full range of relationships and responsibilities, human and otherwise, that necessarily characterize a good life.

Few saw the contradictions of environmentalism's failure to

engage in serious ethical and political thinking as early, or described that failure as eloquently, as Richard John Neuhaus. Already by Earth Day 1970, Neuhaus, then a Lutheran pastor at a poor New York City congregation, saw the problem. He wrote about it in a too-little-remembered book called *In Defense of People: Ecology and the Seduction of Radicalism* (1971).[101] At that time in his career, Neuhaus was perhaps just beginning his shift from what was called "the movement," the anti-Vietnam War Left, to what is usually labeled the neoconservative camp. His main concern in the book was the possibility that the radical politics needed to renew America would be derailed by the Left's willingness to ally itself with the growing environmental movement. He pictured environmentalism's concern for natural purity as a distraction from the social justice issues that should have been of primary concern to the movement, and as an issue too likely to play into the hands of corporate capitalism, which would be only too happy to profit from pollution control, as it had profited from pollution.[102]

In Defense of People is no left-wing tract. Its enduring value is in its analysis of the moral failings that the environmental movement had already fallen into. Environmentalism sought "the ultimate revolution, the revolution to end revolutions, the reordering of man's place in nature." Yet while exhibiting "moving reverence for 'the seamless web of life,' " it could also exhibit "shocking indifference to the weaker and less convenient forms of human life" and "an almost cavalier readiness to disrupt the carefully woven web of civility and humane values." The weak among "extra-human nature" are to be preserved even at the expense of "threatened and oppressed forms of human existence."[103]

While speaking against environmentalism on behalf of civility, Neuhaus's passionate concern for the poor and dispossessed prevented him from thoughtless advocacy of either the status quo or progress as conventionally conceived. "One does not wish to praise civilization too highly," he wrote, lest one overlook its injustices and flaws. "At the same time, we dare not despise and reject the assumptions that have made possible whatever good there is in it." And what are these assumptions, generally speaking? A "reverence and delight in humanity itself." " 'Man is the measure of all things' was never entirely satisfying. But it is a thousand times preferable to 'Nature is the measure of all things'—especially if by 'Nature' one means everything apart from man."[104] Neuhaus reasonably asks whether "man will be more conscientious if he thinks himself less important than Western civilization has taught him to think of himself." His answer is no: "dignity and accountability exist in symbiotic relationship to one another."[105]

Neuhaus overstated the extent to which the environmental popularizers drew inspiration from nature without regard to human concerns and values, as we have seen throughout this book. Their misanthropy, if that is the right term, is that of the social reformer, not of the hermit. Therefore, it is not clear Neuhaus should be comforted by the fact that today's environmentalists are paying ever more explicit attention to the social justice and spiritual issues that Neuhaus found lacking in the early 1970s. If human dignity needs less protection than he thought from a concept of "Nature" that excludes human concerns, it needs all the protection it can get from the popularizers' utopian schemes. Neuhaus eloquently reminds us that when such schemes are placed in a context where "survival"—be it of humans or of all life on earth—is at stake, they will readily become excuses for immorality.[106] And the same is true, as our own century teaches, when the vision is of a hitherto unknown human perfection.[107]

To suggest that a concern for nature is best grounded in some explicit understanding of the human good is not merely to fall into mindless anthropocentrism. Indeed, it prevents some of the absurdities of antianthropocentrism that are becoming all too evident in environmental debates. The ethic of human withdrawal from nature, of maximizing "wilderness," depends on a highly artificial pretense that human beings are somehow so "unnatural"—one might even say unworldly—that we need to be ghettoized lest we compromise nature's purity. We likewise err when in the name of eco-egalitarianism we expect some simplistic translation to nature of complex ethical categories. Speaking, for example, of animal or tree "rights" is a form of radical egalitarianism that will end up either denigrating human dignity or holding animals to absurd responsibilities.

On the other hand, if we think even a little about human affairs, we will likewise see the flaws in such anthropocentric rubrics as "environmental management" and "stewardship." Both at least have the advantage of suggesting that we can give nature its due in a way that is appropriate to our, and its, needs. Yet given the notorious difficulty of being a "good manager" even in small organizations, with what level of confidence should we take on "Managing Planet Earth"?[108] The difficulties would only be greater, since at least human organizations can have clear (if artificial) hierarchies and well-defined (if changeable) purposes. As for stewardship, is it really so clear that such relationships among human beings always involve benefit to those they are designed to serve? Why would stewardship over nature tend to promote more honest or self-sacrificing stewards? In any case, to be a good manager or a good steward is, in most instances, likely to mean one has to be a good human being first.

Thus, we see for the last time how environmental popularizers have not been *wrong* in founding their work on moral and political judgments; these matters are not mere intruders into scientific or technical discussions but the necessary foundations for any serious concern with nature. Popularizers have been wrong in allowing these judgments to be obscured by a careless use of science, and in failing to recognize the utopian and totalitarian character of the principles they have relied on.

Neither is there anything intrinsically ignoble or unreasonable about the desire to improve the world that forms an important part of environmentalism. Sometimes, such an aspiration can lead to welcome changes in the conduct of our affairs, sometimes to a more contemplative appreciation of why things are as they are. We should not forget that by calling ourselves "modern" (or "postmodern") we acknowledge that we are heir to an ambitious project of improvement, a project that only a very few can honestly claim they would have rather seen fail. The various aspects of this project—be it the development of science and technology, secularization, democratization—were in their origins as controversial and in their intentions as far-reaching as anything we see environmentalism advocating today. For all that, however, the modern project is not, and was not in its origins, utopian. For better and for worse, it relied on known human imperfection and promised no ultimate harmonies.

The environmental effort to recreate the world is another matter, with its rejection of the "painful, impermanent, open and imperfect." I have no illusions that simply pointing this fact out will be enough to make people wary of environmental promises or willing to take a more detached view of environmental problems while considering a more thoughtful approach to nature. But surely our century is an object lesson in what happens when the utopian aspirations of a reforming movement like environmentalism move from the printed page into victorious political programs. We will be lucky if the consequences of the totalitarian regimes of our time, and the wreckage they have left behind in so many parts of the world, pass with the waning of this century. Will we then allow green utopianism simply to replace red utopianism? If so, there is no guarantee that, simply because the first time was tragedy, the second will be farce.

Notes

Introduction. Green in Judgement

1. *The Booklist* (April 1, 1971): 648.
2. Art Kleiner, "Theatre of the McServed," *Garbage* 3 (September/October 1991): 52–56.
3. Eric Felton, "The Times Beach Fiasco," *Insight* (August 12, 1991): 12.
4. Karen F. Schmidt, "Dioxin's Other Face," *Science News* 141 (January 11, 1992): 24.
5. Karen F. Schmidt, "Puzzling Over a Poison," *U.S. News and World Report* (April 6, 1992): 61.
6. Schmidt, "Dioxin's Other Face," 27.
7. Compare the reports of the work of Marilyn A. Fingerhut in Felton, "Times Beach Fiasco," 18, and Schmidt, "Dioxin's Other Face," 24.
8. Art Kleiner, "Flexing Their Mussels," *Garbage* 4 (July/August 1992): 48–51.
9. "Dangerous New Ozone Hole over Hemisphere Feared," *Pittsburgh Press* (February 4, 1992): A5.
10. Michael D. Lemonick, "The Ozone Vanishes," *Time* 139 (February 17, 1992): 60.
11. Ibid., 60.
12. As quoted in Micah Morrison, "The Ozone Scare," *Insight* 8 (April 6, 1992): 8.
13. Ibid., 8, 10.
14. Lemonick, "Ozone Vanishes," 62.
15. Morrison, "Ozone Scare," 10.
16. Ronald Bailey, *Ecoscam: The False Prophets of Ecological Apocalypse* (New York: St. Martin's Press, 1993): 128. The NASA study predicted depletion of as high as 40%; a 5% reduction in ozone layer increases UV exposure at ground level about as much as moving 60 miles south.
17. "Paul Revere of Ecology," *Time* (February 2, 1970): 58.

18. *New York Times Index 1955: A Book of Record* (New York: New York Times Co., 1955). Also cited is information from indexes for 1960, 1965, 1970, 1975, 1980, 1985, 1990.

19. Gallup Poll conducted April 11–14, 1991.

20. Edith Efron, *The Apocalyptics: How Environmental Politics Controls What We Know About Cancer* (New York: Simon and Schuster, 1984): 27.

21. Lester Milbrath, *Environmentalists: Vanguard for a New Society* (Albany, N.Y.: SUNY Press, 1984).

22. Irving Kristol, *Two Cheers for Capitalism* (New York: New American Library, 1978): 40–45. Rael Jean Isaac has questioned whether Kristol is on the right track, noting that "the environmental revolution began as an ecological panic, and thus from the beginning lacked the sense of balance and proportion that is associated with a movement of reform." But the movements Kristol cites were not in all their manifestations equally characterized by balance and proportion, to say the least. Isaac wants environmentalism to be seen fundamentally as an inexplicable panic or mass hysteria, yet at the same time admits that unlike most such cases, "this one had a basis in fact." (Rael Jean Isaac, *The Coercive Utopians: Social Deception by America's Power Players* [Chicago: Regnery Gateway, 1983]: 45, 47.) One does not have to search environmentalism far to uncover the angry moralism that today we so readily associate with Prohibition. Consider Geoffrey Wandesforde-Smith's ruminations that what environmentalism needs is more of the politics of moral outrage (Geoffrey Wandesforde-Smith, "Moral Outrage and the Progress of Environmental Policy: What Do We Tell the Next Generation About How to Care for the Earth?" in Norman J. Vig and Michael E. Kraft, *Environmental Policy in the 1990s*, (Washington, D.C., CQ Press, 1990): 325–47). Then there is Robert W. Loftin, who in reviewing Roderick Frazier Nash's *The Rights of Nature* speculates with some apparent enthusiasm about a "second Civil War waged by radical environmentalists on behalf of trees" (Robert W. Loftin, "Book Reviews," *Environmental Ethics* 12 [Spring 1990]: 83–84).

23. This and all of the following information about the temperance movement is drawn from John Kobler, *Ardent Spirits: The Rise and Fall of Prohibition* (New York: Putnam's, 1973).

24. Abraham Lincoln, "Address Before the Springfield Temperance Society," in Richard C. Current, ed., *The Political Thought of Abraham Lincoln* (Indianapolis: Bobbs-Merrill, 1967): 22–33.

25. Kobler, *Ardent Spirits*, 12.

26. William D. Ruckelshaus, "Risk, Science and Democracy," *Issues in Science and Technology* 1 (Spring 1985): 25.

27. Charles O. Jones, *Clean Air: The Policies and Politics of Pollution Control* (Pittsburgh: University of Pittsburgh Press, 1975): ix.

28. It is instructive to compare Sharon Begley, "The Science of Doom," *Newsweek* (November 23, 1992): 56–60, with "Proceedings of the Near-Earth-Object Interception Workshop" (Los Alamos: Los Alamos National Laboratory, February 1993).

29. Ruckelshaus, "Risk, Science and Democracy," 31. I am indebted to Mr. Ruckelshaus for this concise way of putting the point, which will be echoed many times in these pages.

30. Janet Raloff, "Revamping EPA's Science," *Science News* 141 (April 11, 1992): 234–35.

31. Marc K. Landy, Marc J Roberts, and Stephen R. Thomas, *The Environmental Protection Agency: Asking the Wrong Questions* (New York: Oxford University Press, 1990).

32. Ruckelshaus, "Risk, Science and Democracy," 22.

33. Mark H. Moore and Malcolm K. Sparrow, *Ethics in Government: The Moral Challenge of Public Leadership* (Englewood Cliffs, N.J.: Prentice-Hall, 1990): 11–13, and Landy et al., *EPA*, 35–36.

34. Historian Samuel P. Hays would give a different account of the origins of environmentalism, preferring to present it as a concern evolving out of a whole host of social changes in American society in the post–World War II era. But the development of the environmental values that he chronicles seems so "natural" to him largely because he accepts them uncritically. He is explicitly uninterested in "who is closer to 'the truth'" in the various disputes that he discusses. (Samuel P. Hays, *Beauty, Health and Permanence: Environmental Politics in the United States, 1955–1985* [Cambridge: Cambridge University Press, 1987]: 6, 52.) However much individuals may disagree about just who in particular are the most important figures, Philip Shabecoff, William Tucker, and Edith Efron are more on the right track when they note the significance of particular authors in forming our environmental consciousness, even though they come to the conclusion from different points of view. (William Tucker, *Progress and Privilege: America in the Age of Environmentalism* [Garden City: Anchor Press/Doubleday, 1982]: 87–225; Efron, *The Apocalyptics*, 31–45.) Shabecoff presents a curious chronology, however, when he names a number of environmental authors who became prominent only after Rachel Carson (e.g. the Club of Rome, Paul Ehrlich, and Barry Commoner) as having created the "powder keg" of environmental concern whose fuse Carson lit. (Philip Shabecoff, *A Fierce Green Fire: The American Environmental Movement* [New York: Hill and Wang, 1993]: 110.)

35. Stendhal, *A Roman Journal*, trans. Haakon Chevalier (London: Orion Press, 1959): 9.

36. Compare Bailey, *Ecoscam*, 1–9. Many critics of environmentalism have picked up on its tendency to produce apocalyptic visions, and this theme has produced much interesting comment on op-ed pages. See, for example, Charles Krauthammer, "Apocalypse? Now?" *Washington Post Weekly Edition* (December 7, 1987): 28; William F. Allman, "Fatal Attraction: Why We Love Doomsday," *U.S. News and World Report* (April 30, 1990): 13; S. Fred Singer, "Lowering the Gloom," *Newsweek* (September 14, 1987): 12; Gregg Easterbrook, "Green Cassandras," *The New Republic* (July 6, 1992): 23–25. There is no question that "apocalypse abuse" (as Marc Landy has called it) is a serious problem. It is important to expose how it leads to scientific distortions and public hysteria. But it is a mistake to put too much weight on this one flaw and miss the hopes that are the other side of the same coin. By focusing entirely on dismissing the fears, one risks seeming to say that bad things *cannot* happen. But of course they can. Second, one misses a good deal of what is both attractive and problematic about environmentalism by pretending that it is all about avoiding evils, and not looking into its picture of the good.

37. *Hobbes's Thucydides*, ed. Richard Schlatter (New Brunswick, N.J.: Rutgers University Press, 1975): 381 (V. 103).

38. That there is a political program at the heart of environmentalism, once a charge largely confined to critics, is being ever more widely acknowledged. Bob Pepperman Taylor has a particularly thoughtful way of understanding the implications of the fact that "our political and environmental values are necessarily connected." (Bob Pepperman Taylor, *Our Limits Transgressed: Environmental Political Thought in America* [Lawrence: University Press of Kansas, 1992]: xiii.) Langdon Winner has likewise noted perceptively, "We must learn to read contemporary interpretations of the environment and ecology as we read Hobbes, Locke, or Rousseau on 'the state of nature,' to see exactly what notion of society is being chosen." (Langdon Winner, *The Whale and the Reactor: A Search for Limits in an Age of High Technology* [Chicago: University of Chicago Press, 1986]: 137.) Robert C. Paehlke distinguishes environmentalism from its conservationist forebearer by, among other things, the fact that "from the mid 1960s to the present" the movement has been "largely political and ideological in its perspective." (Robert C. Paehlke, *Environmentalism and the Future of Progressive Politics* [New Haven: Yale University Press, 1989]: 21.)

Some sympathetic observers are likewise prepared to admit that at least some environmental thinkers have a strongly utopian side to them. See Shabecoff on Barry Commoner and E. F. Schumacher, for example (Shabecoff, *Green Fire*, 125). Critics point it out more frequently, but it must be said that they are not always clear about what they mean by the charge, except to imply that the environmentalists want a society different from the one they live in, and that there is something foolish or wrongheaded about that ideal. (Michael Fumento, *Science Under Siege: Balancing Technology and the Environment* [New York: William Morrow, 1993]: 353–55.) A more knowledgeable assessment of the "consistently utopian vision" of "radical environmentalism" is made by Martin W. Lewis, *Green Delusions: An Environmentalist Critique of Radical Environmentalism* (Durham, N.C.: Duke University Press, 1992): 249. Yet as we will see when we look at individual authors, Lewis does not always see the unity of a given thinker's position and therefore will find him radical in some respects, moderate in others.

The possibility that there is in environmentalism a pervasive totalitarian utopianism goes beyond what most critics have explicitly noted, even if they critique environmentalism for one kind of extremism or another. To the best of my knowledge the closest like argument has been made by Richard John Neuhaus, to be discussed in more detail in the final chapter. But his careful remarks on environmental totalitarianism should be noted here:

[A]s much as we may credit the humane sensitivities and democratic convictions of its authors, the totalitarian bias of much ecological literature is inescapable. The essential idea that society should be reorganized around a "single guiding concept" reveals a totalist approach to social structure. All demurrers to the contrary, this assumption is the cornerstone of ideological opposition to the pluralism that most Americans who have thought about the matter claim to cherish. The call for an embracing "coherence" that can overcome chaotically threatening fragmentation has marked all integralist and authoritarian political movements . . . [T]he demand for social coherence suggests an ideological rigidity and political centralism that is, I believe, foreign to the American social experiment at its best . . .

When the call for coherence is joined to the single guiding concept of survival, the implications are particularly grave. (Richard John Neuhaus, *In Defense of People: Ecology and the Seduction of Radicalism* [New York: Macmillan, 1971]: 112–13.)

The charge of totalitarianism frequently brings forth the defense that it could hardly be true of a movement as diverse, eclectic, and even riven by faction as the environmental movement undoubtedly is. Yet one usually hears this claim precisely when environmentalism comes under attack for its extremism; when it is *on* the attack, the movement portrays itself as powerful in its unity. Doubtless the truth rests somewhere between these two characterizations. But what exactly provides the common bond that makes it meaningful to speak of "environmentalism" and not merely "environmentalisms"? This book suggests that totalitarian thinking, developed to a greater or lesser degree, and more or less self-consciously in any given case, provides one thread that unites a great deal of environmentalist thought, even if it cannot bind together each and every instance.

39. Paul Lewis, "Storm in Rio: Morning After," *New York Times* (June 15, 1992): 1 (national edition).

Chapter 1. Brightest Heaven of Invention

1. Marcus Aurelius, *Meditations*, and Epictetus, *Enchiridion* (Chicago: Henry Regnery, 1956): 197.
2. René Descartes, *Discourse on Method*, trans. Laurence J. Lafleur (Indianapolis: Bobbs-Merrill, 1956): 40.
3. Rachel Carson, *Silent Spring*, 25th Anniversary Edition (Boston: Houghton Mifflin, 1962).
4. Paul Brooks, *The House of Life: Rachel Carson at Work* (Boston: Houghton Mifflin, 1972): 227.
5. Rachel Carson, *The Sea Around Us* (New York: Oxford University Press, 1951).
6. Frank Graham, Jr., *Since Silent Spring* (Boston: Houghton Mifflin, 1970): 78–79.
7. Brooks, *House*, xi.
8. Ibid, 77.
9. Rachel Carson, *Under the Sea Wind* (New York: Oxford University Press, 1952).
10. John A. Garraty, *Dictionary of American Biography* Supplement Seven (New York: Scribner's, 1981): 109.
11. Rachel Carson, *The Edge of the Sea* (Boston: Houghton Mifflin, 1955).
12. Carson, *Silent Spring*, 1–3. The book is said to have a "detective-story flavor" in Donald Fleming, "Roots of the New Conservation Movement," *Perspectives in American History*, vol. 6 (Cambridge: Cambridge University Press, 1972): 32.
13. Carson, *Silent Spring*, 12.
14. Ibid., 9.
15. Ibid., 6. Fleming suggests that since the book was written to "persuade

and arouse," Carson had to "calculate her effects as never before, trim her sails to catch the prevailing winds" (Fleming, "New Conservation Movement," 29).

16. Carson, *Silent Spring*, 278–88.
17. Ibid., 75.
18. Ibid., 208–9.
19. Fleming, "New Conservation Movement," 29.
20. Carson, *Silent Spring*, 127.
21. Ibid., 13.
22. Ibid., 259.
23. Rachel Carson, "Rachel Carson Answers Her Critics," *Audubon Magazine* (September/October 1963): 313, 315.
24. Carson, *Silent Spring*, 183–84.
25. See her accounts of the Agriculture Department's gypsy moth and fire ant programs, *Silent Spring*, 157–68.
26. See, for example, Fleming, "New Conservation Movement," 30; Samuel P. Hays, *Beauty, Health and Permanence: Environmental Politics in the United States, 1955–1985* (Cambridge: Cambridge University Press, 1987): 6, 28; Robert C. Paehlke, *Environmentalism and the Future of Progressive Politics* (New Haven: Yale University Press, 1989): 29.
27. Loren Eiseley, "Using a Plague to Fight a Plague," *Saturday Review* 45 (September 29, 1962): 18–19.
28. Lorus Milne and Margery Milne, "There's Poison All Around," *New York Times Book Review* (September 23, 1962): 1.
29. "Elixers of Death," *Christian Century* 79 (December 19, 1962): 1564.
30. James Rorty, "Varieties of Poison," *Commonweal* 77 (December 14, 1962): 320.
31. "Elixers," *Christian Century*: 1564.
32. Marston Bates, "Man and Other Pests," *The Nation* 195 (October 6, 1962): 202.
33. LaMont C. Cole, "Rachel Carson's Indictment of the Wide Use of Pesticides," *Scientific American* (December 1962): 173. Contemporary writers, anxious to maintain Carson's reputation, have a hard time on this point. Her book is "calm and reasoned" but "Carson consciously wrote a polemic intended to stir people to political action." (Philip Shabecoff, *A Fierce Green Fire: The American Environmental Movement* [New York: Hill and Wang, 1993]: 109.) It is both an example of a "'most profound sort of propaganda'" and "scientific evidence" that is "documented in impeccable detail" (Paehlke, *Progressive Politics*, 28).
34. Rorty, "Varieties of Poison," 320.

35. Graham, *Since Silent Spring*, 64–65.
36. Ibid., 58–59.
37. Compare Graham, *Since Silent Spring*, 49, with Elizabeth Whelan, *Toxic Terror: The Truth About the Cancer Scare* (Ottawa, Ill.: Jameson Books, 1985): 64.
38. William J. Darby, "Silence, Miss Carson," *Chemical and Engineering News* (October 1, 1962): 60.
39. "Rachel Carson vs. Pest Control," *The American City* (March 1963): 7.
40. I. L. Baldwin, "Chemicals and Pests," *Science* 137 (September 1962): 1042.
41. Darby, "Silence," 60.
42. Graham, *Since Silent Spring*, 56.
43. Ibid., 56–57.
44. Darby, "Silence," 62.
45. Cole, "Rachel Carson's Indictment," 173.
46. Frank Graham admits that Carson's claim that arsenic is the carcinogenic element in chimney soot is wrong, that she overstated the threat DDT posed to robins, and that she was wrong to think that insect pathogens do not cause disease in higher animals (Graham, *Since Silent Spring*, 67). Far more damagingly, Fleming points out that the whole idea that pesticides are concentrated as one moves up the food chain, which is crucial to Carson's arguments about distant and delayed effects, has "become increasingly dubious in the years that followed" (Fleming, *New Conservation Movement*, 31). There remains an unfortunate tendency to present vague criticisms of the book (e.g., the multipoint indictment in George Claus and Karen Bolander, *Ecological Sanity* [New York: David McKay, 1977]: 10). Unlike most of their impressively documented book, the charges in this instance are left completely unsubstantiated. On the other side, there is an equally unfortunate tendency simply to take her science for granted, as indicated in note 33, above.
47. Graham, *Since Silent Spring*, 69.
48. Gino J. Marco et al., *Silent Spring Revisited* (Washington, D.C.: American Chemical Society, 1987): 9.
49. Ibid., 5.
50. Paehlke's assessment seems just when he notes that one of her contributions "was her articulation of these vital sciences in language accessable to the educated public. Her style, a blend of scientific, political, and moral arguments . . . became the hallmark of popular environmentalism" (Paehlke, *Progressive Politics*, 28). The importance of popularization is also picked up by Claus and Bolander, *Sanity*, 9. Hays exhibits a stunning ability to miss the social forces he wants to describe when he claims that "even more influential" than Carson was a "widely reported

administrative hearing about DDT in Wisconsin in 1968 and 1969" (Hays, *Beauty, Health*, 28).

51. Whelan, *Toxic Terror*, 78–85; Edith Efron, *The Apocalyptics* (New York: Simon and Schuster, 1984): 267–70.

52. Marco, *Silent Spring Revisited*, 8. The Rachel Carson Council is an organization that seeks to further Carson's work by the study of pesticides and chemical contaminants.

53. Ibid., 8.

54. Brooks, *House of Life*, 244.

55. Carson, *Silent Spring*, 207–8.

56. Ibid., 336.

57. "Occupational Oligospermia," *Journal of the American Medical Association* 140 (August 13, 1949): 1249.

58. Carson, *Silent Spring*, 193.

59. W. J. Hayes, Jr., W. F. Durham, and C. Cueto, Jr., "The Effect of Known Repeated Oral Doses of Chlorophenothane (DDT) in Man," *Journal of the American Medical Association* 162 (October 27, 1956): 890.

60. Ibid., 897.

61. Ibid., 893.

62. Carson, *Silent Spring*, 234.

63. Ibid., 234–35.

64. Sir Macfarlane Burnet, "Leukemia as a Problem of Preventive Medicine," *New England Journal of Medicine* 259 (August 28, 1958): 423–31.

65. Ibid., 427.

66. Ibid., 427.

67. Ibid., 429.

68. Marco, *Silent Spring Revisited*, 4.

69. Carson, *Silent Spring*, 197–98.

70. Ibid., 198.

71. S. Gershon and F. H. Shaw, "Psychiatric Sequelae of Chronic Exposure to Organophosphorus Insecticides," *Lancet* (June 24, 1961): 1372.

72. Cole, "Rachel Carson's Indictment," 176.

73. Vera L. Norwood, "The Nature of Knowing: Rachel Carson and the American Environment," *Signs: Journal of Women in Culture and Society* 12 (Summer 1987): 740–60.

74. Carson, *Silent Spring*, 5.

75. Ibid., 6.

76. Ibid., 51.

77. Norwood, "Nature of Knowing," 748.

78. Carson, *Silent Spring*, 262.

79. Ibid., 246.

80. Ibid., 6.

81. Ibid., 6–7.

82. Ibid., 127.

83. Ibid., 10.

84. Paul Colinvaux, *Why Big Fierce Animals are Rare: An Ecologist's Perspective* (Princeton: Princeton University Press, 1978): 123, 209. In general, Colinvaux's book is a highly readable presentation of how a professional ecologist looks at nature, and it is striking how different his view often is from the environmental popularizers who claim to be inspired by ecology. As Colinvaux himself puts it in his Preface, "Ecology is not the science of pollution, nor is it environmental science. Still less is it a science of doom. There is, however, an overwhelming mass of writings claiming that ecology is all of these things. I wrote this book in some anger to retort to this literature with an account of what one practicing ecologist thinks his subject is really about . . . I take the opportunity to brand as nonsense tales of destroying the atmosphere, killing lakes, and hazarding the world by making it simple" (vii). See also Mark Sagoff, "Fact and Value in Ecological Science," *Environmental Ethics* 7 (Summer 1985): 107–10.

85. Carson, *Silent Spring*, 5.

86. Ibid., 5.

87. Ibid., 53.

88. Ibid., 15.

89. Specifically on the issue of carcinogenicity, see Efron, *Apocalyptics*, 123–83.

90. Carson, *Silent Spring*, 17–18, 223.

91. Ibid., 32.

92. Ibid., 32–33.

93. Ibid., 33.

94. Ibid., vi.

95. Ibid., 69–70.

96. Ibid., 296.

97. Ibid., 296.

98. Ibid., 297.

99. Rachel Carson, *The Sense of Wonder* (Berkeley: Nature Company, [1956, 1984] 1990).

100. Philip Shabecoff, "E.P.A. Critic Enters the Lion's Den and Is Showered by Wild Applause," *New York Times* (January 15, 1988): B6.

101. Fleming, "New Conservation Movement," 41.

102. Ibid., 40.

103. Barry Commoner, *The Closing Circle: Nature, Man and Technology* (New York: Bantam Books, [1971] 1974).

104. "Commoner Cause," *Economist* 242 (March 11, 1972): 68.

105. Commoner, *Closing Circle*, 29–44.

106. Ibid., 45–108. Fleming offers a critique of Commoner's presentation of Lake Erie as dead or dying (Fleming, "New Conservation Movement," 47–51), while Claus and Bolander argue that there are serious problems with Commoner's treatment of nitrate pollution of Illinois farmland (Claus and Bolander, *Ecological Sanity*, 159–85).

107. Commoner, *Closing Circle*, 258.

108. Michael Crichton, *New York Times Book Review* (October 17, 1971): 7.

109. *The New Yorker* 47 (December 11, 1971): 23.

110. "The Last Ball Game," *Newsweek* 78 (November 1, 1971): 95.

111. Stephen MacDonald, "Pollution and Free-enterprise Economics," *Wall Street Journal* (November 22, 1971): 14.

112. Christopher Lehmann-Haupt, "Waste Not, Want Not, Die Not," *New York Times* (December 24, 1971): 23.

113. *Choice* 9 (May 1972): 388.

114. *Bookworld* 5 (October 15, 1971): 4.

115. Victor C. Ferkiss, *Commonweal* 96 (May 26, 1972): 292.

116. Henry Beetle Hough, "Ecology and Survival," *American Scholar* 43 (Winter 1974): 154.

117. Eric Ashby, "Survival Against the Odds," *Spectator* 228 (February 5, 1972): 196.

118. Crichton, *New York Times*, 7.

119. Stuart Chase, "The Closing Circle by Barry Commoner," *Living Wilderness* 36 (Spring 1972): 36.

120. *Publishers Weekly* 200 (October 11, 1971): 45.

121. *The New Republic* (November 6, 1971): 29.

122. Paul B. Sears, "The Closing Circle," *Natural Resources Journal* 13 (July 4, 1973): 549.

123. *Library Journal* 97 (March 1, 1972): 833.

124. Ferkiss, *Commonweal* 96: 293.

125. Monroe Bush, "The Closing Circle?" *American Forests* 78 (January 1972): 62.

126. Franklin Russell, "The Totalitarian Ecologist," *Life* 71 (November 5, 1971): 18.

127. Commoner, *Closing Circle*, 29.

128. Ibid., 35.

129. Ibid., 35.

130. Ibid., 39.

131. Ibid., 38.

132. Ibid., 118.

133. Ibid., 118–19.

134. Ibid., 119.

135. Ibid., 283.

136. Sustained attack on the idea that nature knows best has done little to lessen the popularity of the idea. William Tucker critiques "nature knows best" by comparing it with Deism and accuses Commoner of adopting a kind of "Panglossian philosophy." He presents examples where it is hard to see how natural design has worked for the best. (William Tucker, *Progress and Privilege: America in the Age of Environmentalism* [Garden City, N.Y.: Anchor Press/Doubleday, 1982]: 167–68.) Rene Dubos offers a similar critique. (Rene Dubos, *The Wooing of Earth: New Perspectives on Man's Use of Nature* [New York: Scribner's, 1980]: 80–84.) Claus and Bolander contest the notion that nature produces nothing it cannot recycle by noting that there is no natural enzyme to break down so common a thing as plant pollen and spores. (Claus and Bolander, *Sanity*, 516–18.)

137. Barry Commoner, *The Poverty of Power: Energy and the Economic Crisis* (New York: Knopf, 1976).

138. Ibid., 5.

139. Ibid., 235–64.

140. Compare Christopher Lehmann-Haupt, "Thermodynamic Socialism," *New York Times* (May 31, 1976): 13, with Wiley Mitchell, "Is the 'Energy Crisis' Only a Symptom of a Deeper Cause?" *Christian Science Monitor* (May 25, 1976): 18.

141. Commoner, *Poverty of Power*, 31, 213.

142. Ibid., 31.

143. Ibid., 233–34, 256, 258.

144. Study Group on Technical Aspects of Efficient Energy Utilization, "Efficient Use of Energy," *Physics Today* (August 1975): 24.

145. Ibid., 24.

146. Barry Commoner, *Science and Survival* (New York: Viking, 1967).

147. Barry Commoner, *Making Peace with the Planet* (New York: Pantheon, 1990).

148. Commoner, *Science and Survival*, 101.

149. Ibid., 120.

150. See Mary Douglas and Aaron Wildavsky, *Risk and Culture: An Essay on the Selection of Technical and Environmental Dangers* (Berkeley: University of California Press, 1982).

151. Commoner, *Closing Circle*, 83–84.

152. See, for example, Robert Bell, *Impure Science: Fraud, Compromise and Political Influence in Scientific Research* (New York: Wiley, 1992); Michael Fumento, *Science Under Siege: Balancing Technology and the Environment* (New York: William Morrow, 1993); Peter Huber, *Galileo's Revenge: Junk Science in the Courtroom* (New York: Basic Books, 1991).

This crucially important aspect of Commoner's argument is usually overlooked, probably because there is so little tendency to question his science. Paehlke praises Commoner for being one of "the most success-ful" of those who have brought "[s]cientific findings that point to a need for political decisions" to the attention of the public "as soon as possi-ble." There is no hint that the speed, or the assumption that the link between science and politics is obvious, may alike be problematic (Paehlke, *Progressive Politics*, 34).

153. Commoner, *Making Peace*, 63.
154. Ibid., 64.
155. Ibid., 64.
156. Ibid., 71.
157. Ibid., 67.
158. Ibid., 77.
159. *Closing Circle*, 193–96.
160. Ibid., 279.
161. Ibid., 279.
162. *Making Peace*, 220.
163. *Poverty of Power*, 4, 6, 235 36.
164. Commoner, *Closing Circle*, 257–62. Hays acknowledges that Common-er "helped to etch into the minds of many Americans ideas about how biological systems worked and could be overloaded and disrupted to the detriment of human life," but never even hints that that analysis might be connected with Commoner's socialism (Hays, *Beauty, Health*, 212). Shabecoff's treatment of Commoner's socialism is in a way even more curious. He suggests it creates a "wide gulf" between him and the "mainstream national environmental groups, to whom he was [*sic*] a perpetual gadfly." That Commoner is such a gadfly is true; but a gadfly has to get pretty close to sting his victims. Shabecoff is far closer to the truth when he notes that thinking like Commoner's in fact underlies what "kind of world" mainstream environmentalists would like to see (Shabecoff, *Green Fire*, 99, 125). Martin Lewis understands that social-ism is important to Commoner but also makes the mysterious and unex-plained suggestion that he "veers toward anarchism." (Martin W. Lewis, *Green Delusions: An Environmentalist Critique of Radical Environmental-ism* [Durham, N.C.: Duke University Press, 1992]: 41.) Although we disagree on emphasis, Bob Pepperman Taylor has a finely nuanced understanding of the role socialism plays in Commoner's thinking. (Bob Pepperman Taylor, *Our Limits Transgressed: Environmental Political Thought in America* [Lawrence: University Press of Kansas, 1992]: 137–45.) See also James E. Krier, "The Political Economy of Barry Commoner," *Environmental Law* 20, no. 11 (1990): 11–33.
165. Commoner, *Closing Circle*, 257–62.
166. Ibid., 267.
167. Charles T. Rubin, "Environmental Policy and Environmental Thought:

Ruckelshaus and Commoner," *Environmental Ethics* 11 (Spring 1989): 27–51.

168. Samuel McCracken, "Solar Energy: A False Hope," *Commentary* 68 (November 1979): 61–67; Dale Gieringer, "Barry Commoner: The Sunshine Candidate," *Reason* (November 1980): 33–42.

169. Commoner, *Making Peace*, 42.

170. Ibid., 240.

171. Ibid., 171–80.

172. Commoner, *Closing Circle*, 291.

173. Ibid., 286.

174. Ibid., 286.

175. Ibid., 212.

176. Ibid., 212–13.

177. Ibid., 295.

178. Ibid., 295.

179. Ibid., 295.

180. Commoner, *Poverty of Power*, 252.

181. Ibid., 257.

182. Ibid., 258.

183. Commoner, *Making Peace*, 220.

184. Commoner, *Poverty of Power*, 261.

185. Commoner, *Closing Circle*, 280.

186. Commoner, *Poverty of Power*, 261.

187. Ibid., 262.

188. Commoner, *Making Peace*, 227.

189. Ibid., 227.

190. Ibid., 227–29.

191. Ibid., 227–28.

192. Commoner, *Poverty of Power*, 2.

193. Taylor argues that Commoner's chief concern is "to tie his environmentalism to a democratic program of political justice and economic equality," and that it is therefore a mistake to see him as simply a technocrat. (Taylor, *Limits Transgressed*, 137, 144–45.) But, as Taylor admits, "the details of how to prevent the socialist control of production from becoming a bureaucratic leviathan are not well developed in his writings" (a generous formulation of the point). Doubts can be raised about what Commoner understands democracy to be, or how much he values it. There is little or no explicit decoction in Commoner of what he has in mind by social justice. Add to all this the fact that the program for technological change is much more completely worked out, and at the very least you have a situation where, if it is an error to see Commoner as essentially a technocrat, it is an error he calls upon himself.

194. Claus and Bolander, *Ecological Sanity*, 98–99. The authors seem to come to this conclusion because they do not take Commoner's socialism very seriously.

195. Commoner, *Closing Circle*, 289.

196. Ibid., 289.

197. Ibid., 186.

198. Ibid., 283.

199. Ibid., 287.

200. Commoner, *Poverty of Power*, 158–59.

201. Commoner, *Closing Circle*, 280–81.

202. Ibid., 162.

203. George Orwell, *The Road to Wigan Pier* (New York: Harcourt Brace, 1958): 196–211.

204. Commoner, *Poverty of Power*, 258.

205. Lawrence Weschler, "Barry Commoner," *Rolling Stone* 316 (May 1, 1980): 48.

206. Carey McWilliams, "Second Thoughts," *The Nation* (April 26, 1980): 487.

207. Commoner, *Closing Circle*, 281.

208. Michael Harrington, *Socialism* (New York: Dutton, 1972): 344.

209. Bertrand de Jouvenel, *The Ethics of Redistribution* (Indianapolis: Liberty Press, 1952): 38.

Chapter Two. We Happy Few

1. Jean-Jacques Rousseau, *On the Social Contract* (with "Geneva Manuscript" and "Political Economy"), ed. Roger D. Masters, trans. Judith R. Masters (New York: St. Martin's Press, 1978): 96.

2. Alan Gregg, "A Medical Aspect of the Population Problem," *Science* 121 (May 13, 1955): 682.

3. John Tierney, "Betting the Planet," *New York Times Magazine* (December 2, 1990): 76.

4. *Booklist* (May 1, 1971): 740.

5. Paul R. Ehrlich, *The Population Bomb* (New York: Ballantine Books, 1968): 15.

6. Tierney, "Betting the Planet," 76.

7. Ibid., 76.

8. Ehrlich, *The Population Bomb* 1968, 4. Notice to this effect was omitted from revised editions.

9. "Unwanted People," *New Republic* (August 2, 1969): 7.

10. Peter J. Donaldson, *Nature Against Us: The United States and the World Population Crisis, 1965–1980* (Chapel Hill: University of North Carolina Press, 1990): 40.

11. Paul R. Ehrlich, "World Population: Is the Battle Lost?" *Reader's Digest* (February 1969): 137–40; Rep. Morris K. Udall, "Standing Room Only on Spaceship Earth," *Reader's Digest* (December 1969): 131–35.

12. Margaret Mead, "Crisis of Our Overcrowded World," *Redbook* 133 (October 1969): 40+.

13. Joseph J. Spengler, "Overpopulation: Threat to America's Future," *Parents Magazine* 43 (April 1968): 42+.

14. "Problem of People Pollution," *Life* 68 (January 9, 1970): 8–15.

15. J[ames] K. P[age], *Natural History* 77 (October 1968): 78, 80.

16. Thomas Robert Malthus, *An Essay on the Principle of Population*, ed. Philip Appleman (New York: Norton, 1976).

17. Paul R. Ehrlich and Anne H. Ehrlich, *The Population Explosion* (New York: Touchstone Books, 1990): 22.

18. Ehrlich, *Population Bomb* 1968, 13.

19. Ehrlich and Ehrlich, *Population Explosion*, 14.

20. Ibid., 22.

21. James Reed, *From Private Vice to Public Virtue* (New York: Basic Books, 1978): 50.

22. Ibid., 106.

23. Donaldson, *Nature Against Us*, 53.

24. Reed, *Private Vice, Public Virtue*, 340.

25. World Resources Institute, *World Resources 1986* (New York: Basic Books, 1986): 236, 238; World Resources Institute, *World Resources 1990–91* (New York: Oxford University Press, 1990): 254, 256.

26. World Resources Institute, *World Resources 1986*, 9.

27. Reed, *Private Vice, Public Virtue*, 147.

28. Ibid., 199, 201.

29. Daniel J. Kevles, "Controlling the Genetic Arsenal," *Wilson Quarterly* (Spring 1992): 68–76.

30. Reed, *Private Vice, Public Virtue*, 134–36.

31. William Vogt, *Road to Survival* (New York: W. Sloane Associates, 1948).

32. Paul R. Ehrlich, "The Coming Famine," *Natural History* 77 (May 1968): 11.

33. Reed, *Private Vice, Public Virtue*, 369.

34. Ehrlich and Ehrlich, *Population Explosion*, 16.

35. Ehrlich, *Population Bomb* 1978, 12.

36. Ibid., 15.

37. Ibid., 15.

38. Ehrlich and Ehrlich, *Population Explosion*, 15.

39. Ibid., 265.

40. Ibid., 39.

41. World Resources Institute, *World Resources 1986*, 10, 46.
42. Ehrlich, *Population Bomb* 1978, 152. See also *Population Explosion*, 217, where the "central question" is said to be what kind of society we want "one or two centuries from now."
43. Ehrlich, *Population Bomb* 1978, 154.
44. Ehrlich and Ehrlich, *Population Explosion*, 181.
45. Ibid., 182.
46. Ibid., 182.
47. Ibid., 182–83.
48. Ibid., 23.
49. Ibid., 137.
50. Ehrlich, *Population Bomb* 1978, 171.
51. Ibid., 135.
52. Ibid., 135.
53. Julian Simon, *The Ultimate Resource* (Princeton: Princeton University Press, 1981): 312–13.
54. Malthus, *Principle of Population*, 20–21.
55. Ehrlich, *Population Bomb* 1968, 76.
56. Ibid., 72, emphasis in the original.
57. Ibid., 72–78.
58. Ibid., 78–80.
59. *Population Bomb* 1978, 49.
60. Ibid., 50–61.
61. Ibid., 62–72.
62. Ibid., 73–77.
63. Ehrlich and Ehrlich, *Population Explosion*, 9.
64. Ibid., 295–96. Ronald Bailey says that "Ehrlich prefers to use 'scenarios' which he disingenuously calls 'devices for helping one to think about the future.'" (Ronald Bailey, *Ecoscam: The False Prophets of Ecological Apocalypse* [New York: St. Martin's Press, 1993]: 43.) But this is an entirely accurate use of the term, and there is no ground for complaint against Ehrlich for using it. One does not have to think that Ehrlich was trying to back away from predictions to see the point of his having presented the scenarios. They were designed to scare people, in the same way that a ghost story is designed to scare people, without committing the author to a prediction that there are ghosts.
65. Ehrlich and Ehrlich, *Population Explosion*, 296.
66. Ehrlich, *Population Bomb* 1968, 11.
67. Ehrlich, *Population Bomb* 1978, xi.
68. World Resources Institute, *World Resources 1986*, 238–39; *World Resources 1990–91*, 258–59.

69. Ehrlich and Ehrlich, *Population Explosion*, 9.
70. Ibid., 47.
71. Ehrlich, *Population Bomb* 1968, 69.
72. Ehrlich and Ehrlich, *Population Explosion*, 286.
73. Ibid., 69.
74. Ibid., 80.
75. Ibid., 80.
76. Ibid., 80, 105.
77. Ehrlich says the world has turned a deaf ear to his warnings, and for the reasons that follow in the text that is not an unreasonable judgment (*Population Explosion*, 10). But Bailey is also correct to point out that Ehrlich is not above claiming credit (although not sole credit, as Bailey seems to suggest) for vast social and legal changes (Bailey, *Ecoscam*, 42).
78. Ehrlich, *Population Bomb* 1968, 105ff.
79. Ehrlich, *Population Bomb* 1978, 98ff.
80. Ehrlich, "The Coming Famine," 7–8.
81. Ehrlich and Ehrlich, *Population Explosion*, 91–95.
82. Ibid., 109.
83. Ibid., 23.
84. Ehrlich, *Population Bomb* 1978, 18.
85. Ibid., 24.
86. Ehrlich and Ehrlich, *Population Explosion*, 84.
87. Ibid., 157.
88. Ibid., 146.
89. Tierney, "Betting the Planet," 52ff.
90. Ibid., 81.
91. Ehrlich and Ehrlich, *Population Explosion*, 139.
92. Ibid., 23.
93. Ibid., 16.
94. Paul R. Ehrlich and John P. Holdren, "Eight Thousand Million People by the Year 2010?" *Environmental Conservation* 2 (Winter 1975): 241–42.
95. Ehrlich and Ehrlich, *Population Explosion*, 23.
96. Paul Ehrlich, "Eco-Catastrophe!" *Ramparts Magazine* 8 (September 1969): 24–28.
97. Ehrlich and Ehrlich, *Population Explosion*, 23.
98. China's expressed goal of a population of 650–750 million is regarded by the Ehrlichs as too high for the long term; they accept it since they expect that China will have a peak population of double that number. (*Population Explosion*, 206). Still, that goal represents 65 to 75 percent of China's current population. Ehrlich has suggested an appropriate

size for the United States could be less than 50 million (quoted in George Claus and Karen Bolander, *Ecological Sanity* [New York: David McKay, 1977]: 93). But let us assume a target, proportional to the Chinese case, of 150 million, or about 60% of today's roughly 250 million.

In 1981 China had a crude birthrate of about 21 per thousand, and a crude death rate of about 6.5 per thousand. Suppose that at the end of five years, the birthrate had been reduced by more than half, to 9.7 per thousand, and that it was kept at that rate or slightly lower for the next 35 years before being allowed a controlled, slow climb to a stable 14.8 per thousand, when birthrate and death rate would match. (The death rate rises owing to the aging population.) Under these circumstances, it would take some 100 years for the population to reach within a few 10,000s of the goal, or 115 years to reach it with greater precision.

With their long view of history and presently undemocratic political institutions, the Chinese may be able to contemplate with some seriousness such a long-term policy, although it would clearly require measures well beyond the draconian ones that they have used to reduce their birthrate to its present place in the low 20s.

Is the case easier for the United States, with a smaller population to begin with? Not really. In 1985, our crude birthrate was about 15.7 per thousand, and the death rate 9 per thousand. If starting in 1985 we had undertaken to lower the birth rate to 8.5 per thousand, and then allowed it to increase gradually over the next 95 years to a stable 13.4 per thousand (again, where birthrate and death rate would match), we could reach within a few 10,000s of our goal in 105 years, and manage to be down "precisely" to 150 million in 135 years.

To speed things up, we might consider measures that are initially more radical. The Ehrlichs once said, "The greatest gift that the United Nations could ask for the world would be *no* births in 1979." (Paul R. Ehrlich and Anne H. Ehrlich, "International Year of No Child?" *Environmental Conservation* 6 [Spring 1979]: 1–2.) While no births is obviously absurd, what would happen if, in a kind of "shock treatment," we reduced the birthrate to less than 1 per thousand (.2, to be precise) for an initial 5-year period? (The worst would then be over within a span not much longer than one presidential term.) Then we could let it "jump" to nearly 9 per thousand in the next 5 years, before letting it climb back to 13.4 per thousand over 80 years or so. Under this scenario, we could be slightly below our goal of 150 million in "only" 85 years.

These scenarios assume *no* immigration, and U. S. death rate and actuarial characteristics as of 1985. But we don't have to hold the death rate constant. What if we increase the death rate somewhat by assuming that U.S. citizens would have the same life expectancy characteristics as Guatemalans (i.e., allow increased infant and early childhood mortality, along with somewhat shorter life expectancy generally)? In 1985, this change would have meant an increase in the death rate from 9 to 15.4 per thousand, and the point of matching birthrate and death rate would occur at 16.1 per thousand after some 100 years. We would then reach "precisely" our goal after 115 years, having been within a couple 10,000s of it after 95 years.

The "winning" policy, at least for speed of success, would clearly be a combination of this death rate increase and the "quick start" radical initial reduction plan. Then we could be slightly below our goal after some 75 years.

These exploratory calculations were performed by "STATPOP: Stationary State Populations: A Demographic Planning Model," a computer program created by Prof. N. C. Field, Department of Geography, University of Toronto. Demographic data for the United States, China, and Guatemala were drawn from Nathan Keyfitz and Wilhelm Flieger, *World Population Growth and Aging: Demographic Trends in the Late Twentieth Century* (Chicago: University of Chicago Press, 1990).

99. Ehrlich, *Population Bomb* 1968, 91. The point is softened somewhat in the 1978 edition: *Population Bomb* 1978, 87.
100. Ehrlich, *Population Bomb* 1968, 128–45.
101. Ibid., 138.
102. Ibid., 138, emphasis added. The 1978 revision tones this point down somewhat: *Population Bomb* 1978, 132–33.
103. Ehrlich, *Population Bomb* 1978, 163; Ehrlich and Ehrlich, *Population Explosion*, 189.
104. Ehrlich, *Population Bomb* 1978, 130–31.
105. Ehrlich, *Population Bomb* 1968, 138. This suggestion is missing from the 1978 revision.
106. Ehrlich, *Population Bomb* 1978, 151–52.
107. Ibid., 152.
108. Ibid., 146.
109. Ehrlich, *Population Bomb* 1968, 164–65.
110. Ibid., 162–63.
111. Ehrlich and Ehrlich, *Population Explosion*, 216–19.
112. Ibid., 222–25.
113. Ibid., 228.
114. Despite the fact that India and Bangladesh are always held up as horror stories, despite the absolute size of China's population, despite the fact that population control in developing nations is "much harder" than in

the developed world (*Population Explosion*, 203), despite the fact that the momentum for growth is much greater in the developing world because of its youthful population, the Ehrlichs want to "lay to rest the myth that population problems arise primarily from rapid growth in poor countries" (*Population Explosion*, 134). The bad global impact of one additional American, they calculate, is 280 times that of an extra Haitian, owing to our profligate use of resources (*Population Explosion*, 134).

The Ehrlichs reach conclusions like this through a "formula" that says that environmental impact = population x affluence x disruptiveness of technology. A devastating critique of this "pseudo-science" can be found in Martin W. Lewis, *Green Delusions: An Environmentalist Critique of Radical Environmentalism* (Durham, N.C.: Duke University Press, 1992): 237–40. In addition, Lewis speculates that blaming American babies either stems from "a profound distaste for the human species or from an attempt to mollify leftist opinion" that would charge them with racism if they spoke too much about Third World population problems.

115. Ehrlich and Ehrlich, *Population Explosion*, 229.
116. Paul R. Ehrlich and Anne H. Ehrlich, *Healing the Planet: Strategies for Resolving the Environmental Crisis* (Reading: Addison Wesley, 1991).
117. Ehrlich and Ehrlich, *Population Explosion*, 187–88.
118. Ibid., 188.
119. Robert Ornstein and Paul Ehrlich, *New World New Mind* (New York: Simon and Schuster, 1989).
120. Ehrlich and Ehrlich, *Population Explosion*, 189–90, 230.
121. Ibid., 205, 207.
122. Ibid., 206.
123. Ibid., 205.
124. Ibid., 207.
125. Ibid., 207.
126. Ibid., 299.
127. Paul R. Ehrlich and Anne H. Ehrlich, "What Happened to the Population Bomb," *Human Nature* (January 1979): 92.
128. Perhaps it is Ehrlich's willingness to advocate coercion so openly that makes him "too hot to handle" for a number of otherwise sympathetic observers of the environmental crusade. Incredibly, Hays manages to speak about the growth of concern about population in the late 1960s, and even to mention ZPG, without a single reference to Ehrlich. (Samuel P. Hays, *Beauty, Health and Permanence: Environmental Politics in the United States, 1955–1985* [Cambridge: Cambridge University Press, 1987]: 214–15.) Shabecoff more reasonably credits Ehrlich with

being "[t]he most widely known proponent of the view that overpopulation is a catastrophic ecological problem," but omits any discussion of the solutions Ehrlich proposed. (Philip Shabecoff, *A Fierce Green Fire: The American Environmental Movement* [New York: Hill and Wang, 1993]: 95.)

Paehlke's approach is complex. He rightly notes that *The Population Bomb* is "crucial to an appreciation of the intellectual history of environmentalism" and goes on to give a fair summary of its argument. He sees that Ehrlich (and Hardin) are pointing to a government that would be able to reach "into every bedroom on the planet," and that one reason this is so is that their thinking promises us only disaster or paradise, instead of a *"preferable world."* (Robert C. Paehlke, *Environmentalism and the Future of Progressive Politics* [New Haven: Yale University Press, 1989]: 58, 55.) So he wants to reject the pessimistic political conclusions Ehrlich and others like him draw. But he apparently wants to maintain the pessimistic environmental analysis from which those conclusions are drawn. I am less convinced than he that this is possible. At any rate, the only ground he suggests for drawing less drastic conclusions seems to be faith in democracy and altruism (Paehlke, *Progressive Politics*, 75). Ehrlich tried to define the problem in a way coherent with his solutions. Different solutions will come from different definitions of the problem, not from trying to use the fear he creates for somehow more reasonable purposes.

129. Michael Satchell, "The Rape of the Oceans," *U.S. News and World Report* (June 22, 1992): 64–75.
130. Ibid., 70.
131. Garrett Hardin, "The Tragedy of the Commons," *Science* 162 (December 13, 1968): 1243–48. Hereafter, all citations to this essay will conform to the pagination of the reprint in Garrett Hardin, *Exploring New Ethics for Survival/The Voyage of the Spaceship Beagle* (New York: Viking, [1968] 1972): 250–64.
132. Harold Hayes, "A Conversation with Garrett Hardin," *Atlantic Monthly* 247 (May 1981): 62–63.
133. Ibid., 63.
134. G. M. Woodwell, "Inconvenient Alternatives," *Science* 178 (December 15, 1972): 1192.
135. Hardin, "Tragedy," 254.
136. Ibid., 257–58.
137. Garrett Hardin, *Naked Emperors: Essays of a Taboo Stalker* (Los Altos, Calif.: William Kaufmann, 1982): 244. Ophuls and Boyan take Hardin to be providing "an accurate description of the current human predicament." (William Ophuls and A. Stephen Boyan, *Ecology and the Politics*

of *Scarcity Revisited: The Unraveling of the American Dream* [New York: W. H. Freeman, 1992]: 195.) But certainly in terms of population issues, this overstates the case, since the conditions just described that create the tragedy are hardly uniformly present in the world. An ambiguity in Hardin's presentation makes it possible that the commons problem need not obtain widely, even in the question of resource exploitation that Ophuls and Boyan are particularly interested in. As Daniel W. Bromley has pointed out, much discussion of the commons problem fails to distinguish between unowned resources and commonly owned resources. His point is that as soon as a resource is considered as *property*, it is possible for rational behavior not to have the tragic outcome Hardin says necessarily follows. (Daniel W. Bromley, ed., *Making the Commons Work: Theory, Practice and Policy* [San Francisco: ICS Press, 1992]: 4.) Since a good deal of the world's resources are in fact owned, whether by individuals, states, or collectives of one kind or another, Ophuls and Boyan—despite the fact that they make a distinction like Bromley's—may be generalizing far too broadly about the consequences of what is now an unusual state of affairs.

This is not to say that people cannot mistreat their property. But Ophuls and Boyan want to assimilate as many pollution and resource problems as possible to the tragedy of the commons in order to suggest how conclusions drawn from it "radically challenge fundamental American and Western values . . . democracy *as we know it* cannot conceivably survive" (Ophuls and Boyan, *Scarcity Revisited*, 199–200). The environmental problems they cite either do not fit the paradigm of unowned resource exploitation or are not self-evidently unsuitable for solution by the creation of property rights, leading again to the conclusion that the analytical usefulness of the tragedy of the commons may be far more limited than they think. See also Susan James Buck Cox, "No Tragedy on the Commons," *Environmental Ethics* 7 (Spring, 1985): 49–61.
138. Hardin, *Naked Emperors*, 244–45.
139. Garrett Hardin, *Stalking the Wild Taboo*, 2d ed. (Los Altos, Calif.: William Kaufmann, 1978): 158–61; Garrett Hardin, *Promethean Ethics: Living with Death, Competition and Triage* (Seattle: University of Washington Press, 1980): 43.
140. Hardin, *Promethean Ethics*, 45.
141. Hardin, "Tragedy," 259. Paehlke suggests that Hardin assumes "erroneously that people will not come to understand the need for population constraint" (Paehlke, *Progressive Politics*, 58). But this criticism ignores the logic of Hardin's argument, which is that everybody must agree to restraint if restraint is to work.
142. Hardin, *Wild Taboo*, 182–83.

143. Hardin, "Tragedy," 260.
144. Hardin, *Naked Emperors*, 209.
145. Hardin, "Tragedy," 257; Hardin, *New Ethics*, 135–36. Peter Stillman has perceptively noted that Hardin makes the problem of the guardians almost impossible, given the way he understands people to behave. Why should short-term calculators of their interests accept such guardians in the first place? And if most or all people are such calculators, why upon elevation to the position of guardian would one act any differently? (Peter G. Stillman, "The Tragedy of the Commons: A Re-Analysis," *Alternatives: Perspectives on Society and the Environment* 4 [Winter 1975]: 12.)
146. See, for example, Terry Anderson and Donald R. Leal, *Free Market Environmentalism* (San Francisco: Pacific Institute for Public Policy Research, 1991); William C. Dennis, "The Public and Private Interest in Wilderness Protection," *Cato Journal* 1 (Fall 1981): 373–90.
147. Hardin, *Promethean Ethics*, 47.
148. Garrett Hardin, "Living on a Lifeboat," *Bioscience* 24 (October 1974): 561–68; Garrett Hardin, "Carrying Capacity as an Ethical Concept," *Soundings* 59 (Spring 1976): 120.
149. Hardin, "Tragedy," 257–58, 261. It is a stock charge against Hardin that he is against poor people. But in this instance, at least, the charge is misplaced; he rejects a "cruel but effective" system of privatization for "good humanitarian reasons" (*New Ethics*, 188). Of course, these reasons require that everyone accept coercion. Still, it seems an error simply to classify him as a "Social Darwinist," as does Fleming. (Donald Fleming, "Roots of the New Conservation Movement," *Perspectives in American History*, vol. 6 [Cambridge: Cambridge University Press, 1972]: 59.) Social Darwinists in the William Graham Sumner mold, at least, have a far greater concern with liberty, and a far smaller faith in progress, than Hardin.
150. Hardin, "Tragedy," 261. In 1968, however, Hardin could note that while the word "abortion" had "ceased to be a dirty word," people still had trouble with "the *fact*." Hardin, *Wild Taboo*, 28.
151. Hardin, *Wild Taboo*, 201.
152. Hardin, "Tragedy," 260–61.
153. Ibid., 261. As noted above (n. 137), a literature has grown up that suggests how resource destruction *can* be avoided in a commons, understood as a common property arrangement. But what is not fully clear is the extent to which these writers are challenging Hardin. Some of their arguments about how commons work in real life seem to confirm his insights into the management or coercive practices required to prevent overexploitation.

154. Karl Sax, "World Population: Control of Crisis," *Science* 163 (February 21, 1969): 763.

155. Robert E. Drury, "Freedom to Breed," *Science* 163 (February 7, 1969): 518.

156. Hardin, *New Ethics*, x.

157. Ibid., x.

158. Ibid., 4.

159. Ibid., 7.

160. Cf. Kenneth E. Boulding, "The Gospel of St. Malthus," *New Republic* 167 (September 9, 1972): 22, and *Booklist* 69 (October 15, 1972): 162.

161. George H. Siehl, *Library Journal* 97 (July 3, 1972): 2422.

162. Boulding, "Gospel," 25.

163. *Choice*, 9 (February 1973): 1378.

164. *Science Books* 8 (December 1972): 199; Boulding, "Gospel," 24.

165. *Science Books*, 8.

166. Siehl, *Library Journal*, 2423.

167. *Choice*, 1578.

168. Joseph P. Fitzpatrick, "Man and Society," *America* (February 9, 1974): 94.

169. Samuel Mines, "Doomsday Antidote," *Bookworld* 6 (July 30, 1972): 8.

170. *Library Journal* 98 (May 1, 1973): 1442.

171. *Science Books*, 199.

172. Woodwell, "Inconvenient," 1191.

173. Hardin, *Naked Emperors*, 24.

174. Ibid., 172.

175. Garrett Hardin, "Nobody Ever Dies of Overpopulation," *Science* 171 (February 12, 1971): 527.

176. Hardin, *Naked Emperors*, 226.

177. Hardin, "Nobody Ever Dies," 527.

178. Garrett Hardin, *The Limits of Altruism: An Ecologist's View of Survival* (Bloomington: Indiana University Press, 1977): 51.

179. Ibid., 28.

180. Hardin, *New Ethics*, 172.

181. Ibid., 174.

182. Hardin, *Wild Taboo*, 164.

183. Garrett Hardin, *Nature and Man's Fate* (New York: Rinehart & Co., 1959): 212–14.

184. Hardin, *Naked Emperors*, 152.

185. Hardin, *Limits of Altruism*, 57.

186. Hardin, *Wild Taboo*, 173–74.

187. Ibid., 179.

188. Hardin, *Limits of Altruism*, 135.

189. Ibid., 58–59.
190. Hardin, *Naked Emperors*, 126.
191. Hardin, *Wild Taboo*, 196.
192. Ibid., 164.
193. Ibid., 153.
194. Hardin, *Naked Emperors*, 202.
195. Hardin, *Wild Taboo*, 178.
196. Hardin, *Nature and Man's Fate*, 319.
197. Hardin, *Promethean Ethics*, 66.
198. Hardin, *Nature and Man's Fate*, 317.
199. Ibid., 309.
200. Hardin, *Limits of Altruism*, 118.
201. Hardin, *New Ethics*, 160.
202. Hardin, "Tragedy," 258–59.
203. When Hardin tells the story of how the Quotions overpopulate their spaceship, he adds a relatively implausible, quasi-psychological argument about how those Quotions who would have smaller families "give up" in the face of the supposed "success" of their large-familied compatriots and stop having children at all. See *New Ethics*, 160–61.
204. Hardin, *Nature and Man's Fate*, 302.
205. Ibid., 346.
206. Ibid., 309.
207. Ibid., 339.
208. Ibid., 346.
209. Ibid., 346.
210. Ibid., 331.
211. Ibid., 331.
212. Hardin, *Naked Emperors*, 96.
213. See, for example, Hardin, *Wild Taboo*, 3–73.
214. Ibid., 176.
215. Hardin, *Naked Emperors*, 101–27.
216. Ibid., 108–14.
217. Ibid., 102.
218. Hardin, *Limits of Altruism*, 1–3.
219. Ibid., 2.
220. Ibid., 42.
221. Ibid., 135.
222. Ibid., 128.
223. Hardin, *Naked Emperors*, 127.
224. Ibid., 166.
225. Hardin, *Limits of Altruism*, 129.

226. Ibid., 132–33.
227. Hardin, *Naked Emperors*, 170.
228. Hardin, *Nature and Man's Fate*, 324.
229. Ibid., 322.
230. Hardin, *Naked Emperors*, 126.
231. Hardin, *Nature and Man's Fate*, 323.
232. Ibid., 323.
233. Ibid., 324–25.
234. Hardin, *Limits of Altruism*, 69.
235. Hardin, *Promethean Ethics*, 54.
236. Hardin, *Naked Emperors*, 255.
237. Ibid., 256.
238. Hardin, *Limits of Altruism*, 69.
239. Hardin, *Naked Emperors*, 257.
240. Ibid., 261.
241. Ibid., 254.
242. Ibid., 181.
243. Hardin, *Limits of Altruism*, 76.
244. Ibid., 75–76.
245. Ibid., 124.
246. For example, Hardin, *Promethean Ethics*, 9.
247. Hardin, *Naked Emperors*, 177.
248. Ibid., 255.
249. Fleming, "New Conservation Movement," 60.
250. Taylor agrees that "mutual coercion" is a democratic principle. It would produce an "authority that, while extensive, need not infringe on democratic norms." There is no *need* to draw "authoritarian conclusions" from it. And yet it seems Hardin sees more clearly the tendencies of simple, majoritarian democracy, particularly when shorn of rights and the rule of law. (Bob Pepperman Taylor, *Our Limits Transgressed: Environmental Political Thought in America* [Lawrence: University Press of Kansas, 1992]: 46.) Taylor, as do nearly all others interested in Hardin's political thought, focuses too narrowly on the "Tragedy" essay or its themes and hence misses important ramifications of Hardin's thinking.
251. Hardin, *Naked Emperors*, 19.
252. Ibid., 170.
253. Hardin, *Wild Taboo*, 176.
254. Ibid., 189.
255. Hardin, *Nature and Man's Fate*, 321.
256. Hardin, *Naked Emperors*, 170.
257. Hardin, *Limits of Altruism*, 56.

258. Ibid., 57.
259. Hardin claims that this principle merely presents the appearance of his having "fallen into the absolutist trap." What saves him, he believes, is an admission that it may not be valid under all circumstances, although "I do not at the moment know what these might be." *Limits of Altruism*, 56–57.
260. Ibid., 57.

Chapter 3. Small-Knowing Souls

1. Plutarch, *The Lives of the Noble Grecians and Romans*, trans. Dryden and Clough (New York: Modern Library, n.d.): 68.
2. Alexis de Tocqueville, *Democracy in America II*, trans. Henry Reeve (New York: Schocken Books, 1961): 379, 381.
3. Robert Reinhold, "Mankind Warned of Perils in Growth," New York Times (February 27, 1972): 1.
4. Donella H. Meadows et al., The Limits to Growth (New York: Universe Books, 1972).
5. Ibid., 124.
6. Ibid., 127.
7. Ibid., 138.
8. Ibid., 139.
9. Ibid., 163–64.
10. Ibid., 167.
11. Ibid., 174–75.
12. Ibid., 179.
13. Ibid., 175.
14. Ibid., 174–76.
15. Ibid., 194.
16. Ibid., 174.
17. Neither has time produced kinder judgments; indeed, to the contrary. Lewis quotes approvingly that *Limits* has undergone a "number of thorough debunkings." (Martin W. Lewis, *Green Delusions: An Environmentalist Critique of Radical Environmentalism* [Durham, N.C.: Duke University Press, 1992]: 184.) Paehlke says that "the details of the simulation, and even its technical soundness, have been roundly refuted," but he does want to hold open the lesson that continued exponential growth is not possible. (Robert C. Paehlke, *Environmentalism and the Future of Progressive Politics* [New Haven: Yale University Press, 1989]: 50, 52.) For a detailed and careful look at the technical defects of the model, see William Tucker, *Progress and Privilege: America in the Age of*

Environmentalism (Garden City, N.Y.: Anchor Press/Doubleday, 1982): 194–211. Bailey has produced a very lively critique of the notion that we are running out of resources: Ronald Bailey, *Ecoscam: The False Prophets of Ecological Apocalypse* (New York: St. Martin's Press, 1993): 63–74. The classic exposition of the view that resources are not in any meaningful sense limited is Julian L. Simon, *The Ultimate Resource* (Princeton: Princeton University Press, 1981).

18. "Club of Rome a Worldwide Organization," *New York Times* (February 27, 1972): 40.

19. Ibid., 40.

20. Jay W. Forrester, *World Dynamics* (Cambridge: Wright-Allen Press, 1971).

21. Robert Gillette, "The Limits to Growth: Hard Sell for a Computer View of Doomsday," *Science* 175 (March 10, 1972): 1092.

22. Ibid., 1089.

23. Peter J. Henriot, "The Politics of Ecology [. . .]" *America* 126 (June 17, 1972): 636.

24. John Naughton, "A Little Global Difficulty: Reflections on the Doomsday Debate," *Encounter* 42 (January 1974): 76.

25. I adapt an example Naughton quotes from Professor Beckerman: Naughton, "Global Difficulty," 76.

26. Gillette, "Hard Sell," 1090.

27. Ibid., 1091.

28. Anthony Lewis, "Ecology and Politics I," *New York Times* (March 4, 1972): 27; Anthony Lewis, "Ecology and Politics II," *New York Times* (March 6, 1972): 33.

29. Leonard Silk, "On the Imminence of Disaster," *New York Times* (March 14, 1972): 43; the first essay was Leonard Silk, "Questions Must be Raised About the Imminence of Disaster," *New York Times* (March 13, 1972): 35.

30. Peter Passell, Marc Roberts, and Leonard Ross, *New York Times Book Review* (April 2, 1972): 1ff.

31. Ibid., 12.

32. Lester R. Brown, "Computer Printout on the Earth's Ecosystem," *Saturday Review* 55 (April 22, 1972): 65.

33. John E. Koehler, *Journal of Politics* 35 (1973): 514.

34. Eric A. Hirst and Stephen K. Schuck, *The Living Wilderness* 36 (Spring 1972): 38–39.

35. Maurice F. Strong, ed., *Who Speaks for Earth?* (New York: Norton, 1973): 76.

36. Ibid., 74.

37. Kenneth E. Boulding, "Yes, The Wolf Is Real," *New Republic* 166 (April 29, 1972): 27.
38. Steven D. Antler, "The Familiar Specter," *Nation* 214 (May 22, 1972): 666–67.
39. Edward Edelson, "A Computer Views Our Future with Alarm," *Bookworld* (March 26, 1972): 13.
40. Gordon Rattray Taylor, *The Doomsday Book* (Cleveland: World Publishing, 1970).
41. Paehlke, *Progressive Politics*, 53.
42. See, for example, H. S. D. Cole et al., eds., *Models of Doom: A Critique of The Limits to Growth* (New York: Universe Books, 1973); William D. Nordhaus, "Resources as a Constraint on Growth," *American Economic Review: Papers and Proceedings*, 64 (May 1974): 22–26. On the other hand, one can still find people who want to take the study very seriously indeed (e.g., Robert M. Peart, "Relevance of the *Limits to Growth* debate: An Update," *Phi Kappa Phi Journal* [Summer 1988]: 23–26., Hays, as usual understating anything that reflects badly on the environmental movement, manages to leave the impression that the dispute was one among various models of doom for which one was more accurate, not (as is the case) that the fundamental premises of *Limits* came under attack. (Samuel P. Hays, *Beauty, Health and Permanence: Environmental Politics in the United States, 1955–1985* [Cambridge: Cambridge University Press, 1987]: 222.)
43. Gillette, "Hard Sell," 1091.
44. Mihajlo Mesarovic and Eduard Pestel, *Mankind at the Turning Point: The Second Report of the Club of Rome* (New York: Dutton, 1974).
45. Cole, *Models of Doom*, 214–15.
46. Meadows et al., *Limits*, 194.
47. Mesarovic and Pestel, *Turning Point*, 77.
48. Ibid., 39.
49. Ibid., 37.
50. Ibid., 54.
51. Ibid., 55.
52. Ibid., 34–35.
53. Ibid., 35.
54. Ibid., 127.
55. World Resources Institute, *World Resources 1986* (New York: Basic Books, 1986): 243; World Resources Institute, *World Resources 1990–91* (New York: Oxford University Press, 1990): 259.
56. Mesarovic and Pestel, *Turning Point*, 3.
57. Ibid., 6.

58. Ibid., 7.
59. Ibid., 4, 8.
60. Ibid., 8.
61. Ibid., 7.
62. Ibid., 18, 26–27. Tucker may well be right that *Turning Point*'s recognition of the need for trade and development made it a great advance over *Limits*. He recognizes in this connection that there is a strong planning mentality at work, but I'm not sure he sees just how different are the organic interdependence of *Turning Point* and that which is seen in market or trade relations. (Tucker, *Progress*, 213.)
63. Mesarovic and Pestel, *Turning Point*, 7.
64. Ibid., 7, 9.
65. Ibid., 31.
66. Compare ibid., 155.
67. Ibid., 147.
68. Ibid., 111.
69. Ibid., 147.
70. "In essence, sustainable development is a process of change in which the exploitation of resources, the direction of investments, the orientation of technological development, and institutional change are all in harmony and enhance both current and future potential to meet human needs and aspirations." (World Commission on Environment and Development, *Our Common Future* [Oxford: Oxford University Press, 1987]: 46.) Although it is hard to know just what a statement like this means, the importance of bringing everything into harmony seems to be central to what "sustainable" adds to "development," since development is always a process of change in various areas that meets present and future human needs and aspirations. While *Our Common Future* sometimes speaks of avoiding a centralizing, planning mentality, global institutions experience exponential growth in the course of its plan being outlined.
71. Mesarovic and Pestel, *Turning Point*, 146.
72. Ibid., 155.
73. E. F. Schumacher (with Peter N. Gillingham), *Good Work* (New York: Harper and Row, 1979).
74. Witold Rybczynski, *Paper Heroes* (New York: Penguin Books, [1980] 1991): 3.
75. E. F. Schumacher, *Small Is Beautiful: Economics as if People Matter* (New York: Harper and Row, 1973).
76. E. F. Schumacher, *A Guide for the Perplexed* (New York: Harper and Row, 1977).

77. Nicholas Wade, "Congress Buys *Small Is Beautiful*," *Science* 192 (June 11, 1976): 1086.
78. Ibid., 1086.
79. "A Homily for Homecomers," *Times Literary Supplement* (June 28, 1973): 1108.
80. "One-horse Theory," *Economist*, 257 (June 23, 1973): 113.
81. Francis Flaherty, "Schumacher's Guide," *Hudson Review* 31 (Spring 1978): 228.
82. Alvin Denman, "On the Human Condition," *Antioch Review* 36 (Fall 1978): 502.
83. Peter Heinegg, "Holy Simplicity," *Christian Century* 96 (October 17, 1979): 1018.
84. Peter Barnes, "Wise Economics," *New Republic* 170 (June 15, 1974): 29.
85. "Homily for Homecomers," 1108.
86. Harvey Cox, "A Subtreasury of Traditional Wisdom," *New York Times Book Review* (October 2, 1977): 10; Denman, "Human Condition," 501.
87. Nicholas Wade, "Cutting Technology Down to Size," *Science* 189 (July 18, 1975): 199–201.
88. Kenneth Woodward et al., "Thinking Small," *Newsweek* 87 (March 22, 1976): 50.
89. Hazel Henderson, "The Legacy of E.F. Schumacher," *Environment* 20 (May 1978): 35.
90. Michael Ashley, "The Enrichment of Boredom," *Encounter* 54 (March 1980): 60.
91. Henderson, "Legacy," 35 (emphasis added).
92. "Homily for Homecomers," 1108.
93. "Know Thyself," *Economist*, 265 (October 1, 1977): 129.
94. Paul K. Kuntz, "The Metaphysics of Hierarchical Order: The Philosophical Center of 'Small Is Beautiful,'" *Proceedings of the American Catholic Philosophical Association* 51 (1977): 36.
95. Schumacher, *Small*, 146–47.
96. Ibid., 137.
97. Ibid., 148–49.
98. Ibid., 154.
99. Ibid., 153–54.
100. Ibid., 180.
101. Ibid., 184.
102. Schumacher, *Good Work*, 131.
103. Ibid., 54–55. Compare Lewis's claim that "Appropriate technology, in

fact, often turns out to mean little more than well-engineered medieval apparatuses" (Lewis, *Green Delusions*, 7).

104. See Rybczynski, *Paper Heroes*, passim.

105. Schumacher, *Small*, 66. There are dangers in being *too* popularizing. The phrase "small is beautiful" took such hold that otherwise intelligent people never manage to get beyond it to what Schumacher is really saying. Lewis speaks of the "glorification of the small" in Schumacher; "true human values . . . can only be realized in intimate groups." (Lewis, *Green Delusions*, 82.) As we will see, this is wrong on several counts. Paehlke uses the phrase as if its meaning were self-evident. (Paehlke, *Progressive Politics*, 245.)

106. Schumacher, *Good Work*, 21.

107. Rybczynski, *Paper Heroes*, 19.

108. Schumacher, *Good Work*, 56; Schumacher, *Small*, 211–13.

109. Rybczynski, *Paper Heroes*, 4.

110. Langdon Winner suggests that "appropriate" means appropriate to "specific cultural and environmental settings." But this does not tell the whole story, as it does not answer the question of what kind of culture or environment one wants to encourage. (Langdon Winner, *The Whale and the Reactor: A Search for Limits in an Age of High Technology* [Chicago. University of Chicago Press, 1986]: 63.)

111. The transition from discussion of technologies to political and economic criticism is nicely illustrated in Hazel Henderson's essay on "The Legacy of E. F. Schumacher" (see note 89, above). The article is illustrated with lots of pictures of appropriate technology. But Henderson argues that "the essence of his work" is to be found in his political critique, which made him "most meaningful to me as a citizen activist."

112. For example, Schumacher, *Small*, 31–39.

113. Ibid., 13.

114. Ibid., 13.

115. Ibid., 24.

116. Ibid., 24.

117. Ibid., 100–101.

118. Ibid., 31.

119. Ibid., 120–22.

120. Ibid., 112.

121. Schumacher, *Guide for Perplexed*, 11 and passim.

122. Ibid., 9.

123. Schumacher, *Small*, 87.

124. Schumacher, *Guide for Perplexed*, 139.

125. Schumacher, *Small*, 263.

126. Ibid., 53–62.
127. Charles Fager, "Small Is Beautiful, and So Is Rome: The Surprising Faith of E.F. Schumacher," *Christian Century* 94 (April 6, 1977): 325. Fager also quotes Schumacher as saying, "All this lyrical stuff about entering the Aquarian Age and reaching a new level of consciousness and taking the next step in evolution is nonsense . . . What I'm struggling to do is to help recapture something our ancestors had."
128. Schumacher, *Small*, 52.
129. Ibid., 263.
130. Ibid., 262.
131. Ibid., 262.
132. None of the authors whose works we have been regularly turning to so much as mention this point.
133. R. H. Tawney, *The Acquisitive Society* (New York: Harcourt, Brace, 1920): 8.
134. Ibid., 62–63.
135. Ibid., 82.
136. Ibid., 147.
137. Ibid., 139ff.
138. Ibid., 123–28.
139. Ibid., 183.
140. Ibid., 181.
141. Ibid., 160.
142. Schumacher, *Small*, 250.
143. Ibid., 284.
144. Ibid., 261.
145. Ibid., 284.
146. Ibid., 284.
147. Ibid., 283.
148. Ibid., 250.
149. Ibid., 253.
150. Schumacher, *Good Work*, 102–3.
151. Schumacher, *Small*, 259.
152. Ibid., 271.
153. Ibid., 264, 266, 274.
154. Ibid., 276.
155. Ibid., 280, 282.
156. Ibid., 280.
157. Ibid., 242.
158. Ibid., 250–52.
159. Ibid., 245.

160. Ibid., 270.
161. Ibid., 284, 289.
162. Ibid., 289.
163. Ibid., 289.
164. Ibid., 288–89.
165. *Scott Bader Bulletin*, Issue 8 (July 1, 1987): 2–3.
166. Schumacher, *Small*, 33.
167. Ibid., 296.
168. Schumacher, *Guide for Perplexed*, 15.
169. Ibid., 63–65.
170. Ibid., 15–25.
171. Ibid., 45.
172. Ibid., 62–63.
173. Ibid., 79.
174. Ibid., 121–22.
175. Ibid., 126.
176. Ibid., 135.
177. Ibid., 138.
178. Bertrand de Jouvenel, *The Ethics of Redistribution* (Indianapolis: Liberty Press, 1952): 14–15.
179. Yet a kind of global monasticism—seemingly without God—seems to be attractive to environmental authors today. Taylor quotes economist Robert Heilbroner that the future may hold an order "that blends a 'religious' orientation with 'military' discipline. Such a monastic organization of society may seem repugnant to us, but I suspect it offers the greatest promise of making those enormous transformations needed to reach a new stable socio-economic basis." (Bob Pepperman Taylor, *Our Limits Transgressed: Environmental Political Thought in America* [Lawrence: University Press of Kansas, 1992]: 32.)
180. Schumacher, *Good Work*, 118.
181. Schumacher, *Small*, 152.
182. Ibid., 108, 109.
183. Schumacher, *Guide for Perplexed*, 139–40.

Chapter 4. The Mind O'erthrown

1. Hans Moravec, *Mind Children: The Future of Robot and Human Intelligence* (Cambridge, Mass.: Harvard University Press, 1988): 1.
2. William Devall, *Simple in Means, Rich in Ends: Practicing Deep Ecology* (Salt Lake City: Gibbs Smith, 1988): 39.
3. William Devall, unpublished lecture in a series sponsored by the Sym-

posium on Science, Reason and Modern Democracy, Michigan State University, November 21, 1991.

4. Alston Chase, "The Great, Green Deep-Ecology Revolution," *Rolling Stone* (April 23, 1987): 61–68.

5. Warwick Fox, *Toward a Transpersonal Ecology: Developing New Foundations for Environmentalism* (Boston: Shambhala, 1990): 44. Lewis has an interesting discussion of this point. Starting from the observation that "Radical environmentalism enjoys substantial, and growing, intellectual clout," he nevertheless argues that "its influence on the vast bulk of undergraduates will remain minimal" because "young college graduates . . . are notoriously conservative" and cynical. (Martin W. Lewis, *Green Delusions: An Environmentalist Critique of Radical Environmentalism* [Durham, N.C.: Duke University Press, 1992]: 247–48.) Eco-radicals, on the other hand (by which he has in mind a class larger than deep ecologists) are "intense idealists"; indeed, one of their central flaws is that they believe that "the roots of the ecological crisis lie ultimately in *ideas* about nature and humanity" and that they constantly hector about the need for new ideals (248, 11). Although attention Lewis gives to ideas shows he too believes them to be important, the more important things to think about are "specific policies" and "specific political plans" (12). "[G]enuine social transformation" calls for more than "ideological conversion," and "purity of ideals can only lead to the frustration of goals" (18). This is why he believes the radicals are utopians, and this characteristic, along with their simply factual errors, is why their plans will remain "no place" (249).

A good deal is sensible in what Lewis says, but it is not without flaw. Where will social transformation come from if not from a changed vision of how we want the world to be? Why should people change their practices unless they believe there is some reason to do so? What Lewis seems to consider to be his own more pragmatic attitude is no less based on a vision of how the world should be, one in which technology allows us to become more and more "de-coupled" from nature in order to save nature. Whatever the merits of this vision, the only thing that makes it seem to provide more concrete plans and policies than the radicals is that it deals far more in familiar realities—although with his hopes for "nano-technology" Lewis presses against the limits of this point. The fact that Lewis rightly disagrees with so many of the specific plans put forth by the radicals does not mean that they lack them.

Lewis understands that utopianism in theory leads to "dysutopian realities" (249), but he does not understand the passion and power of ideas that, in the face of that obvious point, allow people to continue to be utopians. The easy cynicism that the young affect will be no shield against this appeal if, as is so often the case, it masks a longing for certainties and rectitude. The supposed conservatism of college youth will not protect them from utopian appeals if those ideals are (as Lewis claims) often conservative, or if the conservatism they are familiar with is itself a brand of utopianism (249). Most important, if the basic categories of thinking about humans, nature, and society that are impressed upon them throughout their educations (for it is college teachers who teach precollegiate educators) are substantially informed by the mistaken views that Lewis so rightly criticizes, what grounds will all but the most independent-minded of them have for thinking about those issues in any terms but those that will produce the policies and politics that the radicals aspire to? In the end, the radicals have the clearer idea of what they gain by their ascendancy in the academy.

6. A wonderful example of this tendency is seen in Fr. Thomas Berry, *The Dream of Earth* (San Francisco: Sierra Club Books, 1988). Father Berry tries to distinguish himself from the deep ecologists but again and again accepts their premises, right down to a fundamental mistrust of the Bible.

7. George Orwell, *The Road to Wigan Pier* (New York: Harcourt Brace Jovanovich, 1958): 173.

8. Fox, *Transpersonal Ecology*, 81.

9. Ibid., 81, 83.

10. Ibid., 90.

11. Christopher Manes, *Green Rage: Radical Environmentalism and the Unmaking of Civilization* (Boston: Little, Brown, 1990). 140.

12. Arne Naess, "The Shallow and the Deep, Long-Range Ecology Movement: A Summary," *Inquiry* 16 (1973): 95.

13. Manes, *Green Rage*, 61.

14. Fox, *Transpersonal Ecology*, 91.

15. Ibid., 60.

16. Ibid., 60–63.

17. Ibid., 64.

18. Ibid., 68.

19. Bill Devall and George Sessions, *Deep Ecology: Living as if Nature Mattered* (Salt Lake City: Gibbs Smith, 1985): 74.

20. Fox, *Transpersonal Ecology*, 119–45.

21. Naess, "Shallow," 99.

22. Ibid., 95.

23. Devall, *Simple*, 57.

24. George Sessions, "Spinoza and Jeffers on Man in Nature," *Inquiry* 20 (Winter 1977): 483–84.

25. Ibid., 486–87.

26. Ibid., 487–90.
27. Ibid., 481. The deep ecologists have sometimes been labeled "eco-fascists." There are shallower and deeper reasons for this charge. The shallow reason is that sometimes people associated with the movement say some ugly things, like the infamous remark about AIDS as a hopeful solution to overpopulation (Lewis, *Green Delusions*, 37).

The deeper reasons have to do with the criticism of the history of Western thought that Sessions elaborates here, which has eagerly been taken up not just by deep ecology but by "progressive" forces as diverse as the American left, feminism, and multiculturalists (i.e., by the academy generally). Its serious and not so serious origins are largely to be found in German thinkers usually characterized as right-wing, like Friedrich Nietzsche, Martin Heidegger, and Ernst Jünger. (See, for example, Michael E. Zimmerman, *Heidegger's Confrontation with Modernity: Technology, Politics, Art* [Bloomington: Indiana University Press, 1990].) Some deep ecologists celebrate the connection with Heidegger in particular. In any case, their objections to materialistic progress, to technology, to the Enlightenment, to capitalism, to biblical religion, and to liberalism, combined with their love of rootedness and general nature schwarmerei, would make one expect to see careful distinctions being made between deep ecology and Nazi ideology. Bill Devall presents a curiously maladroit defense against this charge: the Nazis, he observed, were not egalitarians, and deep ecologists would never destroy forests and build autobahns. (William Devall, unpublished lecture in a series sponsored by the Symposium on Science, Reason and Modern Democracy, Michigan State University, November 21, 1991.)
28. Devall, *Simple*, 15.
29. Ibid., 15.
30. Ibid., 15.
31. Arne Naess, *Ecology, Community and Lifestyle: Outline of an Ecosophy*, ed. and trans. David Rothenberg (Cambridge: Cambridge University Press, 1989): 28.
32. Ibid., 165.
33. Ibid., 166.
34. Henryk Skolimowski, "The Dogma of Anti-Anthropocentrism and Ecophilosophy," *Environmental Ethics* 6 (Fall 1984): 287.
35. Paul Shepard, *The Tender Carnivore and the Sacred Game* (New York: Scribner's, 1973): 153.
36. Naess, *Ecology, Community*, 168.
37. Ibid., 195.
38. Ibid., 176.

39. Ibid., 84–86.
40. Ibid., 164.
41. Ibid., 197.
42. Ibid., 175.
43. Ibid., 166.
44. Ibid., 170.
45. Ibid., 171.
46. Devall, *Simple*, 21.
47. Dolores LaChapelle, *Earth Wisdom* (Silverton: Finn Hill Arts, 1970): 30.
48. Devall, *Simple*, 35.
49. Ibid., 39–40.
50. Ibid., 81
51. Devall, *Deep Ecology*, 155–56.
52. Naess, *Ecology, Community*, 29.
53. Ibid., 42–43.
54. Ibid., 187.
55. Ibid., 104–6.
56. Ibid., 72.
57. Devall, *Deep Ecology*, 74–75.
58. Ibid., 148–49.
59. Ibid., 152–55.
60. Ibid., 158.
61. Manes, *Green Rage*, 1–6, 175–90.
62. Devall, *Deep Ecology*, 201.
63. Manes, *Green Rage*, 176.
64. Devall, *Simple*, 49. The reference to the death camps is not some isolated slip on Devall's part. In a subsequent discussion of "a means of earning a living which is not destructive of human lives or the habitat of fellow creatures," he cites Arendt on the banality of Eichmann's evil with approval:

> Although his decisions were evil, they were quite normal and acceptable within the context of the Nazi-run bureaucracy. It was a quite ordinary bureaucracy. Its goal seems bizarre to us—mass extermination of people . . . Administrators of this Nazi bureaucracy dedicated to achieving their production goal—killing more people per day—sought cost-effective means . . .

> Similarly, the goal of administrators of timber mills in my country is to produce wood products as cheaply as possible. (*Simple*, 87–88.)

Perhaps we should be heartened to know that however banal this evil is, it is at least bizarre. But a comparison is in order. Mark Lilla has pointed out that the typescript of Heidegger's famous essay, "The Question Concerning Technology" (to which a good deal of the deep ecology criticism of technology hearkens back), contains a line that never appeared in print; Lilla does not seem to know if the line was ever delivered in any form. That line reads, "Agriculture is now a motorized food industry—in essence, the same as the manufacturing of corpses in gas chambers and extermination camps, the same as the blockading and starving of nations, the same as the manufacture of hydrogen bombs." (Mark Lilla, "What Heidegger Wrought," *Commentary* [January 1990]: 44.) Lilla, not unreasonably, calls this comparison "obscene." For any one of a number of imaginable reasons, Heidegger seems to have decided he could not commit such a statement to print. But it has evidently become the cutting edge of wisdom.

65. Naess, *Ecology, Community*, 193–94.
66. Devall, *Deep Ecology*, 200–201.
67. Al Gore, *Earth in the Balance: Ecology and the Human Spirit* (New York: Plume Books, [1992] 1993): 177.
68. Devall, *Simple*, 82. Naess is not quite so quick to endorse relativism, which in extreme forms he calls "norm hypochondria" (*Ecology, Community*, 68–69).
69. Gary Snyder, *The Practice of the Wild* (San Francisco: North Point Press, 1990): 55 and passim.
70. Lewis provides an impressive argument that eco-radicals are far more antitechnology than these remarks suggest (Lewis, *Green Delusions*, 117–25). While there is no question that the deep ecologists think they want to reject not just modern technology but its premises, it is still striking that most of that support Lewis provides for his analysis consists of criticism of particular technologies. In many instances it is Lewis, not the author he quotes, who generalizes to the rejection of classes of technology or modes of production. Perhaps we could agree on a minimalist proposition that the deep ecologists are, in their picture of how we should live today, far more implicated in the world of modern technology than they like to admit. This point will be discussed more below.
71. Devall, *Simple*, 84.
72. Naess, *Ecology, Community*, 88.
73. Ibid., 87.
74. Devall, *Simple*, 82.
75. Ibid., 83.
76. Ibid., 83.
77. Ibid., 85. Taylor hits the nail on the head when he notes, "It is ironic that the deep ecology criticism of Anthropocentrism and selfishness

leads to such a strong emphasis on personal 'healing' and self-interest."
(Bob Pepperman Taylor, *Our Limits Transgressed: Environmental Political Thought in America* [Lawrence: University Press of Kansas, 1992]: 97).

78. This *ambiance* of deep ecology is captured in Alston Chase, *Playing God in Yellowstone: The Destruction of America's First National Park* (New York: Atlantic Monthly Press, 1986): 344–62. Chase paints with a broad and witty brush but gets to the heart of things when he identifies "everything is sacred," "everything is interconnected," and "Self-transcendence is possible through authentic experience" as central themes (347–48).

79. Devall, *Simple*, 83.

80. Ibid., 105.

81. LaChapelle, *Earth Wisdom*, 76.

82. Ibid., 75.

83. Manes, *Green Rage*, 223ff.

84. Devall, *Deep Ecology*, 18ff.

85. Naess, *Ecology, Community*, 144.

86. Ibid., 144.

87. Ibid., 159.

88. Snyder, *Practice of the Wild*, 25–26.

89. Ibid., 39.

90. Hannah Holmes, "Being Bioregional," *Garbage* 4 (March/April 1992): 32–37.

91. Lewis, *Green Delusions*, 112.

92. The immediate origin of much of the mistrust of biblical religion goes back to a famous essay by historian Lynn White, Jr., "The Historical Roots of Our Ecological Crisis," *Science* 155 (March 10, 1967): 1203. Clearly, however, this kind of criticism goes back as least as far as the Enlightenment.

93. LaChapelle, *Earth Wisdom*, 36, 44.

94. Ibid., 45–49.

95. Snyder, *Practice of the Wild*, 95.

96. LaChapelle, *Earth Wisdom*, 25–26.

97. Ibid., 88.

98. Ibid., 89.

99. Ibid., 79.

100. Ibid., 94. LaChapelle, for all she has been praised by serious Heidegger scholars (see Zimmerman, *Heidegger's Confrontation*, 295), gets most of her Heidegger secondhand.

101. LaChapelle, *Earth Wisdom*, 137–48, 168–70.

102. Ibid., 123–24.

103. Snyder, *Practice of the Wild*, 56.
104. Ibid., 112.
105. Shepard, *Tender Carnivore*, 259.
106. Ibid., 259.
107. Plato, *Republic*, 541a.
108. Devall, *Deep Ecology*, 162.
109. Lewis provides an extremely useful corrective to the primitivism of the eco-radicals (Lewis, *Green Delusions*, 43–81).
110. Shepard, *Tender Carnivore*, 260–78.
111. Devall, *Deep Ecology*, 175–76.
112. Shepard, *Tender Carnivore*, 160–74, 183–84.
113. Snyder, *Practice of the Wild*, 41.
114. Ibid., 41–43.
115. Shepard, *Tender Carnivore*, 123–26.
116. Naess, *Ecology, Community*, 75.
117. Naess, "Shallow," 98.
118. Taylor notes dryly that Sasquatch "is obviously not an auspicious position from which to evaluate the nature of human society and political life" (Taylor, *Limits Transgressed*, 99).
119. Aristotle, *The Politics*, trans. Carnes Lord (Chicago: University of Chicago Press, 1984): 37–38. (1253a9-37)
120. LaChapelle, *Earth Wisdom*, 74.
121. Devall, *Simple*, 74. Langdon Winner puts the matter kindly when he notes that deep ecologists speak to the heart more than to the head, but he does not follow through on the implications of their critique of reason. (Langdon Winner, *The Reactor and the Whale* [Chicago: University of Chicago Press, 1986]: 131–34.) Manes is closer to the truth when he claims that deep ecology is less about ideas than it is about confronting in practice our self-destructive civilization. But his contempt for ideas blinds him to the irony of deep ecology's philosophic pose (Manes, *Green Rage*, 139–41).
122. Snyder, *Practice of the Wild*, 64, 61.
123. Naess, *Ecology, Community*, 163.
124. Ibid., 164.
125. Ibid., 28–29.
126. Skolimowski, "Dogma of Anti-Anthropocentrism," 283.
127. Devall, *Simple*, 39.
128. Naess, *Ecology, Community*, 198–99.
129. Richard A. Watson, "A Note on Deep Ecology," *Environmental Ethics* 6 (Winter 1984): 378.
130. Ulysses Torassa, "Meeting to Stall Timmy's Move," *Cleveland Plain Dealer* (October 10, 1991): B1.

131. Associated Press/Media General Survey conducted September 1–7, 1985 (Public Opinion Online/Roper Center for Public Opinion Research).

132. NBC News/*Wall Street Journal* poll conducted July 26–29, 1991 (Public Opinion Online/Roper Center for Public Opinion Research).

133. *Los Angeles Times* poll conducted November 17–21, 1989 (Public Opinion Online/Roper Center for Public Opinion Research).

134. Snyder, *Practice of the Wild*, 5.

Chapter 5. Something More Than Natural

1. Aristotle, *Nichomachean Ethics*, trans. Terence Irwin (Indianapolis: Hackett, 1985): 9. (1096a30)

2. Nathaniel Hawthorne, *The Blithedale Romance* (New York: New American Library, n.c.d.): 78–79.

3. Donella H. Meadows et al., *Beyond the Limits: Confronting Global Collapse, Envisioning a Sustainable Future* (Post Mills, Vt.: Chelsea Green, 1992).

4. Ibid., xiii.

5. Ibid., 198ff. The authors admit that the differences between adopting such policies in 1995 and having adopted them in 1975 are "subtle." (*Beyond the Limits*, 201.)

6. One of the best parts of this exchange is the MIT team's realization that many of the disagreements over *Limits* come down to different pictures of human nature. But having got that far, unfortunately they concluded, "We see no objective way of resolving these very different views of man and his role in the world," thus ending the discussion just when it got interesting. (H. S. D. Cole et al., eds., *Models of Doom: A Critique of the Limits to Growth* [New York: Universe Books, 1973]: 240.)

7. Meadows et al., *Beyond the Limits*, 118, 261.

8. Ibid., 273–74.

9. Ibid., 228.

10. John Royden Maddox, *The Doomsday Syndrome* (New York: McGraw Hill, 1972).

11. George Claus and Karen Bolander, *Ecological Sanity* (New York: David McKay, 1977).

12. Dixie Lee Ray, *Trashing the Planet: How Science Can Help Us Deal with Acid Rain, Depletion of the Ozone, and Nuclear Waste (Among Other Things)* (New York: Harper and Row, 1990).

13. Ronald Bailey, *Ecoscam: The False Prophets of Ecological Apocalypse* (New York: St. Martin's Press, 1993).

14. Michael Fumento, *Science Under Siege: Balancing Technology and the Environment* (New York: William Morrow, 1993).

15. Julian L. Simon, *The Ultimate Resource* (Princeton: Princeton University Press, 1981).
16. Julian L. Simon and Herman Kahn, eds., *The Resourceful Earth: A Response to 'Global 2000'* (Oxford: Basil Blackwell, 1984).
17. Edith Efron, *The Apocalyptics: How Environmental Politics Controls What We Know About Cancer* (New York: Simon and Schuster, 1984).
18. Elizabeth Whelan, *Toxic Terror* (Ottawa, Ill.: Jameson Books, 1985).
19. Claus and Bolander, *Ecological Sanity*, 49–55.
20. Whelan, *Toxic Terror*, 290–94. Fumento puts the point nicely: "[W]hile the responsible scientists are sweating away in their laboratories . . . the irresponsible ones are calling press conferences" (*Science Under Siege*, 350).
21. Bailey, *Ecoscam*, 20–21.
22. Whelan, *Toxic Terror*, 87–105.
23. Maddox, *Doomsday*, 35–110.
24. Claus and Bolander, *Ecological Sanity*, 277–550.
25. Efron, *Apocalyptics*, 187–383. Shabecoff's comments on Efron are telling about the way these critics are too often treated, when they are noticed at all. He briefly summarizes her argument that natural carcinogens far outweigh human-made ones, and that animal testing is not a fully reliable predictor of human cancer, and continues, "Her list of alarmist 'apocalyptics' included Rachel Carson, Lewis Mumford, Barry Commoner, Rene Dubos, Paul Ehrlich, and a number of Nobel laureate scientists, the staff of the National Cancer Institute, and scientists in government research and regulatory agencies—a rather distinguished group." (Philip Shabecoff, *A Fierce Green Fire: The American Environmental Movement* [New York: Hill and Wang, 1993]: 224.) That is the extent of his "refutation." Thus we have come full circle. It was wrong for Carson's critics to try to dismiss her merely by the weight of authority, and it is no less wrong when the environmental movement answers its own critics merely by calling on its own gods.
26. Fumento, *Science Under Siege*, 19–44.
27. Maddox, *Doomsday*, 9.
28. Ibid., 9–12.
29. Claus and Bolander, *Ecological Sanity*, 14–15. Paul Ehrlich has rightly defended his proposals for "semi-development" and "de-development" by saying that his critics confuse criticism of the misuse of technology for an attempt to "destroy technology." (Paul R. Ehrlich and John P. Holdren, "Technology for the Poor," *Saturday Review* [July 3, 1971]: 46–47.)
30. Claus and Bolander, *Ecological Sanity*, 25–27.
31. Ibid., 11–13.

32. Efron, *Apocalyptics*, 30–31.

33. Ibid., 30.

34. Fumento, *Science Under Siege*, 355–58.

35. Whelan, *Toxic Terror*, 297.

36. Bailey, *Ecoscam*, 12.

37. Ray, *Trashing*, xi, 163.

38. Ibid., 14–18.

39. Compare Fumento, *Science Under Siege*, 370, where he speaks of the importance of a strong economy to have the wealth necessary to fight pollution. Bailey finds the "ongoing politicization of science . . . especially dangerous to a secular liberal society such as ours" (Bailey, *Ecoscam*, 176). But better science is not the only thing necessary to solve this problem. Ray speaks of our human "gift to make conscious choices," but as she applies that thought entirely to the pursuit of knowledge and "understanding that will better the lot of all species on the planet," she comes up with a formulation remarkably like that of Naess (Ray *Trashing*, 171).

40. For all his efforts to develop an environmentalism that is politically thoughtful and progressive (yet moderate), Paehlke is still working toward the elimination of all conflict. After noting the good reasons why environmentalism needs to be suspicious of liberalism, he concludes that what is needed is an understanding of progress defined as *"meeting real needs more efficiently."* (Robert C. Paehlke, *Environmentalism and the Future of Progressive Politics* [New Haven: Yale University Press, 1989]: 211.) Commoner could say precisely the same thing. It is just the advantage liberalism has in relation to its protection of freedom that it is slow to tell people what their "real needs" are.

    That an egalitarian regime such as ours, predicated on material comfort, could lapse into despotism unless it maintains a sufficient appreciation of liberty is hardly a new thought. See Alexis de Tocqueville, *Democracy in America II*, trans. Henry Reeve (New York: Schocken Books, 1961).

41. Fumento, *Science Under Siege*, 351–53.

42. Ray, *Trashing*, 165.

43. Bob Pepperman Taylor, *Our Limits Transgressed: Environmental Political Thought in America* (Lawrence: University Press of Kansas, 1992): 98.

44. Simon, *Ultimate Resource*, 344.

45. Ibid., 333–44.

46. Bernard J. Frieden, *The Environmental Protection Hustle* (Cambridge, Mass.: MIT Press, 1979).

47. Ibid., 37–41.

48. Ibid., 107–18.
49. Ibid., 52–59.
50. Ibid., 95–96.
51. Ibid., 119–21.
52. Ibid., 130.
53. Ibid., 129–30.
54. Ibid., 131.
55. Michael S. Greve and Fred L. Smith, Jr., eds, *Environmental Politics: Public Costs, Private Rewards* (New York: Praeger, 1992).
56. For example, Fred L. Smith, Jr., "Conclusion: Environmental Policy at the Crossroads," ibid., 177–97.
57. William Tucker, *Progress and Privilege: America in the Age of Environmentalism* (Garden City, N.Y.: Anchor Press, 1982).
58. Ibid., xv.
59. Ibid., 3.
60. Ibid., xv.
61. Compare James Ridgeway, *The Politics of Ecology* (New York: Dutton, 1970).
62. Deborah Baldwin, "Tirade Against Elitism," *Technology Review* (January 1983): 84.
63. Tucker, *Progress*, 80.
64. Ibid., 7–19.
65. Ibid., 157–60.
66. Ibid., 128–52.
67. Ibid., 284.
68. Mary Douglas and Aaron Wildavsky, *Risk and Culture: An Essay on the Selection of Technical and Environmental Dangers* (Berkeley: University of California Press, 1982).
69. Ibid., 16–28.
70. Ibid., 16–48.
71. Ibid., 35–40.
72. Ibid., 90–104.
73. Ibid., 102–51.
74. Ibid., 122–23.
75. Ibid., 152–73.
76. Ibid., 187.
77. Ibid., 198.
78. Ibid., 193.
79. Ibid., 193.
80. Fred Pearce, "A Hero for the Greens?" *New Scientist* (September 23, 1989): 64.

81. James Lovelock, *The Ages of Gaia: A Biography of Our Living Earth* (New York: Norton, 1988): 5–7.
82. James Lovelock, *Healing Gaia: Practical Medicine for the Planet* (New York: Harmony Books, 1991).
83. Lovelock, *Ages of Gaia*, 8.
84. Richard A. Kerr, "No Longer Willful, Gaia Becomes Respectable," *Science* 240 (April 22, 1988): 393–95.
85. Lovelock, *Ages of Gaia*, 31–34, 45–48.
86. Ibid., 159–77.
87. Ibid., 153–54, 229–37. As Taylor's excellent discussion of those who have taken the idea of Gaia and run wild with it suggests, Lovelock's position is, for all its problems, preferable to the alternative presented by some of his "followers," who "vacillate between overt hostility toward the human community in general and a vague appeal to the extension of the human community to the broader natural world." (Taylor, *Limits*, 132.)
88. Bernard J. Nebel, *Environmental Science: The Way the World Works*, 3d ed. (Englewood Cliffs, N.J.: Prentice-Hall, [1981, 1987] 1990): 576.
89. It is ironic that once upon a time, Paul Ehrlich had to defend the use of the term "environment" as meaning more than a concern for "national parks and trout streams . . . Slums, cockroaches, and rats are ecological problems, too. The correction of ghetto conditions in Detroit is neither more nor less important than saving the Great Lakes—both are imperative." (Paul R. Ehrlich and John P. Holdren, "Impact of Population Growth," *Science* 171 [March 26, 1971]: 1215.) But with increasing clarity about the comprehensiveness of the term can come increasing doubts about its usefulness.
90. Even Lewis, as sensible as in many respects he is, cannot resist this temptation, as he advocates the development of technologies that will increasingly free us from nature, and thus limit our impact on it. (Martin W. Lewis, *Green Delusions: An Environmentalist Critique of Radical Environmentalism* [Durham, N.C.: Duke University Press, 1992]: 16–17.) It is hard not to think of the various versions of Star Trek in this connection—not because what Lewis proposes is mere fantasy, but because these shows are sustained efforts to consider what it would mean for human beings to overcome the "realm of necessity" in the way Lewis advocates. In order for there to be any "drama" at all under such circumstances—that is, in order for there to be life that is recognizably human—those who inhabit this future must constantly be imposing restraints *on themselves* to substitute for their freedom from all natural constraint. Hence pressing exploration to the point of discovering hos-

tile aliens, or the Prime Directive. As members of Star Fleet, then, one can imagine that life has meaning. But what about everybody else? It is striking how often civilian characters are bad guys; vain, petty, self-absorbed. Of course, these are usual stereotypes about civilians held by military organizations, but they reflect in this instance a larger truth as well.

91. Of course, even without "the environment" to speak of, we would still have to contend with the problem of "nature." This word too is much used, and abused, and it can suffer from the same comprehensive vagueness as "the environment." "Love of nature" no less than "environmental concern" can become an excuse for not paying attention to particulars. Still, "nature" has the advantage over "environment" at least in being a term that can be abused not because it refuses to discriminate but because it holds a long, rich, and perhaps conflicting set of distinctions and meanings. More to the point, it is a word that has long been closely bound up with our thinking about ethics and politics. As much as we may use it thoughtlessly, "nature" stands ready to open doors that remain closed to "environment."

92. Donald Fleming, "Roots of the New Conservation Movement," *Perspectives in American History*, vol. 6 (Cambridge: Cambridge University Press, 1972): 36–39.

93. Efron, *Apocalyptics*, 38.

94. Rene Dubos and Barbara Ward, *Only One Earth: The Care and Maintenance of a Small Planet* (New York: Norton, 1972).

95. Rene Dubos, *Celebrations of Life* (New York: McGraw Hill, 1981): 83–84.

96. Ibid., 84, 86.

97. Rene Dubos, *The Wooing of Earth: New Perspectives on Man's Use of Nature* (New York: Scribner's, 1980): 79–127. While Dubos titles part of his discussion "The Management of Earth," he does not have such far-reaching aspirations of more recent environmental managers. However, it may well be that Michael Pollan's *Second Nature: A Gardener's Education* (New York: Dell, 1991) exhibits a still more thoughtful understanding on this point. Pollan points out that the combination of nature and culture is what is meant by "cultivation," a word that far better acknowledges the constraints arising from nature and human nature than "management."

98. Dubos, *Celebrations*, 83.

99. Ibid., 83.

100. Al Gore, *Earth in the Balance: Ecology and the Human Spirit* (New York: Penguin Books, 1993). As Dubos rightly notes, our "widespread use" of

the word "environment" points to the "poverty" of our present relationships to the earth, precisely because there is lacking in them a serious
sense of our understanding of place (Dubos, *Wooing*, 109–10).

101. Richard John Neuhaus, *In Defense of People: Ecology and the Seduction
of Radicalism* (New York: Macmillan, 1971).

102. Ibid., 83–85.

103. Ibid., 188.

104. Ibid., 190–91.

105. Ibid., 199.

106. Ibid., 92–118.

107. Neuhaus is more kind than blind when he assesses this aspect of the
politics of the environmentalists. He recognizes that "the totalitarian
bias of much ecological literature is inescapable" but tries his best to
absolve particular thinkers of the charge. At any rate, he is sure that
Commoner is not, and professes only to be "not so sure" about Hardin
and Ehrlich (Neuhaus, *Defense of People*, 112).

108. *Managing Planet Earth: Readings from Scientific American* (New York:
W.H. Freeman, [1989] 1990).

Index